WOMEN IN PRINT

The LADIES MAGAZINE.

By JASPER GOODWILL of Oxford, Esqr.

VOL. III

LONDON.

Printed for the Proprietor & Sold the Corner of Elliot's Court Little Old Bailey. 1751.

WOMEN IN PRINT

Writing Women and Women's Magazines
From the Restoration to the
Accession of Victoria

Alison Adburgham

London . George Allen and Unwin Ltd
Ruskin House   Museum Street

First published in 1972

ISBN 0 04 070005 4

Printed in Great Britain
in 12 pt Barbou type
by W & J Mackay Limited
Chatham, Kent

Sure the poor woman is a little distracted, she could never be so ridiculous else as to venture at writing books, and in verse too; if I should not sleep a fortnight I should not come to that.
Dorothy Osborne of the Duchess of Newcastle,
in a letter to William Temple, 1653

I, a woman, cannot be exempt from the malice and aspersion of spiteful tongues, which they cast upon my poor writings.
Margaret, Duchess of Newcastle, in a letter
to her husband, 1667

The penalties and discouragements attending the profession of an author fall upon women with a double weight; to the curiosity of the idle and the envy of the malicious their sex affords a peculiar incitement: arraigned, not merely as writers, but as *women,* their characters, their conduct, even their personal endowments become the subjects of severe inquisition. In detecting their errors and exposing their foibles, malignant ingenuity is active and unwearied.
Public Characters, Vol. IV, 1800

Envy, malice, and all uncharitableness—these are the fruits of a successful literary career for a woman
Laetitia E. Landon, 1836

Foreword

This book should be regarded as rescue work. It salvages pre-Victorian periodicals from the limbo of forgotten publications, and exhumes from long undisturbed sources a curious collection of women who, at a time when it was considered humiliating for a gentlewoman to earn money, contrived to support themselves by writing, editing, or publishing . . . sometimes even supporting husbands and children as well.

The existence in the eighteenth century of these self-supporting women of the middle classes seems to have been disregarded by social historians; and historians of the Press have failed to deal faithfully with early publications addressed to women, referring only in passing to those edited by well-known men or to which they contributed. Of course many of the women who come into this account themselves became famous in their generation and have their honoured place in literary history or the histories of women's emancipation and education. But I have been chiefly interested in their more ephemeral activities in journalistic fields. The boundaries are by no means hard and fast between novelist and journalist, dramatist, diarist, essayist, translator, educationalist, poet, pamphleteer, miscellaneous writer; and many of the more desperate 'scribbling females' had perforce to turn their pens to any hack writing that would earn a few guineas and save them from the debtor's prison.

One of the pleasures of delving around inquisitively in the eighteenth century is finding that literary and publishing circles intersected in a cordially haphazard way. Everyone seems to have known everybody else, to have said something about them, to have written some news of them in a letter to a friend, to have included an anecdote about them in their memoirs, to have made some malicious remark about them at a dinner, or jotted down something about them in a diary. These random references, admittedly unreliable but with their own reality, have been my favourite sources, apart from my characters' own writings and contemporary periodicals.

The women who emerge make a motley gallery; but over the years that I have been getting to know them, they have won my respectful affection. More, indeed. To me they are all heroines: brave and resilient throughout the bludgeonings of fate and the contempt of society, humble over their own weaknesses and 'little inadvertencies', unashamedly pleased with themselves when success came their way. As for the publications addressed to the Fair Sex, my admiration for the information and entertainment contained in them is boundless. They provide an unworked goldmine for social and literary diggers. My prospecting has but broken the surface.

ALISON ADBURGHAM

1972

Contents

I   FROM THE RESTORATION TO QUEEN ANNE   19
Women dramatists: Aphra Behn, Catherine Cockburn, Susannah Centlivre. John Dunton and his Athenian Mercury. *The* Gentleman's Journal. *Innocence and seduction. Attitudes to virginity and marriage. Lord Halifax's* Advice to a Daughter. *Bargains to cohabit. Aristocratic adultery. The protection of purity through ignorance.*

II   FASHIONABLE EDUCATION AND LONELY SCHOLARS   37
Boarding-schools for young ladies; the fashion for all things French. Scholarly eccentrics. Mary Astell's Proposal *for a women's college; her* Reflections on Marriage. *Elizabeth Elstob and her Anglo-Saxon grammar. The* Ladies' Diary. *Its* Rules and Directions for Love and Marriage; *its mathematical questions and poetical enigmas.* Delights for the Ingenious. *Continuing intellectual esteem of the* Ladies' Diary.

III   ESSAY PAPERS AND NEWSPAPER WOMEN   53
Richard Steele's championship of women; his writing for them in the Tatler *and* Spectator. *Journals and essay-papers; the* Spinster *and the* Lover. *Mrs Mary Manley and her* New Atlantis; *her* Female Tatler. *Thomas Baker's* Female Tatler. *Mrs Manley succeeds Swift as editor of the* Examiner. *Women printers, book sellers, and publishers during the reign of Queen Anne. Mrs Elizabeth Powell of the* Charitable Mercury. *Her flight to the Continent and return to publish the* Orphan Reviv'd.

IV   'RECORDS OF LOVE' AND ROMANTIC FICTION   67
A weekly for middle-class women, Records of Love. *Pioneer of magazine serial stories. Steele's* Ladies' Library. *Familiar Letters. Mary Davys, playwright, novelist, and coffee-house proprietor. Eliza Haywood, shameless scribbler and romantic novelist. Approved fiction for ladies. Lofty ideals of the* Freethinker. *First* Ladies' Journal. *The first* Parrot.

V   MAGAZINES AND WRITERS OF THE 1730S   79
The Gentleman's Magazine *and its women contributors: Jane Hughes, Catherine Cockburn, Elizabeth Carter. Its imitators: the* London Magazine *and the first* Lady's Magazine. *The* Country Magazine. *Women and politics; Lady Mary Wortley Montagu. Her propaganda for smallpox inoculation; her* Nonsense of Commonsense; *its campaigns against 'sensibility' and the excesses of society; the necessity for bawdy in promoting sales. Mrs Laetitia Pilkington. Literary patronage, publishing by subscription, jobbing for printers.*

VI   THE 'FEMALE SPECTATOR' AND GOODWILL'S
       'LADIES MAGAZINE'   95
Mrs Eliza Haywood returns to the literary scene. Her Female Spectator;
*its campaign against fashionable vice; its warnings on elopements;
its correspondence column; its attitude to marriage and divorce.* The
Parrot. *Mrs Haywood reverts to novel writing.* The Lady's Weekly
Magazine. *Jasper Goodwill's* Ladies Magazine; *its horror crime
reporting and potted novels.* The Lady's Curiosity *and the* Young Lady.
John Newbury and his Juvenile Library.

VII   CIRCULATING LIBRARIES AND MID-CENTURY
       MAGAZINES   110
Libraries and popular novels. Fanny Hill. *Ralph Griffiths hires Oliver
Goldsmith for his* Monthly Review. *Provincial Libraries. Goldsmith's
satire on library novels in the* Critical Review. *Frances Moore Brooke
and her* Old Maid; *her dramatic criticism. Charlotte Lennox, novelist
and editor of the* Lady's Museum. *Hugh Kelly and the* Court
Magazine. *Chastity for women but not for men. Goldsmith's
contributions to the* Bee *and the* Busy Body; *his editorship of the* Lady's
Magazine. *Smollett's* British Magazine. *First serialization of a
previously unpublished novel. Anna Williams and Dr Johnson.*

VIII   THE 'LADY'S MAGAZINE' AND THE BLUE STOCKINGS   128
Introductory address and contents of the Lady's Magazine *of 1770.
Vogue for oriental tales. Mercenary marriages and runaway romances;
female intelligence defended. Elizabeth Carter and Dr Johnson. Mrs
Montagu and Fanny Burney. The Blue Stockings and Boswell. Hannah
More and her literary earnings. The Blue Stockings code compared with
the moral convictions of contemporary novelists and magazine writers.
Epistolary serials; satires on Court characters.*

IX   PUBLISHING PLAGIARISM: NOVELS AS DRUGS   142
Wheble's pirate Lady's Magazine. *The Rev. Mr Charles Stanhope's*
New Lady's Magazine. *Reader participation. Improprieties and
plagiarism by contributors rebuked. Economical management. Old
Bailey reports. William Lane's circulating libraries. Novels as time-
killing drugs.* The Novelist's Magazine. *Carnan's* Ladies' and
Gentlemen's Diary *edited from the Royal Military Academy.
Tytler's* Gentleman's and Lady's Magazine *edited from a debtors
prison.*

X   POCKET BOOKS, SEASIDE LIBRARIES, AND
       WOMEN DRAMATISTS   159
Harrison Ainsworth on ladies' pocket books. Lane's Ladies' Museum.
The Lady's Daily Companion. *The Austens in Kent. Lane's monthly*
Novelist. *Minerva Libraries in seaside towns. Mrs Radcliffe and her*

Mysteries of Udolpho. *The vogue for Gothic fiction. Jane Austen
satirizes it in* Northanger Abbey. *Elizabeth Inchbald's* A Simple
Story; *her plays and dramatic criticism.* Lover's Vows. *Other women
dramatists: Hannah More; Mrs Cowley; Mrs Robinson.*

XI   JOHN BELL, MARY WELLS, AND MRS JOHNSON   177
John Bell: typefounder, printer, publisher, bookseller. The Life of
George Anne Bellamy. *Charlotte Smith, her poetry and novels. The*
Morning Post. Bell's British Library. *Visits of the Prince of Wales.*
The World, or Fashionable Gazette. *Edward Topham, editor; the
Rev. Charles Este, gossip writer. Mary Wells, actress; her connection
with the* World. *The stage and literature as professions for women. Mrs
Johnson founds the first Sunday newspaper.* Bell's Weekly Messenger;
contemporary advertising.

XII   EDUCATING 'THE POOR' AND FAMILY MAGAZINES   187
Mrs Sarah Trimmer. Sunday schools and charity schools. The first
Family Magazine. *Hannah More and her* Cheap Repository Tracts.
*Attitudes towards educating 'the poor'. Religion at a low ebb.
Absentee clergymen and buck parsons. Sewing instruction for the poor.
Pre-Victorian household magazines. The* Female Preceptor.
*Seduction in prose and verse for the rationally devout. Avant garde
exponents of wider education for women. Reactionary beliefs about
wifely duties.*

XIII   FASHION PLATES AND MAGAZINES OF THE 1790S   204
Nicolaus Heideloff flees from the French Revolution to London. His
Gallery of Fashion. *Emigré hand-colourists of fashion plates. Children
as hand-colourists. The* Fashions of London and Paris. *Madame
Récamier in London. The* Lady's Monthly Museum: *profile of Mrs
Inchbald; lonely heart columns; a visit to Bethlehem Lunatic Asylum;
criticisms of Sir Walter Scott; distractions of women novelists; notices to
contributors; sketches from King's Bench prison.*

XIV   PERIODICALS OF THE NEW CENTURY   218
La Belle Assemblée. *Bright new ideas for magazine make-up.* Le
Beau Monde. Ackermann's *Repository of Arts. Mrs M. A. Bell:
her Magazin de Modes; her connection with* La Belle Assemblée.
The World of Fashion. *John Mitford's journalistic activities. The*
Lady's Magazine *accepts Miss Mitford's* Our Village. *Townsend's*
Quarterly Selection of Parisian Costumes. *The* Lady's Pocket
Magazine. *Sales of bound volumes affected by the 'Annuals'.*

XV   THE ANNUALS, THEIR EDITORS AND CONTRIBUTORS 236
*A publishing phenomenon. Harrison Ainsworth's introduction to the
first* Keepsake. *Frederic Schoberl's editorship of Ackermann's*
Forget-Me-Not *and* Friendship's Offering. *Writing to pictures.*

S. C. Hall and the Amulet. *Famous contributors to the annuals. Sir
Walter Scott's payments. The Hon. Mrs Norton, novelist, journalist, and
editor. The* Book of Beauty *edited by L.E.L. Her poetry and other
writings; gossip breaks her engagement. Marriage on the rebound and
tragic death.*

XVI   WRITING WOMEN OF THE 1830S   249
Lady Blessington edits the Book of Beauty. *Her equivocal ménage at
Gore House; her unceasing literary toil; her earnings. Mrs Gore's
'silver fork' novels. Sydney Owenson's* Wild Irish Girl *and other
writing; her social success and marriage to Sir Charles Morgan. First
literary pension awarded to a woman. Lady Blessington's tact with
contributors. Camilla Toulmin's visit to Gore House. Collapse of the
Gore House establishment: Lady Blessington's death in Paris. Her niece
continues the* Book of Beauty. *Mrs Newton Crosland edits* Friendship's
Offering. *Women's magazines of the 1830s; Victorian domesticity
sets in.*

CHRONOLOGICAL LIST OF PERIODICALS MENTIONED
IN THE TEXT   273

BIBLIOGRAPHY   282

INDEX   291

Illustrations

PLATES

Frontispiece to bound volume of Jasper Goodwill's *Ladies Magazine* of 1751   *frontispiece*

I Title-page and frontispiece to the *Female Spectator,* Vol. I, 3rd edition 1747   *facing page* 32

II Two illustrations by Thomas Stothard to Eliza Haywood's novel *The History of Miss Betsy Thoughtless,* edition of 1783 (first published 1751)   33

III *The Toilette*—engraving from the *Lady's Magazine,* 1776   48

IV Copperplate illustration to *The Mysteries of Udolpho* by Mrs Ann Radcliffe (1794) from 6th edition, 1806   49

V Mrs Hannah Cowley, dramatist; engraving in the *Lady's Magazine,* September 1784
Mrs Charlotte Smith, novelist; engraving in the *Female Preceptor* 1814   80

VI Illustrations to stories in the *Lady's Magazine,* June and October 1816 81

VII Mrs Sarah Trimmer, editor of the first *Family Magazine*
Miss Mary Russell Mitford, from a painting by Miss Drummond engraved for *La Belle Assemblée,* June 1823   96

VIII Illustration to a story called *Seduction*
Illustration to *The Gift of Filial Affection*
Both from the *Female Preceptor,* 1814   97

IX Uncoloured costume engravings from *La Belle Assemblée,* 1806   128

X 'Fashionable Party at the Frascati in Paris'; engraved from a popular French print for *La Belle Assemblée,* April 1807   129

XI Two costume engravings from the *Lady's Magazine,* March and June 1816   176

XII Marguerite, Countess of Blessington; after A. E. Chalon. Reproduced by courtesy of the Trustees of the National Portrait Gallery   177

XIII Two illustrations from the *Keepsake,* 1828, engraved by Charles Heath from paintings by Thomas Stothard, RA   192

XIV Two engravings from the *Lady's Cabinet,* 1838; 'The Village Schoolmistress' and 'The Governess'   193

IN THE TEXT

1 Pages from *Poems upon Several Occasions* by Mrs A. Behn,
   edition of 1684   *page* 21
2 Pages from 6th edition (1718) of *All the Histories & Novels
   written by the Late Ingenious Mrs Behn, entire in One Volume*   23
3 Title-page and dedication to John Dunton's *The Ladies' Dictionary*,
   1694   29
4 Trade card of Mrs Masquerier's boarding school; from the
   collection of Sir Ambrose Heal in the British Museum. Reproduced
   from *London Tradesmen's Cards of the XVIII Century* by
   Ambrose Heal   39
5 Title-page of Mary Astell's *Serious Proposal to the Ladies*, 1697   41
6 Title-page and frontispiece to Judith Drake's *Essay in Defence
   of the Female Sex*, 1697   43
7 Mrs Elizabeth Powell's *Charitable Mercury*, reproduced from *The
   English Newspaper*, 1632–1932 by Stanley Morison, by courtesy
   of the Cambridge University Press   65
8 Title-page and contents list of the *Country Magazine*, October 1736,
   reproduced by courtesy of the Trustees of the British Museum   82
9 Woodcut of 'Coffins for Minced Pies made with Neats' Tongues',
   illustrating a cookery column in the *Country Magazine*,
   November 1736   84
10 Contents list of the *Ladies Magazine* by Jasper Goodwill, No. VI,
   January 25 to February 8, 1752. Reproduced by courtesy of
   Trustees of the British Museum   105
11 Trade card of Francis Noble's Circulating Library; from the
   collection of Sir Ambrose Heal in the British Museum.
   Reproduced from *London Tradesmen's Cards of the XVIII Century*
   by Ambrose Heal   112
12 Library labels in the collection of Dr John Johnson, reproduced
   from *The Minerva Press*, 1790–1820, by Dorothy Blakey; by courtesy
   of the Bibliographical Society at the University Press of Oxford 114
13 The *Lady's Magazine* edited by Oliver Goldsmith; first page
   from the issue of April 1763   120
14 Costume engraving; from the *Lady's Magazine*, 1759.
   Reproduced by courtesy of the Trustees of the British Museum   122

15 Woodcut illustrating cookery section of the *Lady's Magazine*, 1763 124

16 Title-page to bound volume of the *Lady's Magazine*, vol XXIII
for the year 1792 130

17 Contents page of the *Lady's Magazine*, May 1792 140

18 Contents page of the Rev. Mr Charles Stanhope's *New Lady's
Magazine*, May 1789 143

19 The Bay of Weymouth, Dorset; engraving from the *New
Lady's Magazine*, 1789 146

20 First page of a song in the *New Lady's Magazine*, September 1789 151

21 Illustration to a romantic tale in the *Lady's Magazine*, November
1782 152

22 Illustration to a romantic tale in the *Lady's Magazine*, March 1782 154

23 Heading to Harrison Ainsworth's introduction to the first
Keepsake 160

24 Title page to Clara Reeve's *Old English Baron* (1777), edition
circa 1816 165

25 Illustration to a moral tale in the *Lady's Magazine*, October 1782 166

26 Library label in the collection of Dr John Johnson, reproduced
from *The Minerva Press*, 1790–1820, by Dorothy Blakey; by
courtesy of the Bibliographical Society at the University
Press of Oxford 168

27 Illustration to a 'gothic' tale in the *Lady's Magazine*, June 1782 171

28 The first Sunday newspaper, published by Mrs E. Johnson.
Reproduced from *The English Newspaper*, 1632–1932, by Stanley
Morison, by courtesy of the Cambridge University Press 183

29 Initial letter heading the first column of Mrs Johnson's *British
Gazette and Sunday Monitor*, reproduced from *The English
Newspaper*, 1632–1932, by Stanley Morison by courtesy of the
Cambridge University Press 185

30 Hannah More. From *Memories of Great Men and Women* by
S. C. Hall 190

31 Engraving from the *New Lady's Magazine*, June 1789 196

32 Maria Edgeworth in the library at Edgeworthstown 202

33 Embroidery pattern in the *Lady's Magazine*, 1792 209

34 Title-page of *La Belle Assemblée*, January 1807 219

35 First page of the advertisement section of *La Belle Assemblée*,
October 1806 221

36 First page of a ballad in *La Belle Assemblée*, June 1823 225

37 Embroidery pattern in the supplement to the *Lady's Magazine*, 1816   228
38 Embroidery pattern in *La Belle Assemblée*, February 1807   229
39 Contents page from the *Lady's Magazine*, February 1816   231
40 First page of a ballad in *La Belle Assemblée*, 1 April 1823; *The Lament of a Poor Primrose Girl*   233
41 Laetitia Elizabeth Landon, the poetess L.E.L. and MS extract   244
42 The house where L.E.L. lodged in Hans Place, S.W.1   247
43 Sydney, Lady Morgan's residence, Kildare Street, Dublin   254
44 Sydney, Lady Morgan's residence, William Street, London   256
45 Handwriting of Marguerite, Countess of Blessington   259
46 Fashion engraving from the *Ladies' Cabinet of Fashion, Music, and Romance*, May 1838   263
47 Fashion engraving from the *Ladies' Cabinet of Fashion, Music, and Romance*, May 1838   265
48 Fashion engraving from the *Ladies' Cabinet of Fashion, Music, and Romance*, March 1838   268
49 Fashion engraving from the *Ladies' Cabinet of Fashion, Music, and Romance*, April 1838   270

Chapter I
FROM THE RESTORATION TO QUEEN ANNE

*Women dramatists: Aphra Behn, Catherine Cockburn, Susannah Centlivre.
John Dunton and his* Athenian Mercury. *The* Gentleman's Journal.
Innocence and seduction. Attitudes to virginity and marriage. Lord Halifax's
Advice to a Daughter. *Bargains to cohabit. Aristocratic adultery. The
protection of purity through ignorance.*

ᔓᔓᔓᔓᔓᔓᔓᔓᔓᔓᔓᔓᔓᔓᔓᔓᔓᔓᔓᔓᔓᔓᔓᔓᔓᔓᔓᔓᔓᔓᔓᔓᔓᔓᔓᔓ

IN the year William and Mary ascended their tandem throne, Mrs Aphra Behn, author of seventeen licentious plays, was laid to her well-earned rest in the cloisters of Westminster Abbey. Although it was for her plays she was most famed, she was also a novelist, poet, historian, and translator of the *Reflections and Maxims* of la Rochefoucauld; and she was the first Englishwoman to earn her living by her pen. The eulogistic epitaph on the marble slab of her tomb includes these lines:

> Here lies a proof that wit can be
> Defence against mortalitie.

Wit was also, at that time, an acceptable defence against immorality. Aphra Behn's plays were so coarse as to offend many people even in that coarse age. But it was not because they were any worse than those of contemporary dramatists—licentious writing was almost obligatory for the stage. They offended because they were written by a woman.

Nevertheless it seems to have been generally conceded that Mrs Behn lived by her pen and not by the means more usually employed by ladies connected with the Restoration stage; and no one could deny her tremendous talent. Her comedies of intrigue are as clever as could be, crisp and witty. Her *Abdelazar*, a rifacimento of Marlowe's *Lust's Dominion*, contains the magnificent song 'Love in fantastic triumph sat'; and some of her poetry has an extraordinarily unfeminine strength, as *The Libertine*, with its splendid opening lines:

> A thousand martyrs I have made,
> All sacrificed to my desire,
> A thousand beauties have betray'd
> That languish in resistless fire.

Aphra Behn's best known comedy is *The Rover*, first performed in 1677, which ingeniously counterpoints four contrasting pairs of lovers. Her best known novel, *Oroonoko or The Royal Slave* was based on her experiences as a young girl in the South American colony of Surinam, to which a relative she called her father was appointed Lieutenant-General. Her real father was a barber of Canterbury, where she was born about 1640. After her marriage to Behn, a man of Dutch extraction, Aphra gained entry to the Court. King Charles was very taken by her 'handsome voluptuous countenance' and animated conversation; and when war with the Dutch began he thought she would make an excellent political spy. So in 1666 he sent her, now a widow, to Antwerp. This seventeenth-century Mata Hari is said to have 'worked upon the passions' of a merchant of Utrecht named Van der Albert, who agreed to supply her with naval intelligence if she became his mistress. When she had got all the information he could give her about the movements of the Dutch fleet she 'consigned him to his wife, soon after which he died of a fever'. Her mission accomplished, Aphra Behn returned to England.

The unashamed indecency of Mrs Behn's witty plays ensured their enthusiastic reception on the public stage, at Court, and in the private houses of the fashionables who took their cue from the King and his entourage. She interpreted the taste of the Restoration so aptly that she has since been called a female Wycherley. Indeed, if the secret of fashionable success and social survival lies in a capability to adapt to the times one lives in, Aphra Behn is a perfect example. She was very much a creature of her time. But she was also unique in her time in that she was a successful professional woman earning her livelihood in a profession other than prostitution. There were, of course, other women writers in the seventeenth century—poets, scholars, writers on religious subjects; but they were of the aristocracy and did not write for money. If they published their work at all it was usually anonymously or for private circulation among their family and immediate friends. Lady Winchelsea wrote poetry which burns with indignation at the prejudice against women writers. Margaret, Duchess of Newcastle, writer of poems, plays, philosophies, discourses, was thought to be more than a little crazy by her contemporaries. Yet her published literary output added up to twelve folio volumes, and she has had her posthumous admirers. Lamb described her as 'The thrice noble, chaste and virtuous, but again somewhat fantastical and original brained, generous Margaret Newcastle'; but Isaac Disraeli wrote more discerningly in his *Curiosities of*

A TABLE

On a Locket of Hair wove in a True-lover's Knot given me by Sir R. O. 77.
The Dream; a Song 78.
A Letter to a Brother of the Pen in Tribulation 80.
The Reflexion, a Song 83.
A Song to Pesibles Tune 86.
A Song on her loving two Equally set by Capt. Pack 88.
The Counsel, a Song set by the same hand 89.
The Surprise, a Song set by Mr. Farmer 91.
A Song. 92.
The Invitation, a Song to a New Scotch Tune 93.
Sylvia's Complaint, a Song to a fine Scotch Tune 95.
In Imitation of Horace 98.
To Lysander who made some Verses on a Discourse of Love's Fire 101.
A Dialogue for an entertainment at Court between Damon and Sylvia 102.
On Mr. J. H. In a fit of sickness 106.
To Lysander on some Verses he writ, and asking more for his Heart than 'twas worth 109.
To the Honourable Lord Howard, on his Comedy called the New Utopia 113.
To Lysander at the Musick meeting 118.
An Ode to Love 120.
Love Reveng'd, a Song 122.
A Song to a New Scotch Tune 123.
The Caball at Nickey Nackeys 125.
A Paraphrase on the eleventh Ode out of the first Book of Horace 126.
A Translation 127.
A Paraphrase on Oenone to Paris 129.
A Voyage to the Isle of Love 144.

FINIS.

A

VOYAGE

TO THE

Isle of LOVE.

An Account from Lisander *to* Lysidas *his Friend.*

A T last dear *Lysidas*, I'll let thee Free,
From the disorders of Uncertainty;
Doubt's the worst Torment of a generous
Who ever searching what it cannot find, (Mind,
Is roving still from wearied thought to thought,
And to no settled Calmness can be brought:

B² The

1. Pages from *Poems upon Several Occasions* by Mrs Aphra Behn, edition of 1694

Literature: 'Her labours have been ridiculed by some wits; but had her studies been regulated, she would have displayed no ordinary genius. The *Connoisseur* has quoted her poems, and her verses have been imitated by Milton.' In 1667 she wrote a copious epistle to her husband, the Duke of Newcastle, also an author, in which she said,

> 'I, a woman, cannot be exempt from the malice and aspersions of spiteful tongues, which they cast upon my poor writings, some denying me to be the true authoress of them; for your Grace remembers well, that these books I put out first to the judgement of this censorious age were accounted not to be written by a woman, but that somebody else had writ and published them in my name.'

Among those of her contemporaries who had no sympathy with the Duchess of Newcastle's need to express herself in published writing was Dorothy Osborne, who herself had such a graceful turn of phrase in her letters, such evocative descriptions of places and people, that she could well have been an author had she not thought authorship undignified in a woman. Writing to William Temple in 1653, Dorothy said: 'Sure the poor woman is a little distracted, she could never be so ridiculous else as to venture at writing books, and in verse too, if I should not sleep a fortnight I should not come to that.' Lady Newcastle was buried in Westminster Abbey in 1673. This honour was more likely to have been accorded to her as the Duke's wife than as a literary genius. Nevertheless her epitaph gave recognition to her scholarship: 'A wise, witty, and learned Lady, which her many books do well testify.'

In contrast to the aristocratic amateurs in their isolated country houses, Aphra Behn was a middle-class woman and a professional, a city dweller working in a man's world. Her writing appealed to the *beau monde* because it was both witty and licentious. She died in 1689 before women of her own class had acquired a taste for reading, and before the appearance of periodical publications aimed at a middle-brow feminine readership. Even had she lived on into the eighteenth century, it is unlikely she would have been a contributor to them. A high moral tone was almost invariably their editorial policy. They promulgated against fast-living society. Their contributors were required to adapt themselves to the new times following the revolution of 1688—the William and Mary times, and then the Queen Anne times. Mary II was a saintly woman and was admired as such by the

own Shoes and Stockings at their heads, retir'd.
This gave Monarch in Fancy so great a Caution,
that he took his Royal Consort into the Country,
(but above forty Miles off the Place where his own
Lady was) where, in less than eight Months, she
was deliver'd of a Princely Babe, who was chris-
ten'd by the heathenish Name of *Hayoumorecaka
Bantam*; while her Majesty lay in like a petty
Queen.

THE

THE

N U N :

OR, THE

Perjured Beauty.

A True NOVEL.

 O N *Henrique* was a Person of great Birth,
of a great Estate, of a Bravery equal to
either, of a most generous Education;
but of more Passion than Reason: He
was besides of an opener and freer Temper than generally his Countrymen are (I mean, the
Spaniards) and always engag'd in some Love-Intrigue
or other.

One Night as he was retreating from one of
those Engagements, Don *Sebastian*, whose Sister he
had abus'd with a Promise of Marriage, set upon
him

2. Pages from 6th edition (1718) of *All the Histories and Novels written by the
Late Ingenious Mrs. Behn, entire in One Volume.*

majority of her subjects, who had become sickened by the laxity of Restoration behaviour. Queen Anne, although insipid and ineffectual in many ways, was the consistent patroness of all charitable, religious, and educational endeavours. Thus coarseness was out—for ladies, that is. Gentlemen were still libertine. For this was a time of one moral code for men, another for women.

The stage was by no means purged during these two short reigns. But there was one woman dramatist, Catherine Trotter (later Catherine Cockburn), who made a valiant attempt at purification. Originally she had been under the influence of Aphra Behn. Her first dramatic production, in 1695, the tragedy of *Agnes de Castro*, was based upon Mrs Behn's English translation of a French novel. But she steered sharply away from this Restoration influence in her second tragedy, *Fatal Friendship*, which was produced a year after Mrs Behn's death. It was sufficiently pure to be dedicated to the Princess of Wales when it later appeared in print, by which time Catherine Trotter had formed the optimistic intention of reforming the morals of the age by means of an ennobled theatre. She was hailed in verse by John Hughes as 'the first of stage reformers'; and an anonymous poet wrote:

> More just applause is yours, who check the rage
> Of reigning vice, that has debauched the stage,
> And dare show virtue in a vicious age.

Writing in 1861 in her *Literary Women of England*, Jane Williams commented:

'The tragedy thus applauded does not contain a single line of real poetry, and does contain indecorous allusions, which would not be tolerated either on the stage or elsewhere in modern times. Hence may be inferred the low standard of poetry in the year 1698, and the gross profligacy of an age which reputed this play to be a corrective model of propriety. Yet the acknowledgement that human life is a state of probation, the assertion that good should be done, and evil resisted, runs through every scene: and the strength of principle which enabled a young girl publicly to maintain such opinions in the face of rampant scepticism and general depravity, justly commanded respectful admiration.'

At one point Congreve took Catherine Trotter under his protection, and also Mary Pix. According to an anonymous pamphlet *Letter to Mr Congreve* in 1698, he was to be seen 'very gravely with his hat over his eyes . . . together with the two she-things called Poetesses'. Mary Pix, born in 1666 and living until about 1720, was also a dramatist, writing assiduously in very irregular blank verse. Her comedies, although coarse, were considerably less indecent than those of Mrs Behn. The *Dictionary of National Biography* (DNB)[1] says of them 'her comic bustle of dialogue is sometimes entertaining. But her tragedies are intolerable. She was neither such a scandalous nor such a celebrated figure as Aphra Behn, but her fatness and love of good wine were matters of notoriety.'

Susannah Centlivre, about fifteen years younger, was another famous writer of plays from the beginning of Queen Anne's reign. Born about 1680, orphaned by the time she was thirteen, twice widowed before she was twenty, 'she had recourse to her pen as a means of subsistence'. She also took to the stage. And when dressed as a man in the part of Alexander the Great captured the heart of Joseph Centlivre, Yeoman of the Mouth to Queen Anne. Marriage ended her career as an actress, but not as a writer. She wrote nineteen successful plays in all, the wittiest being the comedies although, as a later critic put it, they were strongly tinctured with the indelicacy of her times. Her times, of course, were not so indelicate as those of Aphra Behn. They were times of social change, the most significant change for writers being the new interest in reading taken by a growing middle class. With increasing prosperity they were beginning to employ more servants; and in any case many of the traditional domestic tasks such as baking, spinning, and weaving, were no longer done in middle-class homes. There was more leisure for the womenfolk; and to fill this leisure they wanted reading matter that was not too taxing for their intelligence and education. They were ready for light novels and periodicals.

The idea of publishing periodicals addressed solely or in part to women readers can be traced back to John Dunton, an idealistic and eccentric bookseller. Dunton was called 'lunatick' by his contemporaries, and the elder Disraeli referred to him as a 'crack-brain scribbling bookseller, who boasted he had a thousand projects, fancied he had methodized six hundred, and was ruined by the fifty he executed'. He was the son of a country clergyman and at the age of fourteen described himself as being 'wounded by a silent passion for a virgin in my father's house'. Perhaps this passion, though silent, was observable. At any rate his father packed him off to London to be apprenticed to a bookseller called Parkhurst. Later he fell in love in church with Elizabeth Annesley, daughter of the Reverend Dr

[1] Dictionary of National Biography hereafter abbreviated to DNB.

Annesley, eminent non-conformist preacher, and became brother-in-law to Samuel Wesley, father of John Wesley the founder of Methodism. Samuel Wesley joined him in his first publishing venture. This was named the *Athenian Gazette, or Casuistical Mercury*, a penny weekly consisting of a single leaf or half-sheet, started in 1690, which after its first issue was renamed the *Athenian Mercury*. When it had been going successfully for about a year, Dunton began to introduce issues, at first once a month and later once a fortnight, 'supplied with queries from the Fair Sex' and called the *London Mercury*—after No. 8 renamed *Lacedaemonian Mercury*. And the popularity of these led him to bring out, in 1693, an entirely separate publication for women, the *Ladies' Mercury*, in which he promised to answer 'all the most nice and curious Questions concerning Love, Marriage, Behaviour, Dress and Humour of the Female Sex, whether Virgins, Wives, or Widows'. Ladies were 'desired to send in their Questions to the Latin Coffee House in Ave Mary Lane'.

In his memoirs, *Life and Errors*, Dunton wrote that the *Athenian Mercury* was intended to 'open the avenues, raise the soul, and restore the knowledge of truth and happiness that had wandered so long unknown and found out by few.' In its form it was a forerunner of *Notes & Queries*, but dealt with philosophical, ethical, metaphysical and scientific ideas instead of antiquarian topics. It also dealt with personal problems, thus pioneering the 'lonely heart' column, that perennially popular feature of all the women's magazines to come. The personal problems were then, as now, for the most part to do with love and marriage:

> 'I have lately courted a young Gentlewoman and she is now in mind to marry me. Lately died a Relative and left me £100 a year, on condition, moreover, that I never would marry the afore-mentioned Lady. Query, whether to take the Lady and leave the Money, or take the Money and leave the Lady.'

The reply of the *Athenian Mercury* was in the romantic spirit of the seventeenth century: take the lady. It would have been sympathetically approved by one of the *Athenian Mercury*'s most frequent contributors, Sir William Temple, whose own marriage to Dorothy Osborne had been one of love against the prolonged opposition of both their families upon financial grounds. And certainly the counsel was in keeping with John Dunton's aspirations to 'restore the knowledge of truth and happiness'. It was in a very different spirit from the worldly eighteenth-century advice that Lord

Chesterfield wrote for his son three-quarters of a century later. But on the other hand, the *Athenian Mercury's* answers to letters sent in by ladies (or purporting to be sent by ladies) tended to be either patronizing or facetious:

> 'When we are in Love, and the Man won't or can't understand our Signs and Omens; what in Modesty can we do more to open their Eyes ?
> 'Alas poor Lady! Your Case is very hard. Why, pull 'em by the Nose, write to 'em; or if neither of these will do (as you have been formerly, advised) show 'em this Question and Answer in *The Athenian Mercury*.'

Dunton had two other associates besides Samuel Wesley working with him on the *Athenian Mercury*: Richard Sault and Dr Norris. And in his *Memoirs* he mentions various women contributors: Mrs Nutt, Mrs Curtis, Mrs Mallet, Mrs Croom, Mrs Grover, Mrs Barnes, Mrs Winter, Mrs Taylor, Mrs Baldwin. Mrs Baldwin was the wife of a bookbinder and book-seller, 'a man of generous temper, who would take a cherishing glass to oblige a customer'. When he died, his widow, who had been his helpmeet in business, took over all his publishing work. Other women whom Dunton claimed to have had as contributors were 'Divine Astell; refined Lady Masham; that angel in flesh and blood Madam Gwillim; the conscientious and dutiful Maxfield; heavenly Richards; unknown Almira; beautiful Tempest; discreet Whitchurch; good humoured Shute; chaste Bolton; gay and witty Mrs Johnson of Kensington; rhyming Stacey; polite Davis; diverting and always new Mrs Wavil; charming Gill; the modest and beautiful Mrs Grace Cheek; Madame Tipper, who is a philosopher, a poet, and a good Christian'. There was also Madame Singer who was known as 'The Pindaric Lady of the West'. According to Dunton 'she obliged the Athenian Society with a variety of inimitable poems. She has certainly the richest genius of her Sex; she knows the Purity of our Tongue, and con-verses with all the briskness and gaiety that she writes. Her Style is noble and flowing, and her Images are very vivid and shining. To finish her Character, she is as beautiful as she is witty.'

It is not surprising, considering Dunton's evident susceptibility to all these ladies, that one of his projects did not go as planned. This project was 'a Design to expose Vice', a monthly paper issued under the title of the *Night-Walker, or Evening Rambles in Search after Lewd Women, with the Various Conferences Held with Them*. His idea for extirpating lewdness from London was to sally forth in the evenings armed with a constable's staff, accompanied by a clerical companion, and follow the prostitutes home, or to a tavern, where 'every Effort was used to win the erring Fair to the paths of Virtue'. But alas, as he observed, 'these were perilous adventures, as the Cyprians exerted every art to lead us astray, in the height of our spiritual exhortations'. The *Night-Walker* ran from September 1696 until February 1697, but Dunton had evidently done some journalistic research on the same lines for the *Athenian Mercury* some years earlier, since there is this entry in his *Ladies' Dictionary* of 1694; '*Six Nights Rambles* of a Young Gentleman through the City, for the Detection of lewd Women, as I find them inserted in the *Athenian Mercury* Vol. 3 Number 3, in the Manner following'. What follows in the *Ladies' Dictionary* is an account of six nights' rambles, in each of which he details his encounters with various types of prostitutes.

The Ladies' Dictionary was subtitled: *Being a General Entertainment for the Fair-Sex: A Work Never Attempted Before in English*: and it was more of an encyclopaedia than a dictionary. Alphabetically arranged, the entries dealt with a wide range of topics, but all of them were in some way connected with love and marriage. It included the names of men and women of myth, legend, and history whose names are associated with romance or eroticism; and there were entries for all those aspects of health and sickness, beauty and blemishes, behaviour between the sexes and behaviour of servants, which were presumed to occupy the minds of women to the exclusion of all else. These are a few examples: BEAUTY IN GENERAL, its alluring to Liking and Love; BEAUTY of an itchy or scabby skin repaired; SMALL POX, its fears or marks how to obliterate them; LOVE, fully treated on; VIRGINS, their State and Behaviour, particularly those in years; OBEDIENCE OF VIRGINS, to Parents in matters of Marriage; LETTERS, direction to Young Ladies in writing them; HUSBAND, whether lawful for a Young Lady to pray for one, and when shall she obtain one; HUSBAND, indifferent; HUSBAND, a good one, his character; CONFESSION of a New Married Man; SECRET LOVERS; CONCEPTION, the signs to know it, and whether Male or Female, and if false Conception; LYING-IN.

Another of John Dunton's many publishing projects was directly connected with his *Athenian Mercury*. This was a series of letters appearing regularly in the periodical and later published under the title of *The Athenian Spy*. The sub-title to this volume summarizes the contents: *Secret Letters of Platonic Courtship between the Athenian Society and the most*

THE
LADIES DICTIONARY

Being a

General Entertainment

For the

Fair=Sex:

A

WORK

Never attempted before in *English*.

Licens'd and Enter'd according to Order.

LONDON:

Printed for JOHN DUNTON at the Raven
in the *Poultrey*, 1694.

Price Bound Six Shillings.

TO THE

Ladies, Gentlewomen, and Others,

OF THE

Fair=Sex.

The Author Humbly Dedicates this
following Work.

Ladies,

THIS *Project of Composing a* DICTI-
ONARY *for the use of the* Fair=Sex,
(which may serve as a Secret Oracle,
*to Consult in all difficult Cases) being
the First Attempt of this kind that has appeared
in English, 'tis hoped 'twill meet with a Courteous
Reception from all, but more Especially from you,
for whose sakes 'twas undertaken; and if it re-
ceives any Favour at your Hands, I shall Attri-
bute its Success in the World, to the* ILLU-
STRIOUS SUBJECT *it Treats on;* viz. *The
Virtues and Accomplishments of your Sex;
which are so many and Admirable, that no
Volume can contain them in their full Extent.*

Her-

A 2

3. John Dunton's *Ladies Dictionary*, title page and dedication, 1694

ingenious Ladies in the Three Kingdoms; with the Form of solemnizing pla-tonic Matrimony, invented by the Athenian Society. To which is added their Amorous Quarrels on the Disputable Points relating to Love and Wedlock. The Copy of an Act to provide Maids with Husbands. As also a method for un-marrying those that are unequally yoked. Published to direct Bachelor and Virgin in their whole Amour. Clearly Dunton knew how to whet the appetite of women readers.

Although letters and replies, notes and queries, provided most of the material for the *Athenian Mercury*, Dunton included miscellaneous scraps of news. The paper continued for six years until, in February 1696, he proposed publishing the *Mercuries* in quarterly volumes, saying 'as the coffee-houses have the Votes (*of the House of Commons*) every day and nine newspapers every week' there was hardly room for his periodical, al-though he intended to resume his weekly half-sheet 'as soon as the glut of news is a little over'. This was at the time when William III had to con-tend with the plots of St Germain. High treason was a more exciting sub-ject for coffee-house patrons than the solutions given by the Athenians to 'the nice and curious questions proposed by the ingenious'.

Nevertheless, the reading public had appreciated Dunton's introduction of reading matter other than news and political mud-slinging, and this eccentric printer's principal contribution to the history of journalism can be seen to have been his realization of the power and influence that period-ical publications could have when applied to other subjects than news. The nineteen volumes of the *Athenian Mercury* were the precursors of a pub-lishing revolution that turned pamphlets and broadsheets into magazines, miscellanies, reviews, and journals. The *Athenian Oracle* (a selection from the periodical work) maintained that the aim was 'to advance all know-ledge and diffuse a general learning through the many, and by that civilize more men in a few years than Athens itself did of old during the ages it flourished'. There is no record of what number of *Athenian Mercuries* were printed each week, but whatever the size of its circulation there is no doubt it had a *succès d'estime*. Poems in honour of the periodical 'were written by the chief wits of the age', says Dunton. 'The Marquis of Halifax perused it; and the late Sir William Temple, a man of clear judgment and wonderful penetration, was pleased to honour me with frequent letters and questions.' Jonathan Swift, then secretary to Sir William Temple, sent an ode which was prefixed to the fifth supplement of the *Athenian Mercury* in 1691. This was the poem which begins:

30

Pardon ye great unknown, and far-exalted men,
The wild excursions of a youthful pen.

And it was accompanied by a very humble letter begging the honour of its
being printed and 'submitting it wholly to the correction of your pens'.
Jonathan Swift was a far from humble man by the time he became the
vitriolic Dean Swift, whereas the editor to whose judgment he so modestly
deferred, John Dunton, was to end his life in poverty and dire wretched-
ness. In an appeal to George I which he called *Dying Groans from the Fleet
Prison, or Last Shift for Life,* Dunton claimed to have had the most distinguished share in bringing about 'the general deliverance accomplished
by the accession of the House of Brunswick'. But his appeal was of no
avail to improve his desperate plight. The ingratitude of kings is proverbial,
and in any case it is unlikely that George I's estimation of John Dunton's
pamphlets as a power in the land was equal to that of their publisher.

Two years after the first appearance of the *Athenian Mercury*, and one
year before its sister publication the *Ladies' Mercury* was launched, there
appeared a monthly miscellany edited by Peter Anthony Motteux which,
although named the *Gentleman's Journal,* included features that were to
become very popular in women's magazines to come. The sub-title of the
Gentleman's Journal was *By way of a Letter to a Gentleman in the Country*;
but its contents clearly aimed to please the ladies of his household also.
Motteux himself claimed that his journal was 'patronized by the Queen
and much favoured by the ladies generally'. Besides news, history, philosophy and translations, it included anecdotes of the Town, gossipy paragraphs intended not only to entertain and titillate, but also to give useful information about the manners and modes of the *beau monde* to country
dwellers who might have occasion to visit London, Bath, or any other
fashionable city. It also published the words and music of currently popular songs, a feature which was adopted by many women's publications in
the second half of the eighteenth century. Motteux's *Gentleman's Journal*
offered indeed, in spite of John Dunton's high-minded claims for his
Ladies' Mercury, a more satisfying bill of fare for women than Dunton's
publication, which was mainly made up of the *cris de coeur* of correspondents. Moreover, some of the *cris* in the *Ladies' Mercury* were clearly intended to attract gentlemen readers as well as ladies. The more intimate
problems tended to be dealt with in a manner sufficiently bawdy to beguile
coffee-house customers at their most relaxed.

31

There was one question and answer in the first issue of the *Ladies Mercury* which is interesting in view of contemporary attitudes to virginity. It purported to come from a lady of quality who had been so seduced as to give up 'the very Soul of Beauty, my Honour, to a lewd and infamous Rifler'. Since this incident, she had met with the good fortune to marry a rich and worthy man, and she wanted the *Ladies' Mercury* to advise whether she should tell all to her husband. She was counselled to keep her peace. Sensible advice in any century, but in the eighteenth century, surely, the only possible advice. This deflowered young lady of quality was, indeed, most singularly fortunate in that she had secured a husband. Eighteenth-century fiction, whether in book form or in the guise of 'true tales' in a magazine, always carried the warning that one false or even foolish step invariably meant irrevocable ruin. A seduction or elopement never ended in marriage, neither with the seducer nor with any subsequent admirer. There were only two outcomes: desertion followed by death in childbirth; or childbirth, then desertion, followed by near starvation, prostitution, and death by a wasting or unnamed disease. The message and the moral were always the same: doomed is she who follows her heart and not her parents' wishes. Her parents never forgive her, she is forbidden to return to the family home, and no man ever looks on her afterwards as anything but fair game. As surely as night follows day, if a man persuades you into his 'protection' first, he will never marry you afterwards. And neither will anyone else when your protector has, inevitably, deserted you. This was the absolute rule in fictions about girls of the upper and middle classes. The humble village maiden, seduced in innocence, was occasionally allowed, after many years of shame and repentance, to marry a good honest working man, who, in the generosity of his heart, was prepared to overlook her past.

It is all too easy, from this present century, to look back and smile. But the fiction of a period always reflects the facts. And the facts of life for an eighteenth-century girl who defied the social code and the marriage mores of her class were unmercifully, unrelentingly harsh. Even if your 'protector' did not desert you before the birth of your inevitable baby, the chances of dying in childbirth were high. If you and your illegitimate child survived, the baby was the visible sign of your inward and spiritual disgrace. You were 'ruined' and branded for life. The world did not condemn the man. For a man, the code was quite different. He was expected to take what he could get. His prowess in seduction was a proof of virility and to be ad-

THE

Female Spectator.

VOL. I.

Ill Customs, by Degrees, to Habits rise,
Ill Habits soon become exalted Vice.
DRYDEN.

THE THIRD EDITION.

DUBLIN:

Printed for GEORGE and ALEXANDER EWING at the
Angel and *Bible* in *Dame-street*, Booksellers.
M.DCC.XLVII.

1. Title page and frontispiece to the *Female Spectator*, Vol I, 3rd edition, 1747.

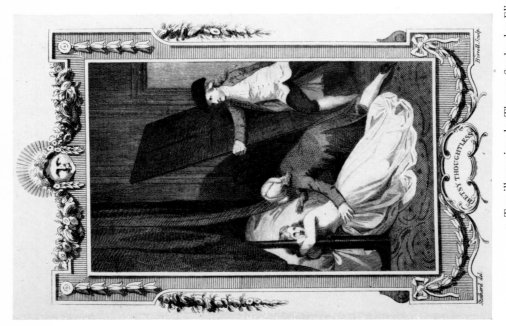

11. Two illustrations by Thomas Stothard to Eliza Haywood's novel *The History of Miss Betsy Thoughtless*

mired. Lord Chesterfield wrote to his son 'distinguish carefully between the pleasures of a man of fashion and the vices of a scoundrel'. The distinction seems in our eyes to have been altogether too fine, for most eighteenth-century gentlemen appear to have exercised the vices of scoundrels to all women socially their inferiors.

To the modern reader, the astonishing thing about Richardson's *Pamela, or Virtue Rewarded*, is how a man who has played every card in the pack to seduce Pamela, a man who has made more than one attempt to rape her, hiding in her wardrobe while she undresses and then following her into bed, a man who sends his servants to abduct her by force, and only offers her matrimony when every dishonourable strategy has failed to penetrate her virtue, is regarded by Pamela, from the moment he offers marriage in the last resort, as being all goodness, sweetness, and light, the very soul of honour. It is true that some people condemned this moral hypocrisy at the time the book was published; but there is a mass of evidence to show that seduction was a sport that was tacitly approved, even admired—a sport that kept rich and leisured gentlemen amused and exercised out of the fox-hunting season. No one expected them to marry their quarry, even if the victim were a girl of gentle birth who had been persuaded to elope in the belief that she was going straight to a marriage ceremony after climbing over her father's garden wall.

Every girl was at risk, since seduction was so often their only encounter with romance. Parental pressure on a girl to marry the man of their choice was ruthless. Wealth and position was the criterion for an eligible husband, not character, disposition, intelligence, or suitable age. Certainly not personal appearance—he could be ugly, gross and raddled. Under such pressure a girl could easily fall in love with any personable young man who attempted to seduce her, and elopement was her only escape from a marriage which she might well regard with horror and loathing. There is no more shocking revelation of this parental approach to marriage than in a book written in 1700 by the Marquis of Halifax and called *The Ladies' New-Year's Gift, or Advice to a Daughter*. This little treatise was an immediate and continuing success. It was admired by people as sensitive and intellectually avant-garde in their attitude to women as Richard Steele and Lady Mary Wortley Montagu—despite the fact that the Marquis was of the firm and unalterable conviction that 'there is Inequality in the Sexes and that for the better Oeconomy of the World, Men, who were to be the Law-givers, had the larger-Share of Reason bestow'd upon them'.

Lord Halifax wrote the book for his own daughter, then a girl of fifteen. It contains common sense in practical matters and the daily concerns of home-life, and shows broad tolerance on religious questions, unusual insight into the minds of children, penetration and considerable wisdom on the relations of mother and child. Yet when it comes to the subject of marriage, this tolerant, enlightened scholar and philosopher offers no other advice to Elizabeth than to 'submit' to the husband chosen for her by her parents. Having submitted, she was advised to observe carefully certain rules by which a humiliating position could best be turned to advantage: 'It is one of the Disadvantages belonging to your Sex, that young Women are seldom permitted to make their own Choice; their Friends' Care and Experience are thought safer Guides to them than their own Fancies'. This being so, he tells Elizabeth that there is nothing to be done but to endeavour 'to make that easy that falleth to their Lot, and by a wise Use of every Thing they may dislike in a Husband, turn that by degrees to be very supportable, which, if neglected, might in time beget an Aversion'. There is no escape, even if aversion is there to start with. And there will be no escape in the future—'Causes of Separation are so very Coarse'. And he tells her that 'the Supposition of your being the weaker Sex having without doubt a good Foundation, maketh it reasonable to subject it to the Masculine Dominion'. He then goes on to outline various kinds of husband she may have to submit to: the man who from the beginning is persistently unfaithful (she must affect ignorance of this); the cholerick or ill-humoured husband; the miserly 'Close-handed Wretch'; the feeble-minded husband; these can all be handled to her advantage in various ways. As to the man who is an habitual drunkard—'be wise and patient, and his Wine shall be on your Side; it will throw a Veil over your Mistakes. When he comes home, no Storms, no reproaching Look, and the Wine will naturally work out all in Kindness, which a Wife must encourage, let it be wrapped up in never so much Impertinence'.

When Elizabeth was nineteen, her father married her off splendidly and ruthlessly to the third Earl of Chesterfield, of whom W. E. Browning, his son's biographer, wrote: 'Little more need be told than that he was a man of morose disposition and violent passions.' She had four sons and two daughters and died while her eldest son, the writer of the famous *Letters to my Son* (1774) was still a child. His grandfather's *Advice to a Daughter* no doubt influenced the fourth Lord Chesterfield's cynical and worldly comments on women and marriage, but the general attitude was little altered at the end of the century from what it had been at the beginning, despite the many intellectual and scholarly women who concerned themselves with improving women's education and status—despite even the Blue Stockings, whose place in society was in fact achieved by their intellectual brilliance and wit more than by birth. Their coterie was by most people regarded as rather ridiculous, a target for jokes. Lord Halifax's *Advice* continued to be reprinted throughout the century, running through twenty-five editions, until in 1774 it was superseded in the same strain by Dr Gregory's *A Father's Legacy to his Daughter*—an astonishingly popular work that was savagely attacked by Mary Wollstonecraft in her *Vindication of the Rights of Women*, published in 1792.

It is very strange that Richard Steele should have admired the Marquis of Halifax's book, since he himself described the arranged marriages of his day with their settlements and jointures as 'bargains to cohabit', and wrote that if the system could be reformed 'a fine woman would no more be set up to auction as she is now'. It is even more odd that it should have been admired by Lady Mary Wortley Montagu, who herself had rebelled against the system. When Edward Wortley was wooing her, he tried to discover from her what were her father's exact financial terms, especially the size of her dowry. In her letter of reply she denied knowing it: 'People in my way are sold like slaves, and I cannot tell what price my master will put on me.' Wortley did not want to commit himself until he knew the price, and again he asked her. He even calculated for her how her father and brother could raise the price to £25,000, but then anxiously feared that his impertinence might raise the settlement demanded of himself. In the event his mercenary preoccupations resulted in a very bad bargain, since the negotiations were so long drawn out that Mary's father brought forward the elderly, unattractive, Lord Dorchester and forced him upon Mary to the point of fixing the wedding day. This brought things to a head, and the young couple eloped, thus forfeiting any settlements at all from either her father or his.

An illustration of the strength of social conventions and class differences in the eighteenth century can be found in Michael Sadleir's *Bulwer and his Wife*. He relates how General William Earle Bulwer of Heyden, when a young officer, carried off a beautiful girl from boarding-school and made her his mistress—'she was not of his class; and he could not so far throw off the conventions of his kind as to avow her his wife. But with a delicacy rather unexpected at such a time (the 1780s) he steadily refused during her life-time to consider regular marriage with anyone else.' A girl at boarding-school would certainly not have been of the artisan or labouring classes. She was most probably a prosperous tradesman's daughter.

The rules of society were ostensibly formed for the protection of women and girls. If they broke the rules they automatically lost that protection. Until a girl was safely married to a man of suitable position and fortune her father, legal guardian, or brothers, were the protectors of her inno-cence and virginity. Once married, the code was changed—at any rate in high society. Adultery was condoned as long as it was reasonably discreet. And any results of adulteries, whether acknowledged to be illegitimate or not, were quite happily absorbed into the family. There were irregularities in many of the greatest houses. At Devonshire House later in the century there was quite openly a *ménage à trois* of the Duke and Duchess and Lady Elizabeth Foster; and her illegitimate St. Jules and Clifford offspring were brought up with the legitimate Cavendishes, Fosters, and Ponsonbys. Society, that is aristocratic society, was mainly concerned with the preservation of impeccable surfaces. It was all part of the Age of Reason. But beneath the worldly wit and sophisticated conversation, beneath the calculated conduct that polished the social surface of their civilized exis-tence, the human heart was as vulnerable as in any other age. And al-though, amongst men, women were spoken of with coarseness and levity, there was at the same time a romantic, chivalrous sentimentality about feminine ignorance, innocence, purity and helplessness. Even Dr Johnson considered portrait-painting and the 'public practice of any art very in-delicate in a female', and later on in the century, the Rev. R. Polwhele's *The Unsex'd Females* (1798) made a furious attack on the indelicacies of botany. Botany was generally not considered a decent subject for young ladies to study, so one can assume that they were unlikely to have been taught the facts of life through the habits of birds and bees. The lower classes living in crowded dwellings cannot have escaped the facts, and country children would be familiar with the mating of animals. But girls of good family may well have been screened in innocence and ignorance until the day they were married—or seduced.

Chapter II

FASHIONABLE EDUCATION AND LONELY SCHOLARS

Boarding-schools for young ladies; the fashion for all things French.
Scholarly eccentrics. Mary Astell's Proposal *for a women's college; her*
Reflections on Marriage. *Elizabeth Elstob and her Anglo-Saxon grammar. The*
Ladies' Diary. *Its* Rules and Directions for Love and Marriage*; its*
mathematical questions and poetical enigmas. Delights for the Ingenious.
Continuing intellectual esteem of the Ladies' Diary.

ᘒᘒᘒᘒᘒᘒᘒᘒᘒᘒᘒᘒᘒᘒᘒᘒᘒᘒᘒᘒᘒᘒᘒᘒᘒᘒᘒᘒᘒᘒᘒᘒᘒᘒ

IGNORANT and innocent though girls of good family might be, they were not illiterate. They were taught French, reading, writing, and sufficient arithmetic to be able to keep household accounts; but the greatest importance was placed upon 'accomplishments': singing, dancing, painting, needlework. In 1703 a pamphlet was published named 'The Ladies' Catechism, useful for all Eminent Females, and Necessary to be learnt by all Young Gentlewomen that would attain to the Dignity of the Mode.' In effect it was an attack upon the manner in which girls were educated and in which married women conducted their lives. In particular it poured scorn on the fashion for all things French—'nothing will go down with the Town now but French Kickshaws, and now and then French Sauce comes in among them.'
The Catechism asks:

'How was you educated?'
　'At a Boarding-School.'
'After what manner?'
　'By the help of a French Dancing Master, a French Singing Master, and a French Waiting Woman. Before I could speak English plain, I was taught to jabber French; and learnt to Dance before I could go; in short, I danced French Dances at eight, sung French at ten, spoke it at thirteen, and before fifteen could talk nothing else.'
'And how do you govern your Family?'
　'As other ladies do: I love Gaming myself, and tolerate it among my

Servants; I leave them to their own licentious Appetites, to swear and curse, riot, drink and do what they please; I give 'em a great deal of Liberty and little Wages; and if the Steward gets the Housekeeper with Child, I make the Coachman marry her, and turn away the Footman for aspiring at my Woman; who I marry to my Lord's high-fed Chaplain, and give her six Changes of cast Cloathes for a Dowry; and sometimes fancy the Butler myself, because he is handsomer than my Husband.'

The daughters of merchants and rich tradesmen were almost invariably sent to boarding schools; and very often less rich tradesmen scraped and saved to send their daughters to schools where they would mix with girls in a better social position than their own, hoping that would give them a better chance in the matrimonial market. One of the most favoured boarding-schools was in Marylebone, kept by a Mrs Bellpine from about 1670 until well into the eighteenth century. She was the daughter of a French Minister, Monsieur La Marre, so everything was considered very *bon ton*. James Peller Malcolm in his *Anecdotes of the Manners and Customs of London during the Eighteenth Century* (published in 1810) wrote:

'Even in the year 1759 two or three houses might be seen in almost every village with the inscription *Young Ladies Boarded and Educated,* where every description of tradesmen sent their children to be instructed, not in the useful attainments necessary for humble life, but the arts of coquetry and self-consequence—in short, those of a *young lady*. The person who received the children had then the sounding title of Governess; and French and Dancing-masters prepared the girl for the hour when contempt for her parents' deficiencies was to be substituted for affection and respect. Instead of reading their native language with propriety and just emphasis, it was totally neglected . . . while the lady repeated familiar words of the French language with a sound peculiar to boarding schools, and quite unintelligible to a native of France.'

This may have been true of many boarding schools, but the weekly periodical *Records of Love* carried an announcement in its issue of 10 March 1710, of an establishment where the fashion for all things French was not followed to the exclusion of other subjects. The advertisement emphasized that the reading and writing of English was given first priority:

'At Mrs Carey's School in Old Bosvit Court near Temple Bar, young

4. Trade card of Mrs. Masquerier's boarding school, from the collection of Sir Ambrose Heal (*British Museum*)

Gentlewomen are carefully and expeditiously taught that so necessary, though so much neglected part of Education, *Orthography*: or the Art of Reading, and Writing true *English*—by Methods so successful and familiar that the Scholars' Improvement is shown in a very short Time, as several Parents have found by happy Experience for above these twenty Years past. All manner of Needle-works are likewise taught to the nicest Degree of Perfection; as also French, Latin, Writing, Arithmetick, Singing, Dancing, and Musick, with all other necessary Accomplishments too numerous to insert.'

Girls of aristocratic birth were almost always educated in their own homes. They would have a governess for the 'necessary accomplishments' and she would also instruct them in the elements of reading, writing, and arithmetic. If they showed any real eagerness to learn, and their brothers had a tutor, they might be allowed to join them in rather more advanced studies.

39

But the amount of education they received chiefly depended upon whether their parents considered anything more than 'accomplishments' of any importance. Many daughters of aristocratic families living in great country estates ran practically wild in their childhood, and were only brought in from the garden and polished up when they got near marriageable age. On the other hand, a girl with a scholarly father or mother, living in a home which contained a well-stocked library, would be taught by her parents and encouraged to study far more than she would ever have done if sent to a boarding-school. The late seventeenth and early eighteenth century is remarkable for the number of talented women who, despite the general assumption that women were born with lesser intellects than men, and despite the very severe social prejudice against women who published work under their own names, did manage to employ their gifts to some purpose and leave behind them a legend of learning—in many cases with published proof of intellectual gifts of the highest order.

Damaris Cudworth, for example, who became Lady Masham, was the daughter of a Regius Professor of Hebrew at Cambridge. John Locke, the philosopher and educationalist, wrote of her in 1690: 'The Lady is so well versed in theological and philosophical studies, and of such an original mind, that you will not find many men to whom she is not superior in wealth of knowledge and ability to profit by it.' And Lady Masham was not the only female disciple of John Locke to study in regions of learning generally considered quite beyond the bounds of female comprehension: philosophy, the sciences, and higher mathematics. But these scholarly women studied in their own homes, in all humility and quietness, for their own pleasure and satisfaction. They did not stir up any controversy over accepted attitudes to women. They did not openly challenge the assumption that the destiny of women was to be subservient to men, and above all to be amiable to them, to bear and rear their children, to conduct their households, and to restrict their activities to the confines of their own homes.

The only challengers of this assumption were the Quakers. Margaret Fell, wife of George Fox, advocated women preachers in the early 1650s. Barbara Blangdon was persecuted and imprisoned in 1654 for preaching in the West Country. Outside the Society of Friends, the first shot in the feminist campaign, which was to be waged for the next two hundred years and more, was fired by Mary Astell in 1694 with *A Serious Proposal to the Ladies for the Advancement of their True and Greatest Interest*.

Her proposal, which she published under the pseudonym of 'Lover of

A Serious

PROPOSAL

TO THE

LADIES,

FOR THE

Advancement of their

True and Greateſt

INTEREST.

In Two Parts.

By a Lover of her S E X.

L O N D O N:

Printed for *Richard Wilkin* at the *King's-Head* in St. *Paul's Church-Yard,* 1697.

5. Title page of Mary Astell's *Serious Proposal to the Ladies,*
4th edition, 1697

her Sex', was no less than to start a College for women, that would provide an escape from the only alternatives open to so many girls at that time: a mercenary marriage or a humiliatingly dependent spinsterhood. It was said that Lady Elizabeth Hastings offered £10,000 to start the project but that Bishop Burnet contrived to stop it because he suspected a Popish plot to revive the nunneries. Mary Astell's declared purpose in founding a seminary was 'to stock the Kingdom with pious and prudent Ladies', which seems to have been a declaration open to different interpretations by different people. At any rate, the offer of £10,000 was withdrawn. It was another century and a half before the first college for women was founded: Queen's College in Harley Street, London, in 1848. This was planned as a College for Governesses—pious and prudent governesses, of course.

Three years after Mary Astell's *Proposal* came Judith Drake's *Essay in Defence of the Female Sex*, 1697, and also Daniel Defoe's *The Education of Women* which included 'An Essay on Projects on an Academy for Women'. Defoe criticized Mary Astell's plan on the ground that it would impose too great a restraint on the levity of youth, and savoured too much of the nunnery. The plans he outlined himself were designed to establish good discipline, but without spying or execessive supervision. At the same time 'Intrigue must be guarded against and an Act of Parliament should make it a felony without Clergy for any Man to enter by Force or Fraud . . . or solicit any Woman, though it were to Marry, while she was in the House'. Defoe was a stout champion of the principal of equal opportunity for women. He felt it a 'barbarity' to deny them learning . . . 'I would have Men take Women for Companions and Educate them to be fit for it'. Instead of which 'their Youth is spent to teach them to stitch and sew or make baubles. They are taught to read, indeed, and perhaps to write their names or so, and that is the height of a woman's education'.

Even writers with advanced views on women's education at this time still in the main concurred with the accepted customs of marriage. Astonishingly, Mary Astell looked upon marriage as a divinely appointed state of subjection for women, not intended for their happiness. It should be regarded as an institution which gave them unique opportunities for exercising the qualities of patience and endurance that were the best preparation for Heaven. She stated that no lady of quality should fall in love. Modesty required 'that a Woman should not love before Marriage, but only make Choice of one whom she can love hereafter: she who has none but innocent Affections being easily able to fix them where Duty requires'.

THE COMPLEAT BEAU

This vain gay thing sets up for man, But see ni fate attends him
The pow'dring Barber first began, The Barber Surgeon ends h.

AN

ESSAY

In Defence of the

FEMALE SEX.

In which are inserted the

CHARACTERS

OF

A Pedant,	} {	A Vertuoso,
A Squire,	} {	A Poetaster,
A Beau,	} {	A City-Critick, &c.

In a Letter to a Lady.

Written by a Lady.

The Third Edition with additions.

Since each is fond of his own ugly Face ;
Why show'd you when we hold it break the Glass?
Prol. to Sir *F. Flutter*

LONDON,
Printed for *A. Roper* at the *Black Boy,* and *R. Clavel*
at the *Peacock,* both in *Fleetstreet,* 1697.

6. Title page and frontispiece to Judith Drake's *Essay in Defence of the Female Sex,* 1697

The ladies of her Seminary would refuse unsuitable offers of marriage, but if friends provided 'a Christian and ingenious Gentleman, equal in all ways to the Lady whom he addressed', she assumed that he would be accepted. Indeed, virtuous and prudent gentlemen would be encouraged to apply to her seminary for wives, and this was put forward as an inducement to fathers of small means to place their daughters with her. A gentleman who chose one of them would, for his part, get a good bargain since 'Such a Lady, if she brings less will not waste so much'; and since they would all be ladies of quality he would have the satisfaction of 'preserving the Purity of his Blood', rather than gaining 'a weighty Bag' with a 'wealthy Upstart'. A father should consider five or six hundred pounds to the seminary easily spared, although it would be a negligible marriage dowry for a Lady of Birth. And if a daughter should reach a mature age unmarried, the seminary was still an inexpensive solution for her parents since 'so often the Daughter who despairs of a Husband will fly to some dishonourable Match as a last Resort, and the Father finds himself with an idle Fellow and perhaps a Race of beggarly Children to hang on him and provide for'.

In 1700 Mary Astell wrote a tract entitled *Reflections Upon Marriage*, giving some original arguments regarding the birthrights and privileges of women, or rather the lack of them. It was said that she wrote so feelingly on the subject because she had been disappointed in a marriage contract with an eminent clergyman. She certainly had her friends in high church places. Although Bishop Burnet had remonstrated so strongly—and so effectively—against her proposed Academy, Bishop Attenbury was an admirer of her scholarship. He expressed astonishment at such learning in a woman, an astonishment hardly complimentary to the sex as a whole. He was immensely impressed by a sheet of notes she wrote when she returned to him his sermon delivered on the election of the Lord Mayor, which she had requested him to send her—a request that no doubt flattered his vanity. Whether it was Bishop Attenbury whom the gossips decided had jilted her, or some other eminent cleric we do not know, but Mary Astell was probably the first of the feminists to be martyred by sneering suppositions that it was only women who failed to get a husband who bothered themselves about women's rights. Courageously, when her critics were at their most loquacious, she published a second edition of *Reflections Upon Marriage*, adding a long Preface in answer to some of their objections. This book and its preface were praised by Ballard as being written with 'a vast deal of wit and smartness: making perhaps the strongest defence that ever yet appeared in print of the *rights* and *abilities* of the fair sex'.

Mary Astell was not only courageous in publishing her unpalatable opinions and running the gauntlet of social scorn and derision; she was also brave in bearing physical suffering. Ballard tells how, when she had a cancer of the breast that she had for a long time dressed and managed as best she could for herself, she finally went to the Rev. Mr Johnson, a gentleman very eminent for his skill in surgery, and entreated him to take it off. There were, of course, no anaesthetics then, 'but regardless of the sufferings and pain she was to undergo she refused to have her hands held, and went through the operation without the least struggling or resistance, or even so much as giving a groan or a sigh'. It is easy to forget, until one comes upon such an anecdote, how much women had to contend with physically in those early days of medicine and surgery.

Elizabeth Elstob (1683–1756) was less of a crusading feminist, more of a scholar, than Mary Astell. She specialized in Anglo-Saxon and Teutonic languages, and was one of the most learned scholars of her time, male or female. She was taught at first by her mother 'who was a great admirer of learning, especially in her own sex', and later went to live with her brother William Elstob, Fellow of University College, Oxford. John Nichols reports in his *Literary Anecdotes of the Eighteenth Century* that she was the 'first woman that ever attempted that ancient and obsolete language Anglo-Saxon. An excellent linguist in other respects, mistress of her own and the Latin tongue, and seven other languages, a good antiquary and divine.' She published an Anglo-Saxon grammar; but after her brother died, led an uncomfortable and penurious life teaching children at Evesham and later the children of the Duchess of Portland. Nichols quotes a description of Elizabeth Elstob by Rowe Mores: 'Companion of her brother's studies, a female student in the university . . . a Northern lady of an ancient Family and a genteel Fortune; but she pursued too much the Drug called Learning, and in that Pursuit failed of being careful of any one Thing necessary. In her latter Years she was Tutoress in the Family of the Duke of Portland, where we have visited her in her sleeping-room at Bulstrode, surrounded with Books and dirtiness, the usual Appendages of Folk of learning.' Clearly Mr Rowe Mores was not a feminist; and if he looked upon learning as a drug he will hardly have approved of the *Ladies' Diary*, or *The Woman's Almanack* which first appeared at the end of 1703 for the year 1704. The particular speciality of this publication was its mathematical problems, really tough problems that could only be tackled by those well advanced in the study of geometry and algebra. There were also abstruse literary enigmas to be solved, and paradoxes of geography and astrology to be pondered over.

The *Ladies' Diary* was an annual publication edited by John Tipper, who was a mathematician of distinction and Master of Bablake School, Coventry. It was published by the Stationers' Company, and was at first only a four-page sheet, but it was the forerunner of all the ladies' pocket books and diaries which became such an elegant feature of eighteenth-century publishing. These little books included a calendar and the usual information found in almanacks; and in addition all kinds of domestic information, cookery receipts, medicines, hints on the toilet. They gave space for their owner's own daily entries and household accounts; and they often included a few verses or moral tales, occasionally one or two engravings. Their contents were a small-print précis of the most popular features in women's periodicals—they were magazines in miniature.

The Stationers' Company, who had a monopoly of almanack publishing, priced this first ladies' diary at 'dearer by one half' than any other almanack they were preparing for 1704. Yet by New Year's Day they were able to claim that they had sold out their entire printing of 4,000 copies. The editor, in setting out his intentions in the preface to the first issue, shows a keen conception of the kind of features likely to appeal to the intelligent women readers he hoped to attract:

'Under the Reign of so great and glorious a Woman as our Queen Anne, I hope the Woman's Almanack is not unseasonably published: a Book designed on purpose for the Diversion and Use of the Fair Sex, which shall contain (besides those things common to other Almanacks) something to suit all Conditions, Qualities, and Humours. The Ladies may here find their Essences, Perfumes, and Unguents; the Waiting-women and Servants, excellent directions in Cookery, Pastry, and Confectionery; the Married shall have Medicines for their Relief, and Instructions for the Advancement of their Families; the Virgin directions for Love and Marriage; the Serious be accommodated with instance of Virtue and Religion; the Jovial with innocent Amusements and pleasant Adventures; Mothers shall have Rules for the Education of their children; and those that delight in Gardening, Painting, or Music, shall not want Assistance to advance their Pleasures; in sum, the Ingenious shall have something exalted to exercise their Art, and the meanest some Subjects adapted to their Level . . . Nothing shall be inserted that is mean and trifling; nothing to raise a Blush or intimate an evil Thought. To conclude, nothing shall here be, but (what all Women ought to be) innocent, modest, instructive, and agreeable.'

Cookery, cosmetics, medicines, innocent amusements; love and marriage, virtue and religion; children's education, gardening, painting, music; everything innocent, modest, instructive, and agreeable . . . this summary of contents, so fascinatingly similar to the contents of so many women's magazines to come, does not sound like a syllabus to tax the intelligence. It was a few years later that Mr Tipper introduced the harder stuff. Playing his publication in gently, he led off with Perfections of the Fair Sex: Of the Beauty, Excellency, and Perfections of the Fair Sex; of Love and Marriage, with Directions relating thereto; of Marriage Ceremonies in divers Countries; with divers other very delightful Subjects, intermixed with a variety of Poems, collected from the choicest and best Authors.' And follows with:

Rules and Directions for Love and Marriage

1. Never marry a vicious Man in Hope of reclaiming him afterwards.
2. Agreeableness of Humour and Affection, with an equality of Birth, and Fortune, are the surest Foundations of a lasting Happiness in Marriage.
3. Never entertain a Man very much above your Quality and Fortune for your Lover, he having in all probability an ill Design upon your Honour; a sad Instance of which we have in Cloe.

There follows a moral tale entitled 'The Philanderer and Cloe'.

In 1706 the editor advertised for readers' contributions in the form of 'verses, enigmas, and pleasant stories'; but in 1707 he wrote that he was convinced by a multitude of letters that enigmas and mathematical questions gave the greatest satisfaction and delight to the obliging Fair, and substituted for the cooking receipts two easy arithmetical problems and some paradoxes, an amendment which in the next issue he claimed had proved highly acceptable to his lady readers. Nevertheless, in this issue he also pursued the eternal topic of love and marriage, giving some 'curious Remarks and important Advice towards the Conduct of the Fair in their time of Courtship, that wicked and designing Men may not impose upon, and ruin them'. He began by

'taking Notice of the Hardship the fair Virgin is reduced to, in that she may not court the Man she loves, but only accept in Marriage one of those who happens to court her, whereas the Men may address themselves to whom they please; this, I must confess, is very unequal, and nothing is more just than the Maid's complaint in the following verses:

> Custom, alas! does partial prove,
>   Nor gives us even measure;
> A pain to maids it is to love,
>   But 'tis to man a pleasure.
>
> They freely can their thoughts explain,
>   But ours must burn within;
> We have got eyes, and tongues in vain,
>   And truth from us is sin.
>
> Men to new joys and conquests fly
>   And yet no hazard run;
> Poor we are left, if we deny,
>   And if we yield, undone.
>
> Then equal laws let custom find,
>   Nor thus the Sex oppress;
> More freedom give to woman-kind,
>   Or give to mankind less.'

There follows a description of 'those Methods and cunning Artifices which designing Men take, to decoy and ruin the Honour and Reputation of the Fair'. First comes the flattery of wit and beauty, 'then will they tell you how fading Beauty is, and that in a few years it will undiscerned steal away'. This point is made more poignant by a poem of four verses, the last verse being:

> Night's shades do pass, and Day comes on,
>   But Beauty has no second Dawn;
> The Sun returns, but Beauty never,
>   When Beauty sets, it sets for ever.

The next inducement to disaster comes in the shape of gifts: 'when no other Ways can overcome the Affections of Women, Gold, Money, Gifts,

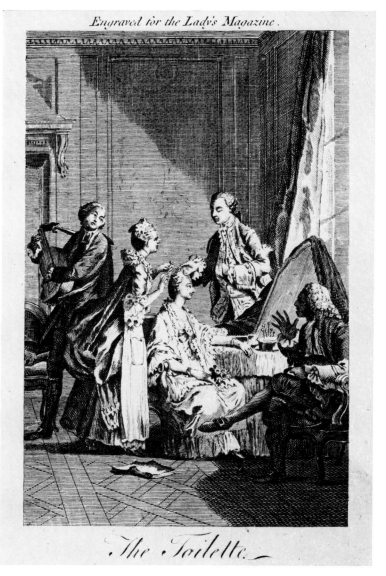

The Toilette

III. Engraving from the *Lady's Magazine*, 1776

Mysteries of Udolpho.

Fate sits on these dark battlements, and frowns,
And, as the portals open to receive me,
Her voice, in sullen echoes, through the courts
Tells of a nameless deed.

and Bribes have done it.' And the writer continues: 'When the incautious Virgin is thus prepared by her Lover's Praises and Gifts, then he pursues her with Prayers, Vows, Tears, Promises, Oaths, Flatteries. He pretends he cannot forbear thinking of her divine Perfections day nor night, and that he cannot rest in his Bed for dreaming of her. These are the Wiles and Strategems laid to betray the Fair; these are the chief of those Methods that are made use of to sully their Honour, and despoil them of Innocence:

> Thus the sly Monsters of the Wood beguile
> Their heedless Prey: a while they kill they smile;
> The Basilisk, with poisoned Glances kills,
> The Crocodile, her fraudful Tears distills;
> Unwary Passengers, they thus decoy,
> And fawn on those they purpose to destroy.'

By 1710, Tipper had dropped most of the domestic features in the *Ladies' Diary* and was devoting most of the almanack to mathematical questions and poetical enigmas, although he also included 'A Discourse on the Nature of Love, of the various Passions it raiseth in the Soul, particularly in the Absence and Presence of the beloved Object, and the Disorders it causeth the Body.' The diary for 1711 presented the 'beautiful and charming Females' with six enigmas, six arithmetical questions, and two geographical questions. There was also a prize enigma, with the promise of twenty diaries to the lady who sent in the first correct answer, and 'likewise a prize Question, with the affluence of twelve Diaries to that Person (whether Man or Woman) who sends me the first Answer thereto'. These competitions proved so popular that in the next issue of the *Ladies' Diary* the editor was able to tell his readers that in one day he received twenty-eight letters, and above a hundred during the year. He now filled the diary exclusively with questions, enigmas, and answers, and in 1714 was claiming 'its Usefulness is conspicuous considering it is profitable, commendable, and diverting, and has excited and won the Fair Sex to a Love for mathematical Learning; the Utility of which laudable Science I need not describe'.

The success of the *Ladies' Diary* had encouraged John Tipper to launch in January 1711 a monthly called *Delights for the Ingenious, or A Monthly Entertainment for both Sexes*. This publication took on a lighter tone, setting out to provide 'a vast Variety of pleasant Enigmas, delightful arithmetical Questions, witty Epigrams, surprising Adventures, and amazing Paradoxes, together with Songs, Anagrams, Emblems, Dialogues, Elegies, Epitaphs, and other useful and diverting Subjects in Prose and Verse'. The editor urged all gentlemen and ladies to 'contribute original Copies of Verses or any other Thing proper to carry on this Design'. They were also invited to compete for prizes in the same way as in the *Ladies' Diary*, and John Tipper seems to have relied to a large extent on his almanack readers to provide him with material for his monthly periodical. Unfortunately they did not come up to his expectations in this matter, and after the first six months he had to restrict *Delights for the Ingenious* to quarterly issues. Two of these were produced, but the end of the year saw the end of the publication. In contrast, Tipper's *Ladies' Diary* continued for over a century and a half, until 1871, changing its title in 1840 to the *Ladies' & Gentlemen's Diary*. During the second half of the eighteenth century various Appendices, Companions, and Supplements to the *Ladies' Diary* were published. The first of these was the *Palladian, or Appendix to the Ladies' Diary, 1749*. The next was the *Gentlemen's and Ladies' Diary* and *Palladian*, 1757, of which there were a variety of editions up to 1779. And from 1788 to 1806 there was *A Supplement to the Ladies' Diary, containing a List of all the Enigmas, etc.*

To return to the early years of the *Ladies' Diary*, Henry Beighton, who succeeded to the editorship on John Tipper's death in 1713, wrote in 1718:

'I believe that the Diary has the good Fortune to fall into a multitude of Hands which mathematical Books seldom or never would and that rather because Almanacks are generally bought, and at a small price; and especially at such a Season of the Year when almost everybody may have Leisure from Sports or Gaming to try their Skill in the Enigmas and Questions.

'The Enigmas cause the Ladies to read much Poetry and History, as may be seen by their Composition; the answering of them puts Persons into a serious and methodical Way of thinking on any Subject, which by all is allowed no small Advantage to the Mind. And that the Rest of the Fair Sex may be encouraged to attempt Mathematics and philosophical Knowledge, they here see that their Sex have as clear Judgements, a sprightly quick Wit, and penetrating Genius, and as discerning and sagacious Faculties as ours. Foreigners would be amazed when I show them no less than 400 or 500 several Letters from so many several Women, with Solutions geometrical, arithmetical astronomical, and philosophical.'

The readers' letters published in the Diary show from their addresses that the publication reached the farthest parts of the country. To take a small sample, we find letters and solutions to problems coming from St Ives, Heyshot, Portsmouth, Lynn, Northampton, Carmarthenshire, Cumberland . . . they even came from Ireland, and the Canary Islands. Some people evidently had difficulty in obtaining the Diary, because the Editor wrote in the issue of 1717: 'I generally find a Complaint from most Parts of the want of Diaries, which is their Booksellers fault only. I am confident they might dispose of many more if they could. To remedy this, those Persons waiting need only send by any Hand to Stationers' Hall, Ludgate, and be furnished at any time. There is indeed an excuse by them urg'd, that the Stamps* have hindered the Sale, which, though true, the Diary out-sells the rest, there scarce any besides selling above 6,000 or 7,000 yearly.'

A sales figure of over 7,000, even if exaggerated by the proud editor, was indeed remarkable considering that the population of England and Wales at the beginning of the eighteenth century was only about five-and-a-half million all told, including illiterates, babies, the blind and the insane. The *Ladies' Diary* was not only a pioneer, but also a best seller. It had a *succès d'estime* as well as financial success, two things that do not usually go together. Furthermore, it deserves a place in the long drawn out saga of women's education. And not only women's. A correspondent to the Diary in 1717, a Mr Meredith Jones who had been a tutor of mathematics and sciences, wrote: 'I know this Day many eminent Men that owe (as I have heard them confess it) their Knowledge in these Mysteries to the ingenious Mr Tipper deceas'd. I mean owe it so far as his Diary was the first Occasion of applying themselves in that way.' And its permanent value was recognized by a compilation made from it in 1775 by Charles Hutton FRS, Professor of Mathematics in the Royal Military Academy. He called it *The Diarian Miscellany*, and it contained 'all useful and entertaining Parts, both Mathematical and Poetical, extracted from the *Ladies' Diary*, from the beginning of that Work in the year 1705, down to the end of the Year 1773'. In his preface, Mr Hutton quotes 'the late ingenious Mr Thomas Simpson, who was one of the worthy Compilers of the original *Ladies' Diary* . . .':

'For upwards of half a Century this small Performance, sent abroad in

* Stamp Duty on newspapers, pamphlets, and periodical publications imposed from 1712 at 1d a sheet, increased progressively to 4d by 1815, and not finally abolished until 1855.

the poor Dress of an Almanack, and under a Title not calculated to raise the highest Expectations, has contributed more to the Study and Improvement of the Mathematics than half the Books professedly written on the Subject. The most celebrated Authors now among us, have contributed to promote the Reputation of the *Ladies' Diary*.'

Indeed the *Ladies' Diary* is proof that home-bound women of the eighteenth century did not all have homely wits by any means. The preface to the issue of 1721 is a revealing summary of the general attitude to women's education prevailing at the time and to the new thinking about it that was just beginning to break through:

'They say Learning makes a Woman proud and impertinent; 'tis not the business of their Sex; the Management of their Families, and Religion, ought to be their Study. But for my Part, I cannot see that the Search after Truth and Reason, the Improvement of the Mind and duly rectifying the Judgements by these rules, and by the unerring Opinions of the wisest Men, should any more conduce to the bringing a Woman into Errors, than the Search for Virtue should be thought the only way to teach us Vice. Nor can I conceive that a Woman who does mathematically demonstrate that the Whole is equal to all its Parts, or two and two make four, is less capable of managing her Household, governing her Servants, and giving her Children due Education. Nor will she be less a Christian for understanding the System of the Universe; but on the contrary, admire that infinite Wisdom in the Creator, who alone could make and govern Things so vastly surpassing our Comprehension. . . . Ignorance never sets a Value on any Person, but has always been found a constant Attendant on Self-conceit and Impudence; when Learning is the Way to Modesty and good Manners. Ignorance is forever incapable of doing Right; but Knowledge like a Diamond polished, more illustriously shines.'

Chapter III

ESSAY PAPERS AND NEWSPAPER WOMEN

Richard Steele's championship of women; his writing for them in the Tatler *and* Spectator. *Journals and essay-papers; the* Spinster *and the* Lover. *Mrs Mary Manley and her* New Atlantis; *her* Female Tatler. *Thomas Baker's* Female Tatler. *Mrs Manley succeeds Swift as editor of the* Examiner. *Women printers, booksellers, and publishers during the reign of Queen Anne. Mrs Elizabeth Powell of the* Charitable Mercury. *Her flight to the Continent and return to publish the* Orphan Reviv'd.

ᔧᕪ

RICHARD STEELE was one of the very few male writers of the early eighteenth century who believed a woman could be as intelligent as a man—or nearly. Although in later life he veered round to the orthodox attitudes of the male establishment, in the first flush of his young manhood and writing vigour he entered the lists as a chivalrous exposer of women's wrongs. Many of his essays in the *Tatler* and the *Spectator* attacked accepted attitudes towards the education of young ladies and the contemporary fashion of treating with contemptuous badinage women's hopeless legal position in marriage, their humiliating position in spinsterhood. He wrote indignantly of the dependence of unmarried women upon relatives, saying that there was no reason why it should not be open to them 'to go into a Way of Trade for their Maintenance'.

Steele also wrote of the evil effect upon young girls of enforced idleness and ignorance, saying that if they were better educated 'the unnatural Marriages which happen every Day' would be prevented. He attacked the custom of jointures and settlements: 'The World is mercenary even to the buying and selling of our very Persons.' One cannot help feeling that his own marriage placed him in no position to joust at mercenary marriages. In 1705 he had married an elderly widow with extensive estates in Barbados. She confirmed his expectations by dying the year after their marriage. At her funeral he made the acquaintance of his second wife, the daughter of a Welsh landowner, who according to Mrs Manley was 'a cry'd up beauty'. They were married a few months later. The DNB records that the lady, 'although genuinely attached to her husband, was imperious and exacting; the gentleman ardent and devoted, but incurably erratic and impulsive'. If he was genuinely ardent and impulsive, we can forgive him his haste in marrying her so swiftly after burying his property-owning widow; but we cannot discount her being the daughter of a man with large properties.

However hypocritical he may seem in his denouncement of mercenary marriages, Steele was a courageous journalist in his demand that there should be compassion for prostitutes. Most prostitutes, he suggested, had got into their tragic way of trade through small fault of their own: 'Many are taken into such Hands without the least Suspicion, previous Temptation, or Admonition, to what Place they are going'. And again: 'Regard is to be had to their Circumstances when they fell, to the uneasy Perplexity under which they lived under senseless and severe Parents, and the Importunity of Poverty, to the Violence of Passion at its Beginning well grounded.' Of course he aroused virtuous wrath in some quarters. One outraged reader wrote to the *Spectator*: 'Your Papers which regard the fallen Part of the fair Sex are, I think, written with an indelicacy which makes them unworthy to be inserted in the Writings of a Moralist who knows the World.' Nevertheless, from the first number of the *Tatler* on 12 April 1709, Steele found a new reading public whom he continued to interest and amuse, scold, cajole, and beguile, until the end of his connection with the *Spectator*, three years and nine months later.

The *Tatler* came out three times a week to catch the country mails, and its readers were largely drawn from the increasingly numerous middle class. It purposed

> 'to bring Philosophy out of the Closets Schools and Colleges to dwell in Clubs and Assemblies, at Tea-tables and in Coffee-houses . . . to unite Merriment with Decency . . . no obscene Ideas, no Satires upon Priesthood marriage, and the like popular Topics of Ridicule; no private Scandal, nor anything that may tend to the Defamation of particular Persons, Families, or Societies.'

And Steele made no secret about setting out to please the 'Fair Sex'—in whose honour, he said, 'he had chosen the title of his publication'. This could be considered a somewhat back-handed compliment, implying that it was mainly females who indulged in the tattle of idle gossip and frivolous chatter. It would not have pleased those readers who were more feminist than feminine. But then Steele made no pretence of being high-brow. In the first half-dozen *Tatlers* he included a 'Poetical Tale for Ladies', an account of two captivating belles, a discourse on a lover, and a report of a feminine conclave presided over by fair Sappho. Later he introduced Jenny Distaff, Bickerstaff's half-sister, as the mouthpiece for feminine views on love and marriage. Sometimes she was even characterized as editor of the paper, and published awful warnings from her own experience about the results of straying from the path of prudence. In the two-hundredth number of the *Tatler* Steele claimed, with justice, to have devoted the greater part of his time 'to the service of the Fair Sex'. And it was women of the middle classes whom he most benefited, because it was they who were most humiliatingly at risk from the immorality and extravagance of the self-elected ruling society which provided the prototypes for social success. The 'wits' were all-powerful. Their ridicule was ruthless. They could damage a woman's reputation equally whether she provided a target by her prudery or by her licence. Clerics and religious bodies thundered against the morals and mischiefs of Society, but Steele and Addison attacked what they called 'Fop Men' and 'Fop Women' by the far more effective weapon of satire and ridicule. Addison, like Steele, wrote for women readers as well as men; and in *Spectator No. 10* he claims 'there are none to whom this Paper will be more useful than to the female World'.

Three months after the *Spectator* ceased publication, Steele announced in the *Guardian* that one of his objects was 'the Improvement of Ladies', and that he proposed to offer for their entertainment 'what passes at the Tea-table of Lady Lizard'. Under the pseudonym of Nestor Ironside he discoursed upon female poets, the education of young ladies, their introduction to the world, their reading, their use of leisure, with sketches of Lady Lizard's daughters in which his readers might recognize themselves, and elevating instances of women who had so 'improved their Minds by Books' that they 'attained to Posts of Honour'.

Steele and Addison not only wooed and won a new kind of reader, but they also created a new form of journalism. This form had, it is true, to some extent been anticipated by John Dunton's *Pegasus* (1696), which provided, 'with News and a Jacobite Courant', what he called an Observator—a dissertation or serialized instruction upon some moral, political, or historical subject of topical interest. These Observators were not unlike the *Tatler* essays but were more heavy going. It was the light, witty essays in the *Tatler* that led to the 'journals'. These first journals were six-page publications whose main feature was an essay on exact *Tatler* lines; but they included more news, foreign affairs, and London intelligence. Addison in the *Spectator* had declared 'my Paper has not in it a single Word of News, a Reflection of Politics, nor a Stroke of Party'. The back page of the journals printed advertisements and 'Stop Press' news. It was the essay that made them journals as distinct from newspapers. There were also a number of slighter 'essay-papers' consisting of virtually nothing but an essay, of which Steele himself produced several: the *Reader* (1714); the *Englishman* (1715): the *Plebeian* (1719); the *Spinster* (1714); the *Lover* (1714); *Town Talk, In a Letter to a Lady in the Country* (1715–16); *Chit-Chat* (1716), in which Steele wrote under the pseudonym of Humphrey Philroye. As can be gauged from their titles, these essay-papers were addressed foremostly to women.

In the first number of the *Spinster*, Steele wrote under the name of Rachel Woolpack, and excused the title of his publication by reminding his readers that spinster was not originally an opprobious term, but referred to the highly laudable 'Industry of female Manufacturers', in other words spinners. The OED dates from 1719 the use of the word spinster for 'an unmarried woman; especially an "old maid" ', but only from 1823 the word 'spinsterhood' as 'the condition of being an unmarried woman, especially one advancing in years'. As the eighteenth century advanced, the unmarried woman of a family ceased to be an economical asset in her capacity of spinner, weaver, and seamstress, because less of these labours were done in the home. Also it was becoming fashionable for gentle-women to leave all household tasks to the servants.

The most long-lived of these 'essay-papers' was the *Lover*, published during 1714, which ran to forty numbers. In this publication Steele wrote under the pseudonym of Marmaduke Myrtle, Gent., with the motto *Virginibus puerisque canto*, and regaled his readers with accounts of the 'Province of Love and all Transactions relating to that Passion'. A later edition entitled *The Lover, to Which is Added the Reader*, came out in 1715 'by the same Author'. In 1718 there was a second edition of the *Lover and Reader*, this time 'By the Author of the *Tatler* and *Spectator*'. In the *Theatre* (1720) Steele continued his courtship of women by presenting his views through the medium of the illustrious Sophronia and her tea-table companions, and this ran for twenty-seven numbers.

Steele and Addison can be said to have achieved what Addison claimed to be his object in the dedication to the first volume of the *Spectator*: 'to offer a Work which endeavours to Cultivate and Polish Human Life'. And later, in *Spectator 58*, 'to establish among us a Taste of polite Writing'. This they undoubtedly did; and their influence pervaded much of the subsequent writing of the eighteenth century. Their style, 'writing in an air of common speech . . . familiar, not stylized in any way', was consciously or unconsciously followed—not only in the two hundred odd periodicals started in imitation of the *Tatler* and the *Spectator*, but in the lucid, easy, unpurpled prose of later eighteenth-century novels, belles-lettres, journals and correspondence. It seems ironical that Jane Austen in *Northanger Abbey* could, in referring to the bound volumes of the *Spectator*, say that it was unlikely any young lady would 'be occupied by any part of that voluminous publication of which either the matter or manner would not disgust a young person of taste . . . and their language, too, frequently so coarse as to give no very favourable idea of the age that could endure it'. Yet Miss Austen's severity towards the *Spectator* underlines how greatly taste had altered by the end of the eighteenth century; and it is beyond question that Addison and Steele played a very influential part in starting the trend away from coarseness towards a more graceful manner of expression.

Not all the publications created in the image of the *Tatler* and *Spectator* had their good-natured, healthy outlook. Perhaps the least healthy was the *Female Tatler*, which had begun to appear three times weekly from 8 July 1709. Whereas the original *Tatler* was entirely non-political, the *Female Tatler* was a vehicle for the violently Tory invective of 'Mrs Crackenthorpe, a Lady that knows Everything'. Mrs Crackenthorpe's real name was Mrs Mary de la Rivière Manley, daughter of Sir Roger Manley, governor of Guernsey. Leigh Hunt in his autobiography attributes to Sir Roger Manley the authorship of the first volume of the *Turkish Spy*: 'a sort of philosophical newspaper, in volumes which, under a mark of bigotry, speculate very freely on all subjects'. Dr Johnson said that Mrs Manley claimed her father wrote the first two volumes, and that Dunton's associate Richard Sault wrote the rest at two guineas a sheet, under the direction of Dr Midgeley. At any rate, Sir Roger was an unusual father in that he realized his daughter had considerable mental abilities, and therefore provided her with a good education. Her mother had died when she was a small child; and before she was fully grown up Sir Roger also died, leaving her to the guardianship of a kinsman.

Mary Manley was described by many of her contemporaries as a woman of easy virtue; but Sir Richard Steele, if he knew her early history, must surely have included her among those innocents whose feet were first guided to the slippery path through their own total ignorance of where it would lead them. Her cousin, the kinsman who had become her guardian, was John Manley, Member of Parliament for Bossiney, and then Camelford in Cornwall. He made love to her and married her, and only later did she find he had a wife still living. He took her to London and, in the manner of the fiction of the time, deserted her 'to disgrace and poverty'. After about three years of we know not what, she went to live with the notorious Duchess of Cleveland, who soon quarrelled with her on the grounds that she was intriguing with her son. Whether this was so or not, other intrigues in high life followed her banishment from the Duchess's household. There was an affair with Sir Thomas Skipton of Drury Lane Theatre, and with John Tilley, Warden of the Fleet; and there was a scandal about a forged entry of marriage in a church register, an attempt to obtain money from the estate of a man called Pheasant. She may very well have made an attempt to support herself before these affairs, because her association with Sir Thomas Skipton began after her first attempts at play-writing in 1696—a tragedy called *The Royal Mischief,* which found fashionable favour. Her next play, a comedy called *The Lost Lover or Jealous Husband,* was produced the same year with much less success, and it was followed in 1707 by another tragedy: *Almyna, or the Arabian Vow.* In 1705 she had published *The Secret History of Queen Zarah and the Zarazions,* the first of a series of volumes dealing with current politics and personal scandals in the form of a romance. This kind of thing had been familiar in France for some years, but was new to England; and it was the literary form in which Mary Manley, who by now had considerable connections in political society, found her malicious métier. In 1709 her most famous, most scandalous book was published under the title of *Secret Memoirs and Manners of Several Persons of Quality of Both Sexes. From the New Atlantis.*

The New Atlantis, as it came to be popularly called, was a sensation from the start, and initiated the fashion for scandalous 'memoirs' in which gossip was thinly veiled as fiction. It was chiefly, although not exclusively, directed against the Whig party, then in power. Mrs Manley let ramp her taste for intrigue, impudently satirizing many prominent people and recklessly including in her attacks such dangerous enemies as the diarist Colley Cibber. In form, *The New Atlantis* was a compendium of anecdotes about

Stauratius and Thracian, Thracian being clearly recognizable as the Duke of Marlborough. It was a goulash of gossip and innuendo, mixed with heavy moralizing about life in an imaginary kingdom that was quite evidently England. Mrs Manley followed up with a second volume in the same year, and *The New Atlantis* went into seven editions as well as a French one. It was great fun while it lasted, but retribution caught up with the opprobrious author in the form of libel actions, and she was arrested on 29 October 1709, together with the printers and publishers of the book. She was admitted to bail on 5 November, and finally discharged by the court of the Queen's Bench on 13 February 1710, getting off more lightly than she deserved or can have hoped. She had been examined before Lord Sunderland, and replied to his interrogations with flippant falsehoods. But she proved herself to be a loyal friend, since she carefully screened from censure, not only the printers and booksellers who had also been arrested, but everyone who had supplied her with information. A professional journalist, she refused to reveal her sources. Her discharge was probably due to her relations with some powerful Tory politicians being intimate, to use an equivocal word, and she herself being a useful tool of the party.

All the publicity of these legal proceedings no doubt boosted the sales of Mrs Manley's *Female Tatler*. And at one point in 1709 she was thought to be also the author of the *Whisperer*, 'by Mrs Jenny Distaff, Half-sister to Isaac Bickerstaffe, Esq.', a publication that was described by Fox-Bourne as 'an equally scurrilous outcome of female journalism'. It would indeed have been an heroic output that could feed the *Female Tatler* on Mondays, Wednesdays, and Fridays, and the *Whisperer* on Tuesdays, Thursdays, and Saturdays—even with Mrs Manley's prodigious facility and fine disregard for accuracy. Jonathan Swift said in a letter to Addison that Mrs Manley's writing seemed 'as if she had about 2,000 Epithets and fine Words packed up in a Bag, and that she pulled them out by Handfuls, and strewed them on her Paper, where about once in 500 times they happen to be right'.

Perhaps Mrs Manley's writing deserved this description when at its most virulent; but to be fair, some of her sketches on non-political and non-scandalous subjects in the *Female Tatler* were lively and clever, she had a light descriptive touch which makes them very readable. She describes a shopping expedition to Ludgate Hill, and the manners of the men who served in the drapery establishments:

'The Shops are perfect gilded Theatres, the variety of wrought Silks so many Changes of fine Scenes, and the Mercers are the Performers in the Opera; and, instead of *vivitur ingenio*, you have in gold Capitals, NO TRUST BY RETAIL. They are the sweetest, fairest, nicest, dished-out Creatures; and, by their elegant Address and soft Speeches, you would guess them to be Italians. As People glance within their doors, they salute them with: "Garden silks, Ladies, Italian Silks, Brocades, Tissues, Cloth of silver, or Cloth of gold, very fine Mantua Silks, Geneva Velvet, English Velvet, Velvet embossed."

'We went into a Shop which had three Partners: two of them were to flourish out their Silks; and, after an obliging Smile and a pretty Mouth made Cicero-like, to expatiate on their Goodness; and the other's sole Business was to be Gentlemen usher of the Shop, to stand completely dressed at the Door, bow to all the coaches that pass by, and hand Ladies out and in.

'We saw abundance of gay fancies, fit for Sea-Captains' Wives, Sheriffs' feasts, and Taunton-dean Ladies. "This, Madam, is wonderful charming. This, Madam, is so diverting a Silk. This, Madam,—ye Gods! would I had 10,000 yards of it!" Then gathers up a Sleeve, and places it to our Shoulders. "It suits your Ladyship's face wonderfully well." When we had pleased ourselves, and bid him ten shillings a-yard for what he asked fifteen: "Fan me, ye winds, your Ladyship rallies me! Should I part with it at such a Price, the Weavers would rise upon the very Shop. Was you at the Park last night, Madam? Your Ladyship shall abate me sixpence. Have you read the *Tatler* today?"

'These Fellows are positively the greatest Fops in the Kingdom; they have their Toilets and their fine Night-gowns; their *Chocolate in the Morning*, and their *green Tea two hours after*; Turkey-polts for their Dinner; and their Perfumes, Washes, and clean Linen, equip them for the Park Parade.'

From 17 August to 17 October, 1709, a rival *Female Tatler* was produced by Thomas Baker, a dramatist whose plays are described by the NDB as being 'up to the not very exalted level of the comedies of the period'. This must have been the same Baker who published, according to Swift in a letter to Stella, a spurious number of Steele's original *Tatler*, No. 272, on 4 January 1711, at the Black Boy, Paternoster Row. His *Female Tatler* was published by A. Baldwin at the Oxford Arms in Warwick Lane. It was on Crackenthorpe lines, and was described by Lowndes as 'a scurrilous periodical paper'. Mrs Manley's *Female Tatler* was also published by A. Baldwin. The two papers hurled abuse at one another, the original one asserting that Mrs Crackenthorpe's man Francis had deserted her services 'seduced by a scandalous lewd Wench, a cast-off of a quondam quack Doctor in the City', and that he had taken with him 'Letters and Papers of moment'. The allegation was obvious—that he had handed them over to the spurious *Female Tatler*. The authorship and vicissitudes of the two *Female Tatlers* are by no means clear, and some authorities suggest that Baker was responsible for the original one. But at any rate, the author of one *Female Tatler* was silenced by the threat of legal proceedings, and the author of the other *Female Tatler* found it prudent to alter its character. The Grand Jury of Middlesex had sent up a presentiment on 19 October 1709, in these terms:

'Great Numbers of Printed Papers are continually dispersed in and about this City, under the names of the *Female Tatler*, sold by A. Baldwin. The *Review of the British Nation*, and other Papers under other Titles (the Authors of which are unknown to the Jury) under feigned Names, by describing Persons, and by placing the first and last Letters of the Words and otherwise, do reflect and scandalously abuse several Persons of honour and quality, many of the Magistrates, and abundance of Citizens, and all sorts of People; which Practice we conceive to be a great Nuisance, does manifestly tend to the Disturbance of the public Peace, and may turn to the Damage, if not Ruin, of many Families if not prevented.'

It appears that proceedings were commenced, although no prosecution resulted. At any rate it was enough to scare 'Mrs Crackenthorpe' who, in No. 51 of the *Female Tatler*, dated 2 November 1709, gave notice that she 'resented the Affronts offered to her by some rude Citizen' and resigned her editorship in favour of a Society of Modest Ladies, who would in their turn 'oblige the Publick with whatever they should meet with that was diverting, innocent, and instructive'.

The Modest Ladies with their innocent and instructive writings proved to be a very insipid bunch in comparison with Mrs Crackenthorpe. The paper now went in for harmless, almost edifying features such as a 'Table of Fame', made up of biographical accounts of women noted for their achievements—a feature intended 'for the Encouragement of the Sex . . . to demonstrate that Women are as capable as Men of sublimity of Soul'.

There were little tales with moral messages, little verses with pretty sentiments. The *Female Tatler* was indeed changed, and her old admirers deplored her lack of spirit. One correspondent complained, 'Of late the Authors have set up for Morality, and are as insipid as anything in Print'; another warned, 'Depend upon it that as Scandal was the Rise of your Paper, so whenever that fails 'twill sink . . . There's no tattling without some Satyr. If you are afraid to be kicked or indicted, knock off and save Paper, for none of my Acquaintances would give a Pin for Scandal where the Parties are not sufficiently described to be known'. The *Female Tatler* minced along in its new strait-laced manner until No. III, issued on 30 March 1710, and then disappeared into the limbo of bankrupt publications.

Mrs Manley had been employed by Swift from time to time in writing pamphlets (including *The Duke of Marlborough's Vindication*), and we next hear of her in June 1711 when she took Swift's place on his relinquishing the editorship of the *Examiner*, a weekly paper started by Lord Bolingbroke. Swift resigned at the forty-seventh issue because he 'could no longer be anonymous, and because the enmities he had provoked made his life unbearable, and even rendered it dangerous for him to go out after dark'. Mrs Manley did not fear the dark. She took over from Swift 'with much spirit and little conscience' and carried on, under the general editorship of Dr William King, until the end of the reign of Queen Anne. By that time she had become the mistress of John Barber, Printer to the City of London and a High Tory, who became an alderman and then Lord Mayor of London. Her savage pen scratched relentlessly on and, as Fox-Bourne says, 'If Mrs Manley no longer poured out her malicious and scandalous trivialities in the *Female Tatler*, it was a doubtful benefit that she should be free to exaggerate Swift's vices of style in the *Examiner*.'

In politics licence had sunk to licentiousness and a contemporary writer deplored that 'the present Gain from recent Progress in political Journalism is marred by the outrageous Coarseness indulged in by those who make it their Trade'. The sub-title of *The Examiner* was *Remarks upon Events and Occurrences*, and according to Addison five years later, 'it baited all the great Men who had done eminent Services to their Country but a few years before. No Sanctity of Character or Privilege of Sex exempted Persons from this barbarous Usage. Several of our Prelates were the standing Marks of public Raillery, and many Ladies of the first Quality branded by Name for Matters of which, as they were false, were not heeded, and, if they had been true, were innocent. The dead themselves were not spared.'

Mrs Manley, however, was thick-skinned and without conscience. Moreover she had her supporters. In July 1711 when she was editing the *Examiner* she attempted to get some sort of pension or reward from Lord Peterborough for her services to the Tory Party in writing *The New Atlantis*, and as compensation for her subsequent prosecution. This appeal was seconded by Swift; and when later that year Mrs Manley became very ill he wrote to Stella, 'Poor Mrs Manley the Author is very ill of a Dropsy and sore Leg. The Printer (John Barber) tells me he is afraid she cannot live long. I am heartily sorry for her; she had very generous Principles for one of her sort; and a great deal of good Sense and Invention; she is about forty, very homely and very fat.' So, she had her friends as well as lovers, admirers as well as detractors. It depended upon which side you were backing, Whig or Tory. Journalist to the end, she died on 11 July 1724, in John Barber's office. She had brought out another successful tragedy, *Lucius*, in 1717 and published an autobiography under the title of *Memoirs of Rivella*. Her *New Atlantis* lived on after her and a seventh edition was published in 1736, in spite of it being considered—or possibly because it was considered—'a compilation of the vilest refuse'.

Another woman journalist of the scurrilous scribbler breed was Mrs S. Malthus, daughter of a bookseller and wife of a bookseller who went bankrupt. His death followed on the bankruptcy, and John Dunton at first commended his widow to friends in the trade as being 'free from all that Pride and Arrogance that is found in the Carriage of some Publishers'. He claimed to have helped her to start the *Wandering Spy, or the Way of the World inquired into*. This weekly, issued as by S. Malthus, only ran for four numbers from 9 June to 30 June, 1705. Later, John Dunton did not have a good word to say for Mrs Malthus, nor any bad enough. He called her his 'scribbling Enemy', and wrote of,

'. . . that spiteful Woman that hired those Fellows to slander me in the *Grub Street News*. She copies her Religion and Honesty from hackney Authors; and if she have any *Ears*, it is more than I dare assert of any one that writes for her. She sets up for a Wit; and if she can say no ill of a Man, she seems to speak Riddles as if she could tell strange Stories if she would; and when she has wreaked her Revenge to the uppermost, she ends, "But I wish him well, I therefore hold my Peace". She is a private Slanderer, I am not the only one she has deceived.'

63

However, retribution evidently caught up with the malicious Mrs Malthus. Dunton was able to record with pleasure that '*Malthus*, my ungrateful Enemy, as a just judgement on her, has now neither Books nor Moderators, etc. to publish; and, after all her Bounce, can hardly pay 2s. 6d. in the pound'.

John Dunton mentions two other women in the printing, publishing, and bookselling world. He wrote of Mrs Stacy Sowle: 'She is both a Printer as well as a Bookseller, and the Daughter of one, and understands the Trade very well, being a good Compositor herself'; and he described Mrs Elizabeth Harris as 'the beautiful Relic of my worthy Friend, Mr John Harris. She printed my *Panegyrick on the Lord Jeffreys*, and other Copies that sold well.' There were even women newspaper proprietors during the reign of Queen Anne. Sarah Popping of *The Dunciad* was joint proprietor with Benjamin Harris of the *Protestant Post-Boy*, a Whig newspaper started in 1711 that constantly attacked Swift, calling him 'an ambitious Tantivy'— Tantivity being a post-Restoration nickname for High Churchmen and Tories. In October 1711 Swift procured the committal to Newgate of Mrs Popping for printing an attack on him in the *Protestant Post-Boy*. Another newspaper proprietor was Mrs Elizabeth Powell, founder of the *Charitable Mercury and Female Intelligence, being a Weekly Collection of all the Material News, Foreign and Domestic; with some Notes on the Same*. This was a six-page paper published every Saturday, and was launched on Saturday, 7 April 1716.

Mrs Elizabeth Powell, like Mrs Mary Manley, managed to get on the wrong side of the law, but for a very different reason. Her crime was not libel but tax evasion. A very heavy Stamp Duty had been imposed in 1712 upon all newspapers of a whole sheet or a half-sheet—that is, of four or two pages, these being the two usual sizes for newspapers. Mrs Powell conceived the idea of making hers a six-page newspaper, made up of a sheet and a half-sheet. She found herself very hard-pressed to fill six pages every week, but spread herself in the heading which took up four-and-a-half inches and helped to fill up the space on the front page. But her six-page strategy was seen by the eye of the law to be the tax evasion quibble that it was, and to escape from arrest she temporarily fled the country. Her name crops up next in the *Weekly Medley or the Gentleman's Recreation*, which was founded in 1719, a periodical claiming to contain *An Historical Account of all News Foreign and Domestick*. This weekly only lasted until the issue of 16–23 January, 1720, which contained a farewell 'Letter from

The Charitable Mercury,

A N D

Female Intelligence.

Being A

Weekly Collection

O F

All the Material N E W S, Foreign and Domeſtick:

With ſome NOTES on the ſame.

To be Publiſhed Every Saturday.

Saturday, April 7. 1716.

Chi biaſima i Grandi ſcorre pericolo ; chi li loda ſpeſſo dice la bugía.

IT *is well enough known to the Publick, that I intended lately to entertain 'em with a Paper under another Title ; and I need not tell by what means I am prevented from purſuing my Deſign. However, the ſame Reaſons ſtill prevailing with me to accept of that Encouragement the Publick then intended me, and ſome worthy Gentlemen generouſly offering their Aſſiſtance in carrying on a Weekly Paper for my Benefit, emboldens me to attempt this Publication, and I hope for better Succeſs with this than I had with my other Undertaking. Theſe Gentlemen bid*

7. Mast head to Mrs Elizabeth Powell's *Charitable Mercury*, 1716

the Author of the *Medley* to his readers', asking them to transfer their custom to another periodical:

> 'There is one Mrs Powell of the Printing Trade who is fallen unluckily under the Displeasure of the Government, and is (according to Report and all probability) fled to France, for what occasion I don't exactly know. In her House that was are two pretty Children whose Father has been lately buried and whose Mother is now dead to them, so that they remain helpless Orphans and in this House, the Sign of which is the Prince of Wales's Arms in Blackfryers, is printed a Paper called *The Orphan*. It is a Journal of all the News, Foreign and Domestick; it is perfecter and better than any of the others; and besides the Writer of it does, what no other Journalist does. He forms pretty Tracts upon Religion and Morality, and attacks those Enemies of Both, the Dissenters, with a great deal of Spirit and Vigour. I desire, therefore, that now the *Medley* is ceased, the *Orphan* may live in the Esteem of all my Readers.'

The full title of this weekly was the *Orphan Reviv'd—The State of Europe, Embellish'd and Intermix'd with Observations, Historical, Political, and Philosophical, concluding with the 'Tea-table Tatler or the Ladies' Delight'*. By number XVI the title had shortened to the *Orphan Reviv'd or Powell's Weekly Journal, Containing all Remarkable Occurrences Foreign and Domestick together with a Tatler*. The name of Powell appearing in the headline seems to suggest that Mrs Powell had returned from her expedient exile towards the end of 1719. Certainly she was back in time to see the final issues through the press, because the last known, that of February 1720, made no secret of her having set up in business again. Under the shortened title of the *Orphan Reviv'd, or Powell's Weekly Journal* the imprint was 'Printed and Sold by Elizabeth Powell, at Mr Clifton's, in the Old Bailey'. These lady journalists, scribbling females, were of a tough, surviving species.

Chapter IV

RECORDS OF LOVE AND ROMANTIC FICTION

A weekly for middle-class women, Records of Love. *Pioneer of magazine serial stories.* Steele's Ladies' Library. *Familiar letters. Mary Davys, playwright, novelist, and coffee-house proprietor. Eliza Haywood, shameless scribbler and romantic novelist. Approved fiction for ladies. Lofty ideals of the* Freethinker. *First* Ladies' Journal. *The first* Parrot.

ᔑᔑᔑᔑᔑᔑᔑᔑᔑᔑᔑᔑᔑᔑᔑᔑᔑᔑᔑᔑᔑᔑᔑᔑᔑᔑᔑᔑᔑᔑᔑᔑᔑᔑᔑ

ALTHOUGH the *Orphan Reviv'd* ran a *Tea-table Tatler or Ladies' Delight* in each issue, this was only a small concession to the fair sex and it would be quite incorrect to class it as a woman's weekly even though it was edited by a woman. The new middle-class feminine readership that Steele and Addison had created with the *Tatler* and *Spectator* was offered much lighter fare in a weekly periodical called *Records of Love, or Weekly Amusements for the Fair Sex,* which appeared in 1710. This had an unpretentiously popular and sentimental appeal. It made no intellectual claims. It had no political adhesions, and contained no enigmas nor mathematical problems to exercise the mental powers of its readers. There was no almanack or diary section, no foreign or domestic news service. Its modest aims were set out in the first issue of Saturday, 7 January 1710:

> 'Each Paper will contain something new and diverting according to the example of the first Novel, without any Personal Reflections or Immodest Obscenities, being chiefly designed to promote a Love of Virtue, by insinuating Examples and diverting Passages. It is therefore to be hoped the Ingenious part of the World, especially those of the Fair Sex, will be pleas'd to continue that Encouragement, which many Honourable Persons of the first Quality have nobly begun.'

By this one can assume that the paper was subscribed for in advance of its first issue, thus assuring a known circulation; and the distribution arrangements reveal an efficient management:

> 'This Paper will be Published every *Saturday* and Deliver'd to each

Subscriber by four in the Afternoon. The Price for Subscribers is but 1s 6d per Quarter; 6d of which is to be paid at the time of the Subscription, and the Remainder at the end of the Quarter. But to those who are not Subscribers, the Paper will not be sold under 2d each Sheet; by which means every Subscriber will save 6d per Quarter, besides the Conveniency of having the Paper brought home to their Houses.

'Subscriptions are taken in by Mr Brown Bookseller, at the Black Swan without Temple Bar; Mr Milner Bookseller, at Lincolns Inn Back Gate in Lincolns-Inn Fields; Mr Robotham, at the M. and Dagger in Pope's-Head-Alley against the Royal Exchange; Mr Pidgeon Perriwig-Maker against Surrey-Street in the Strand; Mr Grantham Printer in St Bartholomew's Close near West-Smith Fields; and by the Men who carry the Papers about. N.B. Any person, by sending their Name and Place of Abode, with the 6d advance, by the Penny Post etc. to any of the aforesaid Places, may have the Paper sent them without further Trouble.'

Each issue consisted of a story and a poem. The first issue had The Fashionable Quaker' and 'An Ode in Praise of Coffee', of which the first verse was in French, and the next two were 'The Same in English'. The following week the story was 'The Romantick Lady', and the next issue had 'The Gentleman Gardener', 'done out of French by a Lady', and also a charming little verse:

OH, THE COLDNESS OF THE SEASON
For now the Hero leaves the rough Alarms
Of horrid War, to die in Celia's Arms.
The Warrior now his Tent securely folds,
And quits the open Field for warmer Holds.

By this time the Editor is evidently getting unsolicited contributions, for there is an announcement from 'The Record Office':

'Upon reading this Day at the Board the ingenious Translation of an unknown Lady. It is ordered that Thanks be returned the Author for her kind Assistance. And Notice is hereby given, that if any of the Ingenious of either Sex will be pleased to communicate anything worthy of Notice to this Design, it shall be thankfully received, and not thrown by with the unmannerly Disdain of our modern Scribblers. Persons are desired to superscribe their letters for Endimion Gossip, Esq.'

There is no indication that contributions would be paid for. Some of the poems were by John Reading, and in issue No. 5 there is a 'Proposal for printing (by subscription) a Book of Songs, Composed (after the Italian manner) by Mr John Reading. That the said Book shall contain twelve new Songs, with Symphonies, and a thorough Bass, fitted to the Harpsichord etc. all transposed for the Flute, curiously engraved with copper Plates, and printed on very good Paper. That the price of the Book, to Subscribers, will be 3s; 1s 6d to be paid at the time of subscription and 1s 6d at the delivery of the Book. That to those who buy six Books, a seventh shall be given *gratis*, as usual. That after the Books are delivered to the Subscribers, they shall not be sold under 4s each Book. Subscriptions are taken at the Author's house in Arundel Street, against St Clement's Church in the Strand.' It is satisfactory to learn in the issue of 25 March 1710 that 'Mr Reading's Book of Songs will be publish'd in six weeks time without any farther delay'.

Records of Love was a pioneer of magazine serial stories. 'The Generous Heiress' appeared in two parts, in No. 6 and No. 7; and 'The Wandering Dancing Master' was serialized in three consecutive issues. Other features began to be introduced. This was the time of the long Peninsular Wars and there was a humorous feature entitled 'Proposals for a Matrimonial Lottery':

'Whereas several disconsolate Damsels have, during this time of War, laboured under the Torments of an insupportable Solitude . . . a Lottery is now in agitation . . . tickets at 5 gns. each from our Record Office in Panton Street, Haymarket. The Lottery to be drawn three Weeks after Proclamation of Peace. Ten thousand Officers in her Majesty's service by Sea and Land shall be selected and set apart as Prizes . . . all single Men, young, handsome, and vigorous, the Glory of their Country and the Terror of their Enemies. N O T E None are to be Adventurers in this Lottery but Maids, Widows, and Single Women.'

There follows in the same issue, presumably to damp down the excitement, an essay entitled 'In Praise of Chastity'. Two weeks later the Record Office made another announcement:

'Whereas by reason of the great numbers of Maids, Widows, and Single Women, who daily resort in great numbers to our Record Office in Panton Square for Tickets in the Matrimonial Lottery, this is to give

Notice to all Coachmen, Carmen, Draymen, Horsemen, that all the Ways will be blocked, so that none shall pass within two furlongs of our Record Office under pain of 5 gns. for the use of such distressed Damsels as shall be judged in most need of Husbands.'

In spite of all its circulation building ideas and efficient management, there is no trace of *Records of Love* having lasted beyond twelve issues.

The feminine appetite for light fiction and romance which had been whetted by *Records of Love* would certainly not have found anything to satisfy its sentimental taste in the *Ladies' Library* of 1714 which came out in three volumes, 'Written by a Lady and published by Sir Richard Steele', who supplied an introduction. In his sponsoring of this prim compilation, Steele seems to have deserted the advanced position *vis-à-vis* women that he took up in his essays in the *Tatler* and *Spectator*. For there is nothing in the *Ladies' Library*, or in his preface to the first volume, to suggest any widening horizons. All is dutifully domestic. The lady author (who is given as Mary Wray in the *Cambridge Bibliography of English Literature*) says in her Introduction: 'The Writings are those she has compiled from the Writings of Eminent Divines for a Guide to her own Conduct to be of some Service to Others of her Sex, who have not the same Opportunities of searching into various Authors for themselves.' There is little variation of style throughout, and some literary historians seem to assume that there was no lady author but that Steele himself produced all three volumes, borrowing unacknowledged but recognizable slices from other people's work, not all 'Eminent Divines'. But whatever its exact origins, the *Ladies' Library* set a fashion for compilations of elegant extracts which supplied the young ladies of two or three generations with education in literary taste combined with moral instruction.

The first volume of Steele's *Ladies' Library* contained fourteen essays of an improving kind with titles such as 'Chastity', 'Modesty', 'Meekness', 'Wit', and 'Delicacy'. The second volume consisted of five long essays entitled 'The Daughter', 'The Wife', 'The Mother', 'The Widow', 'The Mistress'. This last meant the mistress of the household and servants, not of a lover. The third volume contained eight religious essays. And Richard Steele supplied an eulogistic dedication to each volume: 'to the Countess of Burlington'; 'to Mrs Bovey'; and to his own wife. Alas for the *avant-garde* young man who had voiced his revolutionary opinions about the status and education of women! Success and prosperity were making him a pillar of the Establishment. He became a Member of Parliament in 1715, and in the same year procured a Baronetcy by the presentation of an Address to the King. His interests now lay in supporting the *status quo*.

No periodical took the place of *Records of Love* in supplying ladies with light fiction, but there was at this time a form of book publication which went under the general heading of 'Familiar Letters' and was extremely popular. Between 1660 and 1740 there appeared in England nearly two hundred of these books in which a correspondence between two people was largely, or more often entirely, the narrative medium. A great number were translations from the French, the best selling being *Lettres Portugaises*. They show that Richardson was by no means the originator of epistolatory fiction. The informality of some of these brief fictional correspondences, their restrained narrative quality which yet contained little or no plot, gave them a kind of quiet day-to-day realism that Richardson's lengthy letters with all their dramatic happenings never achieved. Many of the 'familiar letters' were written by women; and it is women, generally speaking, who make the best letter writers. They tend to be more personal, more intuitive, more observant of the daily detail of living—and also of the little peculiarities of personality which betray the character of a man or woman. The minutiae of everyday life *is* life to them, and nothing is too small or unimportant to escape notice. Hannah More once wrote to a friend, 'I have a particular notion about correspondence. I would not give much for what is called a fine letter even from those who are most gifted in writing. What I want in a letter is a picture of my friend's mind and the commonsense of his life . . . I have the same feeling in writing to him.'

The 'Familiar Letters' were always elegant. They never contained anything coarse or 'impolite', but placed an emphasis upon 'sensibility' and the minute analysis of the emotions. Such plots as they had tended to be simple, quite credible, and without any exaggeration or sensational romanticism. Robert A. Daw, in an introduction to an Augustan Reprint Society's edition of Mary Davys's *Familiar Letters Betwixt a Gentleman and a Lady* (1725) points out that it is principally remarkable not for beaux sentiments, the technical manipulation of correspondence, or tearing a passion to tatters, but for its atmosphere of British middle-class realism . . . 'Although it retains the high-flown names of outworn tradition, 'Artander' and 'Berina' are obviously Thomas and Jane. And this realism of furniture, food, and the difficulties of day-to-day life is as rare as a sense of humour in the early English novel. This refreshing realism—a pair of lovers who manage to be witty instead of passionate while conveying the impression that they entertain tender feelings . . . together with her eye for physical detail, gives Mrs Davys a claim to be a pioneer in the approach to fiction improved by Fanny Burney and perfected by Jane Austen.'

Mrs Mary Davys (1674–1732) was the wife of an Irishman, the Rev. Peter Davys, who was a friend of Dean Swift. On her husband's death in 1698 she left Ireland and went to Cambridge, where she had some acquaintances in university circles. There she started to write for her living, and also established a coffee-house. Her first novel, *The Reformed Coquet,* had some success, and also a play called *The Northern Heiress. Familiar Letters Betwixt a Gentleman and a Lady* appeared in her *Works* of 1725. This volume was published by subscription, a fact that indicates she could depend upon a certain following.

She seems to have been a determined and tiresome correspondent to Jonathan Swift. Writing in his Journal to Stella on 21 February 1712, he says of Mary Davys, 'She took care to have a letter delivered for me at the Lord Treasurer's; for I would not own one she sent by post. She reproaches me for not writing to her these four years, and I have honestly told her it was my way never to write to those whom I never am likely to see, unless I can serve them, which I cannot her.' Tiresome Mrs Davys may have been, but she was a pioneer in more ways than one. She was a pioneer in establishing a coffee-house, coffee-houses being looked upon as entirely masculine preserves. And she was a pioneer in adopting the medium of 'familiar letters', a form of fiction peculiarly suited to women writers and to women readers. She wrote for her living, which puts her among the professionals. Indeed, she was one of the most desperate female scribblers of her day. In a letter written in 1725 she remarks she had been left to her own endeavours for twenty-seven years together.

The course carved out for herself by Mary Davys was followed by Mrs Eliza Haywood (1693–1756), romantic novelist, who in her early days was a prolific writer of 'familiar letters'. She was socially in a lower stratum than Mary Davys, and her reputation was not so unblemished. Of course it did not take much to blemish a woman's reputation at this time—the 'wits' could attack on the most slender evidence, or indeed without a shred. Mrs Haywood's social rating was not sufficiently high for her to be much of a target for the fashionable 'wits'; but the fact that she had been on the stage was enough to tarnish her in the eyes of the class into which she was born. She was the daughter of a London tradesman called Fowler, and must have had a reasonably good education, which included French. Nothing is known about her husband Haywood except that he deserted her when her children were small. Rumour had it that they were illegitimate, the one by a peer and the other by a bookseller. Her friends loyally asserted that Haywood was the father of both; but she herself in *The Female Dunciad* seems to admit to 'little inadvertencies'.

At any rate, she was obliged to support herself and the children; and after an unsuccessful skirmish on the stage set about becoming a literary woman. Unfortunately she followed the example of Mrs Manley by introducing into her romances contemporary scandals about the leaders of Society, their names only transparently veiled. Her *Memoirs of a Certain Island Adjacent to Utopia, Written by a Celebrated Author in that Country* (1725) related many scandalous episodes and was a direct copy of Mrs Manley's *New Atlantis*. It even went to the length of having a 'key' at the end of the book in which the fictitious names in the narrative were identified with well-known living persons through initials. Pope described her as one of those 'shameless scribblers who, in libellous memoirs and novels, reveal the faults or misfortunes of both sexes, to the ruin of public fame, or disturbance of private happiness'. Swift wrote of her on 26 October 1731, in a letter to the Countess of Suffolk, who seems to have been afraid of Mrs Haywood's pen, that she was a 'stupid, infamous, scribbling woman'. Horace Walpole dimissed her contemptuously as the counterpart of Mrs Aphra Behn; but Mrs Haywood was never as audacious, nor as salacious, as Aphra Behn with her sparkling Restoration wit. Eliza Haywood wrote one or two plays herself, but they were dull things compared with those of the 'female Wycherley'. Swift's invective against her as an 'infamous, scribbling woman' was probably caused by the pamphlets in which she occasionally let herself rip. Her real forte was novel writing, romances, and 'familiar letters'. Hers tended to have a more popular appeal, a lower-brow market, than those of Mary Davys. These are a few of their irresistible titles: *Love in Excess, or The Fatal Enquiry*; *Letters from a Lady of Quality to a Chevalier*, translated from the French; *The British Recluse, or the Secret History of Cleomina, supposed Dead*; *Idalia, or the Unfortunate Mistress*; *The Masqueraders, or the Fatal Curiosity*; *The Rash Resolve, or the Untimely Discovery*; *Bath Intrigues, in Four Letters to a Friend in London*; *Love-letters on all Occasions*. All these titles appeared between 1719 and

73

1724, and Mrs Haywood also wrote a bi-weekly essay-paper on *Tatler* lines called the *Tea Table*, which was published every Monday and Friday for thirty-six numbers from 21 February to 21 June 1724.

Since the Restoration the output of romances other than 'familiar letters' had been steadily growing, but most of them were tainted with Restoration licentiousness, many of them being merely reprints of the more popular books of Charles II's reign. To take the title of one of them, *The Maidenhead Lost by Moonlight,* is to give the flavour of them all. Daniel Defoe's *Moll Flanders* broke new ground, and was written in a totally new style. It appeared in 1722, followed by *Roxana* two years later. But both these would have been considered too coarse for young ladies of middle-class families to read. Defoe's biographer, Wright, makes the point primly by observing 'they are not works for the drawing-room table'. Aristocratic ladies undoubtedly read translations from the French authors of the time: Sieur de Calprenède, Brémond, Mademoiselle de Scudéry, and Scaroon. And there is a story in Lockhart's *Life of Scott* which shows that Aphra Behn's novels were not considered inappropriate to be read aloud, even later in the century. He tells how an old lady asked Sir Walter to obtain for her Aphra Behn's novels which she had enjoyed so much in her youth. He did so, although against his better judgment, and the old lady returned them to him to be burned. She said she had been unable to read through one of them, 'But is it not a very odd thing,' she wrote, 'that I, an old woman of eighty and upwards, sitting alone, feel ashamed to read a book which, sixty years ago, I have heard read aloud for the amusement of large circles consisting of the first and most creditable society in London?' Of course, her sensibilities had changed with the changing climate of opinion upon moral and social codes throughout the century. Nevertheless, the clue to the readings aloud of the erotic Aphra Behn probably lies in that phrase 'circles consisting of the first and most creditable society in London'. High society has always permitted itself more licence than the middle classes. It has never been possible to *épater les aristocrates*. If Lockhart's correspondent had belonged to the bourgoisie, she would not have been allowed, at twenty years old, to know of the very existence of a book by Aphra Behn in the same house as herself.

In periodical publishing there appears to have been a gap of some eight years between the discontinuation of *Records of Love* and the launching of the next publication planned to appeal directly to women readers. And when it came it was a much more serious publication than *Records of Love*. It was intended for the improvement of women's minds rather than their entertainment. It was edited and for the most part written by Ambrose Phillips and was named the *Freethinker, or Essays on Ignorance*. Launched on 24 March 1718, it ran for 159 numbers until 28 September 1719. It was not the first periodical of that title—there had been the *Freethinker* of 1711, published by J. Baker; and it was followed from 1720 until 1721 by the *Free Thinker*. But neither of these were intended as publications especially for women; whereas Ambrose Phillips's periodical was particularly addressed to 'the Sex whose Approbation most flatters the Heart of a Writer'.

He declared himself to be dedicated to the embellishment of women's understanding in order to 'give their Minds as beautiful a Turn as Nature had bestowed on their Persons'. He gave them accounts of women famous for their learning, and deplored the usual low standard of education with which most women appeared to be content. He proposed to exercise their minds with 'Philosophical Lectures', but assured them he would always attempt to deliver his 'abstracted Notions' in terms that would be familiar to them. He urged that the realities of philosophy were an elevating alternative to 'the insipid Fictions of Novels and Romances' in which most women indulged. Anticipating the criticism that excessive learning made women unattractive to men, he assured them that 'Knowledge would in no way disfigure the Features, wrinkle the Skin, or spoil the Complexion'. It is a tribute to Ambrose Phillips that his *Freethinker* should have lasted for 159 numbers—a considerable run for a publication at that time. Four years later, that is in 1723, Daniel Bellamy the Elder edited a collection of various dramatic pieces and moral essays entitled the *Young Ladies' Miscellany, or Youth's Innocent and Rational Amusement, to Which is Prefixed a Short Essay on Pronunciation*—another attempt to improve the education of young ladies. And in the same year, a weekly periodical inspired by lofty ideals was launched under the title of the *Visiter*. This ran for fifty-one numbers, from 18 June 1723 to 31 January 1724.

The anonymous editor of the *Visiter* announced in his first number that he proposed to confine himself 'to those Subjects that tend to the Improvement of the Mind and Manners as they are relative to a Domestick Life'. The ornaments of the mind were to be his chief concern, not feminine conduct nor dress, 'provided the Ladies keep their Hearts free from Blemishes, they may wear what Spots they please upon their Faces'. He

75

was not, of course, meaning spots in the sense of skin blemishes, but 'beauty spots', or 'patches'. He invited correspondents to honour him with their confidences, and the early numbers were mainly made up of correspondence, which may or may not have been from genuine readers. For example, it may well have been an imaginary Captain Bluff who desired the editor to reprove the idle young women who infested encampments, and to impress upon them that females should refrain from visiting soldiers to whom they were not related. The editor seems to have been quite a feminist, for he managed to dib in here and there many comments in support of the unpopular notion that women are possessed of intellects as well as men. He complimented his fair readers on the judgment their letters showed 'in spite of the limited Education we inhumanly confine them to'; and went so far as to declare that if a university should be erected for young women 'it would produce much fewer female Block-heads than Oxford or Cambridge does of the masculine'. One suspects very strongly, in fact, that the editor was a woman.

The *Visiter* started as a weekly, but after sixteen numbers the editor decided to publish it twice a week, on Tuesdays and Fridays. Poetry, essays, and moral tales were introduced. And also sketches of undesirable husbands: the Rake, the Sot, the Crochet, the Grave Man—more and more it seems likely the editor was female. There were discourses on Modesty, on Love grounded upon Reason, on Good Manners, on the Vice of Evil-speaking. It was pointed out that the base wretches who imposed upon credulity and betrayed innocence were most likely to succeed in their artifices with 'Women of a narrow and confined Education'. Those with well-instructed minds, 'rightly formed and adorned with prudent simplicity of Manners', were able to see through the deceivers' arts. The need for women to receive a less narrow education than the customary instruction in 'accomplishments' was a constantly recurring topic in the correspondence columns. The publication included a certain amount of literary and dramatic criticism, and one number castigates Shakespeare's heroines: 'Shakespeare never represents women worthy of a hero's love but only draws them fit to inspire a base sensual passion.' Richard Steele was reprimanded, as well as Shakespeare. The popularity of his *Conscious Lovers* was attributed by the reviewer to a taste for 'low gallantry'—not that the critic desired to reflect upon Sir Richard Steele who, he admitted, 'has wrote a great many Things worthy of himself, but having a just Opinion of the weakness of Mankind, he sometimes chooses to be applauded by the ignorant Many rather than to merit the approbation of the well-wishing Few.' This criticism seems to bear out the feeling we had from the *Ladies' Library* that the young Richard Steele of the *Tatler* was a gentleman of much higher ideals and purpose than the Sir Richard Steele he became when success had made him an urbane man of the world.

A *Ladies' Journal*, the first of the many publications with that title which would appear over the next two centuries, was launched in Dublin on 17 January 1727. It was a weekly, and ran for twenty-two numbers until 29 June. Dublin at this time was quite a literary centre, where witty women sparkled and Jonathan Swift held captious court. Many of the men and women who made their names in journalism, literature and the stage in eighteenth century London came from Ireland. In the first issue of the *Ladies' Journal* the editor announced that it would contain only 'the lighter Affairs of the Ladies, such as the more agreeable subjects of Love and Gallantry'; and at 'the Request of female Acquaintances' it was to be the first paper to be 'devoted entirely to an Exposition of Love, with some poetical Illustrations of its Power'. But in the second issue the editor swung round and urged the ladies to consider 'what Miracles they would be with the advantages of Study and the Knowledge of the liberal Sciences'. He hoped 'by unquestionable Instances to shew that there is an absolute Necessity for the Ladies being as learned as the Gentlemen'. This he was planning to do 'at a more convenient Opportunity'.

In the meantime he recommended to their study the more delightful arts of poetry, painting, and musick as the most suitable to the delicacies of their nature. He was evidently by no means a convinced feminist; rather the reverse, since he seems to have been quite astonished at any instances of a woman having shown herself capable of anything verging on the intellectual. A later issue of the journal proffered some 'undeniable Examples of the Fair Sex who have surprisingly distinguished themselves in all kinds of human Literature', and included some reflections upon music and occasional comments upon plays. But for the most part the publication was made up of little tales and poems on the never-failing topic of love, guaranteed to please the ladies. A few of these tales added the spice of gossip, hinting at society scandals with the names of well-known people thinly disguised, very much in the manner of the 'secret histories' so popular with Mrs Manley's admirers.

In London, an essay-paper appeared in 1728 that was almost certainly edited by Mrs Eliza Haywood. This was a weekly periodical called the *Parrot*, published under the pseudonym of Mrs Penelope Prattle. Certainly something seems to have deflected Mrs Haywood from writing romances after 1725; and this Mrs Prattle of the *Parrot* started out with a crusading pen, showing the same reforming zeal that Mrs Haywood later displayed in her famous *Female Spectator*. Introducing her first issues, Mrs Prattle hoped that the world would 'not be so rude as to demand a Reason at a Woman's Hands why she should set Pen to Paper at a Time when the Number of Journals and News-Letters had become cumbersome even to Coffee-houses'. The reason, she went on to explain, was that she desired to put things right in the world and to comment upon its vices and foibles. Ladies and gentlemen disposed to assist her in this high purpose were requested to send their correspondence through Thomas Edlin, Printer, near Story's Gate, Westminster.

In the four issues of the *Parrot* which remain in the Bodleian Library, the first confines itself to a disposition upon the life and character of Mrs Prattle. The next comes out with 'a Defence of Soldiering and of Satyr'. The fourth wrote of the 'fasionable Evil of Gaming', and pointed out that young women with a fondness for gaming spoilt their chances of good marriages since 'the Apprehension of a gaming Wife was a great Impediment to sincere Addresses'. As well as the essay, there were letters from readers. One of these reported that there was great curiosity among the gossips as to the identity of the editor. Some people affirmed positively that the editor was Mrs H......d; others saw a great likeness between her and Mrs Behn or Mrs Manley. Since Mrs Behn and Mrs Manley were both dead, Mrs Haywood is the obvious candidate. She was the author of a later *Parrot* issued in 1746, and the similarity of style and subject matter in this first *Parrot* to that in her *Female Spectator* leaves little room for doubt as to the true identity of Mrs Penelope Prattle.

Chapter V

MAGAZINES AND WRITERS OF THE 1730s

The Gentleman's Magazine *and its women contributors: Jane Hughes, Catherine Cockburn, Elizabeth Carter. Its imitators: the* London Magazine *and the first* Lady's Magazine. *The* Country Magazine. *Women and politics; Lady Mary Wortley Montagu. Her propaganda for smallpox innoculation; her* Nonsense of Commonsense; *its campaigns against 'sensibility' and the excesses of society; the necessity for bawdy in promoting sales. Mrs Laetitia Pilkington. Literary patronage, publishing by subscription, jobbing for printers.*

꧁꧁꧁꧁꧁꧁꧁꧁꧁꧁꧁꧁꧁꧁꧁꧁꧁꧁꧁꧁꧁꧁꧁꧁꧁꧁꧁꧁꧁꧁꧁꧁

THE term 'magazine', applied to a periodical, did not come into use until the third decade of the eighteenth century. It was the happy thought of a bookseller named Edward Cave to use it in the sense of a storehouse of miscellaneous writings; and in January 1731 he launched a monthly publication called the *Gentleman's Magazine* or *Monthly Intelligence*, which was 'to treasure up, as in a Magazine, the most remarkable Pieces' of writing and news, culled from 'the two hundred or so Half-sheets per Month thrown upon the Press . . . Newspapers are of late so multiplied as to render it impossible, unless a Man make it his business, to consult them all.' Thus Cave's original idea was that of the present-day *Reader's Digest*; but in addition to the extracts from other publications, his magazine included a brief record of events during the past month, some instructive articles, and also conundrums and cookery receipts. These latter show that he realized the value of including features of particular interest to the new middle-class female reader, and he provided them as well with a miscellaneous assortment of practical information and entertainment. One section of the magazine, however, was not expected to be of any interest to the ladies. This was the section containing reports of parliamentary debates, a feature never before included in either newspapers or periodicals.

There had been forerunners of Edward Cave's magazine idea in a publication called the *Monthly Miscellany, or Memoirs for the Curious by Several Hands* which ran from 1707 to 1710, and another called *Bibliotheca*

Literaria, edited by S. Webb, which ran from 1722 to 1724. But these had not attracted a wide readership. If they had been more popular, no doubt the booksellers whom Cave tried to persuade into taking a share in his project might not have been so unenthusiastic. As it was, he had to launch the *Gentleman's Magazine* on his own. It was an immediate success, and many rivals started up. The very same booksellers who before had rejected his proposition, at once got together to produce a very similar *London Magazine, or Gentleman's Monthly Intelligencer*. This ran successfully from 1732 until 1785, but its circulation never outstripped the publication it plagiarized. The circulation of the *Gentleman's Magazine* rose steadily, and in little more than ten years had reached 15,000, helped greatly by its parliamentary reports. These were unique in their time, since no reporting was allowed in the House. They were written by a man with a prodigious memory called Thomas Guthrie, who was smuggled in to sit through the debates and wrote them down afterwards. Dr Johnson, newly arrived in London, was employed by Cave for a number of years as a sub-editor, polishing and re-writing Guthrie's reports. Before the *Gentleman's Magazine* had completed its ninth year, the fifth edition of its earliest numbers was being reprinted; and it continued its extremely influential life for 166 years. A. S. Collins in *Authorship in the Days of Johnson* contends it was the *Gentleman's Magazine* that, by encouraging the growth of a wide reading public and therefore more markets for a writer's work, made unnecessary the old system of patronage by which an author who could not find a patron was likely to starve.

Some of the *Gentleman's Magazine*'s earliest contributors were women. There was a Welsh girl named Jane Hughes, who had been educated by her scholarly father. The consequences of giving this daughter the education of a son were no doubt pointed out as a dreadful warning by those who disapproved of girls being taught anything but 'female accomplishments'. For Jane Hughes married an undergraduate in 1711, a commoner of Brasenose College, Oxford. It is not on record whether Thomas Brereton pursued his studies and achieved a degree in spite of the distractions of marriage with Jane. But it is on record that 'having been imprudent and outrun his pecuniary means' he had to take refuge from his creditors in France for a number of years. And on his return he imprudently allowed himself to be drowned by an incoming tide. His widow, left with two daughters, became a contributor of verses to the *Gentleman's Magazine* under the pseudonym of Melissa. This could hardly have provided a liveli-

v. Mrs. Hannah Cowley, dramatist; engraving in the *Lady's Magazine*, September 1784
Mrs. Charlotte Smith, novelist; engraving in the *Female Preceptor*, 1814

Self-conviction.

Matrimonial Contrition.

VI. Illustrations to stories in the *Lady's Magazine*, June and October, 1816

hood, but will have carried so much prestige that she would not have difficulty in placing other work elsewhere.

Catherine Cockburn, the reforming playwright, was in later life a contributor of poetry to the *Gentleman's Magazine*. And the early compositions in verse of the famous scholar Elizabeth Carter first appeared under the name of Eliza in the fourth volume of the *Gentleman's Magazine* when she was only sixteen years old. Visiting London occasionally with her father, she was introduced by Edward Cave to many literary people, including Dr Johnson; and in 1738 she published anonymously a collection of poems which included those which had previously appeared in Cave's magazine. It was to be a very long time before any lady with social ambitions would publish anything under her own name, although the remarkable learning of Elizabeth Carter made her well known in literary circles while still very young. In 1739, when she was only twenty-two years old, she translated and published with notes the criticisms of Crousaz on Pope's *Essay on Man* and Algarotti's *Exploration of Newton's Philosophy*—anonymously, of course. Her subsequent work, and her circle of friends in the 'Blue Stocking' group, have their place in Chapter VIII.

Inevitably the enthusiasm with which the *Gentleman's Magazine* was received led to many imitators quite apart from the immediate plagiarization of the *London Magazine*; and naturally somebody thought of producing a publication called the *Lady's Magazine*. The first to do so advertised in the *Universal Spectator* on 7 April 1733, announcing that the opening number of a monthly *Lady's Magazine, or Universal Repository*, had been issued in March, price one shilling. It was said to contain a complete review of the 'essays' which had been published during the month. Also included were poetical productions; a summary of foreign and domestic intelligence; prices of stocks, goods, etc; lists of marriages, births, and deaths; and a catalogue of new books and pamphlets—all the features, in fact, of the *Gentleman's Magazine* except the reports of Parliamentary debates. The proprietors of this *Lady's Magazine* even had the impertinence to cast a slur on the magazine they were copying, stating that in *their* publication 'the valuable Lucubrations published throughout the Month in Papers of entertainment' were to be given without being mangled or murdered as was 'objected against all other Collections of the kind'. No copies of this *Lady's Magazine* appear to have survived; and mention of it cannot be found in any of the lists, reference books, or library catalogues consulted. Perhaps Edward Cave contrived to stop it. The first traceable publication

The COUNTRY MAGAZINE:
OR, THE
GENTLEMAN and LADY'S
POCKET COMPANION.
For the MONTH of

OCTOBER, 1736.

(Being a Work of greater Variety, and more Use than any Thing of this Kind hitherto ever published.) Containing,

I. The COOK's KALENDAR, being Rules and Directions in all Parts of COOKERY; with elegant Bills of Fare for the ensuing Month.

II. Choice Receipts in Pastry, Picking, Confectionary, Distilling, and making *English* Wines, Brewing, *&c.* particularly in this Month is the Receipt for making MUM. as recorded in the Town-House of BRUNSWICK.

III. Receipts in PHYSICK and SURGERY, particularly an experienced Medicine for the Cholick, and farther Rules for HEALTH and LONG LIFE from Dr. CHEYNE.

IV. GARDENER's KALENDAR for the coming Month.

V. Observations and Directions in every Part of HUSBANDRY and HORSEMANSHIP; Receipts for curing Diseases incident to HORSES, DOGS, HOGS, and all other Cattle: Also Instructions for managing Bees.

VI. A View of the WEEKLY ESSAYS, *viz.* On Sovereign Princes and States driving their Subjects to Desperation.

Letter from an ugly old Maid in Love. On the terrible Accident at the *Theatre* in *Covent-Garden.* Reflections on the Characters of Courtiers. On the Danger of Princes confiding too much in Favourites. On the Manners of the *French* Court, *&c.*

VII. POETRY. The *Sussex* Clown. *Horace,* Book 1. Ode 5. imitated. Verses on Mrs. *Mellish* and Miss *Carver,* begging for the Poor last Season at *Scarborough.* On Praise of Tobacco, or the Smoaker's Epitome. Mr. *A.* H's Style imitated. To the Author of two Copies of Verses on Lord *B----'s* House. Punch's dying Speech. Verses to the Memory of a Friend, *&c.*

VIII. A CHRONOLOGICAL DIARY of all the most Remarkable EVENTS in the foregoing Month.

X. LISTS of all Preferments, Births, Marriages and Deaths in the foregoing Month; of Bankrupts, the Course of Exchange, Prices of Stocks, and Goods, and Monthly Bill of MORTALITY, *&c.*

LONDON: Printed for the Authors, and Sold by J. READ in *White-Fryars* *Fleet-Street,* and by the Booksellers and Pamphlet Shops in Town and Country: Where the former Magazines may be had. Price Six-Pence.

8. Title page and Contents List of the *Country Magazine*, October 1736 *(British Museum)*

of the title was the *Lady's Magazine or The Compleat Library*, 2 October 1738 to 27 January 1739.

A monthly periodical that had appeared two years earlier under the title of the *Country Magazine, or The Gentleman's and Lady's Pocket Companion* undoubtedly owed a great deal to Edward Cave's original ideas, but it also broke some entirely new ground. It was in fact a compilation of far and away the best features for women readers that had yet appeared—practical without being preaching, informative without being dull. There was even included an occasional woodcut illustration. It is surprising that it did not have a longer life, for it only ran from 1736 until 1737. This was the contents list of the *Country Magazine* for the month of April 1736:

I. The Cook's Kalendar, being Rules and Directions in all Parts of Cookery; with ample and elegant Bills of Fare, for Grand and Private Tables of every Thing in Season for the ensuing Month; in an entirely new and regular Method, the Bills of Fare are placed first, and the Receipts for dressing every Thing mentioned in them immediately following, with Notes explaining all the different and uncommon Terms in Cooking; and giving Instructions for the placing and serving up Dishes.

II. Choice Receipts in Pastry, Pickling, Confectionery, Distilling, making all sorts of *English* Wines, Cordials, etc.

III. Rules and Receipts in Physick and Surgery, with Directions for the Preservation of Health and long Life.

IV. A new and accurate Gardener's Kalender for the coming Month.

V. Observations and Directions in every Part of Husbandry and Horsemanship, with Instructions for all sorts of Culture, and Receipts for any Diseases in Horses, Dogs, and all Cattle.

VI. A View of the Weekly Essays, being Extracts from the Craftsman, Fog's Journal, Grub-street Journal, London Journal, Weekly Miscellany, Old Whig, Weekly Oracle, Daily Gazetteer, and every other Paper of the same Kind.

VII. A Collection of Songs, Epigrams, and other Poems.

VIII. A chronological Diary of all the most remarkable Events in the fore-going Month.

IX. Ample Lists of all Preferments, Births, Marriages, Deaths of Persons in the fore-going Month; of Bankrupts, the Course of Exchange, Prices of Stocks and Goods, and Monthly Bill of Mortality, etc.

The several Fashions of MINCED-PIES.

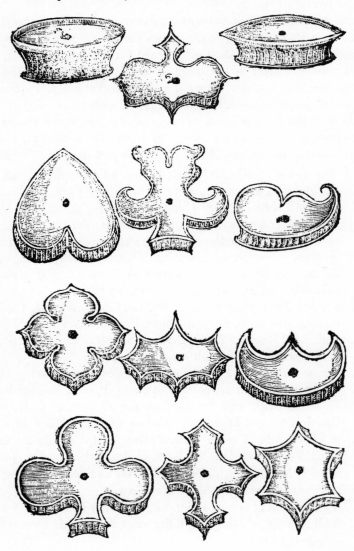

9. Woodcut of coffins for minced pies made with neats' tongues; illustrating cookery column in the *Country Magazine*, November 1736 (*British Museum*)

To be continued monthly. Price Six-pence. London, Printed for the Authors and sold by J. Reed in White-fryars, Fleet-street, and by the Booksellers and Pamphlet Shops in Town and Country where the Magazine for March may be had.

A truly impressive contents list, and there was nothing fragmentary about the features, which gave very comprehensive information. For example, the 'Gardener's Kalendar' was divided into six sections, under the six separate headings of 'Work to be done in the Kitchen Garden', 'Work to be done in the Fruit Garden' . . . in the Nursery, Flower-garden, Green-house, and Stove.

The cookery was equally thorough, and a receipt in the November 1736 issue for 'Minced Pies made with Neats' Tongues' has a full page woodcut illustration of the different shapes of 'coffins' in which they might be baked. A neat's tongue is an ox tongue. The instructions are:

'Take a fresh Neat's Tongue, boil, blanch and mince it, hot or cold; then mince four pounds of Beef Suet by itself; mingle them together; and season them with a quarter of a pound of Sugar, four pounds of Currants, and a little Ver-juice and Rose Water, and a Gill of Sack; stir all together and fill your Coffins. *See the different Shapes and Forms of them in the Cut on the following Page.*'

The monthly Bills of Mortality are interesting for the light they throw upon family life. The figure for those dying under two years old would not include still-births. This is the table for October 1736:

Died under 2 years old	...	...	...	...	...	1,054
Died between 2 and 5	...	...	...	...	...	279
Died between 5 and 10	...	...	...	...	...	103
Died between 10 and 20	...	...	...	...	...	85
Died between 20 and 30	...	...	...	...	...	191
Died between 30 and 40	...	...	...	...	...	240
Died between 40 and 50	...	...	...	...	...	215
Died between 50 and 60	...	...	...	...	...	213
Died between 60 and 70	...	...	...	...	...	156
Died between 70 and 80	...	...	...	...	...	103
Died between 80 and 90	...	...	...	...	...	56
Died between 90 and 100	...	...	...	...	...	9
Died at 100 and upwards	...	...	...	...	...	1

The fact that a household magazine should publish the mortality figures every month is indicative of death being a normal part of everyday family life.

We noted that the first *Lady's Magazine* projected in imitation of Edward Cave's *Gentleman's Magazine* intended to copy faithfully all his features, omitting only the reports of Parliamentary debates. Ladies were not expected to be interested in politics. Certainly middle-class ladies for the most part were not. Newspapers were not brought into the home. Men read them at the coffee-houses, and it was there that they discussed the news of the day. In the country, a weekly news-letter was handed from neighbour to neighbour, and was discussed at village hostelries, but wives and daughters usually gathered their news by hearsay and did not hold opinions on politics. It was different with aristocratic women. They were naturally drawn into the current of affairs by their connections with statesmen, by their distinguished foreign visitors, by their opportunities of travel and contact with circles in which the discussion of politics was an integral part of social intercourse. And it was a lady of aristocratic birth who set up the next milestone in the history of women's journalism by writing a weekly essay paper for political purposes. It was a Whig paper called the *Nonsense of Commonsense*, and was quite different from the political pamphlets of Mrs Manley's day with their malicious injecture. It set itself against lewdness and obscenity, gossip and personal defamation. It was written anonymously, and not for money, by Lady Mary Wortley Montagu.

Lady Mary was a cousin by marriage of Mrs Montagu who was a prominent member of the group of intellectual ladies that became known, soon after the mid-century, as the Blue Stockings. But Lady Mary herself was never a Blue Stocking. She rather despised them as being over-precious and artificial. Her own lively intelligence and wit was backed by considerable learning; but she liked to think of herself as an aristocrat and *bel esprit*, not a scholar. Unlike the Blue Stockings, she never published anything under her own name. She would have felt it incompatible with her position in Society. As for earning money by writing!—that would have been unthinkable. She expressed pity for Sarah Fielding 'constrained . . . to seek her bread by a method I do not doubt she despises'.

Lady Mary's daughter was married to the Lord Bute who became Prime Minister, and she felt the indignity of authorship in women even more keenly. All her life she considered it unseemly for her mother to have been a writer, regardless of the acclaim given to Lady Mary's *Turkish Embassy Letters* which were written when her husband, Edward Wortley, was Ambassador to the Porte, but only published after her death. They were reprinted many times, as were Lady Mary's letters to her sister, Lady Mar, with their cynical comments on London society, and some of those to her daughter which had more philosophical and literary content. Lady Mary wrote poetry throughout her whole life, and the success of the letters led to her verse being collected and published. But Lady Bute destroyed the diary her mother had written from the time of her marriage until her death, determined that posterity should not have the impertinent pleasure of indulging in its private and personal contents. Unless Lady Mary had expressed a wish for her diary to be published, one can understand her daughter's action; but nevertheless the destruction must rank among the great losses of literature, and a great loss to social historians. As Isaac Disraeli said in his *Curiosities of Literature*, 'We have lost much valuable literature by the illiberal or malignant descendants of learned and ingenious persons. Many of Lady Mary Wortley Montagu's letters have been destroyed, I am informed, by her daughter, who imagined that the family honours were lowered by the additions of those of literature: some of her best letters, recently published, were found buried in an old trunk. It would have mortified her ladyship's daughter to have heard that her mother was the Sévigné of Britain.'

Lady Mary's excursions into journalism were not many. There was an essay in the *Spectator*. She wrote one or two verse squibs, and was attributed with many more. She helped to write at least one satire on Pope, who was at first her friend and admirer. Later he became her most malicious enemy, calling her a 'scurrilous scribbler', although scribbler was a term usually employed to denote a paid professional journalist, while Lady Mary was essentially an amateur. Pope denied to Lord Peterborough that he was referring to Lady Mary in his first satire, saying that such women as Mrs Centlivre, Mrs Aphra Behn, and Mrs Haywood were his targets. But the first two of these, after all, were already dead, and Mrs Haywood was no longer writing pamphlets; so Pope's denial seems pretty thin. Lady Mary's most controversial contribution to the press was probably the newspaper letter she wrote in 1721 on smallpox inoculation. When she was in Turkey she had contracted the dreaded disease and, following the practice there, she subsequently had both her children inoculated with the virus to produce a slight attack and subsequent

87

immunity. It was a very courageous thing to do, since nobody in England had experimented with smallpox inoculation before.

The disease was an ever-present peril in the eighteenth century, and was said to be the cause of one-tenth of the total mortality. If you survived an attack, you were likely to have to go through life with a scarred and cicatrized face. There were ladies so disfigured that they habitually wore thick veils when out of doors and sat in dark corners when in society. A girl who had survived an attack without permanent blemish was considered 'beautiful for ever'. In eighteenth-century fiction, smallpox was often made the *deus ex machina* to curb vanity, punish pride, test constancy, cause heart-rending renouncements of marriage. Novelists could draw their fictitious situations from examples in real life of romance standing the test of disfigurement. The best known was that of the Temples. When happiness was at last in sight for Dorothy Osborne and William Temple after long years of family opposition to their marriage, Dorothy was struck down with smallpox a week before the wedding. In *Two Quiet Lives* Lord Cecil writes, 'Oblivious of the risk, Temple stayed with her constantly. By December she was out of danger. But smallpox is a cruel disease: Dorothy rose from her bed with her beauty gone. And though Temple married her the moment she was well enough, yet it is related that he found the change in her appearance too great to leave him wholly insensible'.

On 16 December 1737, Lady Mary Wortley Montagu launched anonymously her political paper called the *Nonsense of Commonsense*. For such a dilettante of extempore although brilliant abilities, this was an astoundingly sustained effort. The *Nonsense of Commonsense* was published every Tuesday in support of the Government, as a retort to the highly successful weekly run for the Opposition under the title of *Commonsense*. Lady Mary neither expected nor received any reward for her work, and in a letter to her disapproving daughter in 1761 she assured her she had never 'taken (in any shape) either Premium or Gratification for any Service that I have rendered to any Acquaintance or supposed Friends.' Most of the essays in the Opposition's *Commonsense* were written by Lord Chesterfield, Lord Lyttleton, and C. Molloy; and it was a much more popular paper than the *Daily Gazetteer* and other Whig publications supporting the Government. Lady Mary was a loyal friend of the Prime Minister, Sir Robert Walpole, and her own political principles were Whig.

The *Nonsense of Commonsense* employed no literary devices except the fictitious letter that comprised issue No. III. All the other papers were straightforward essays without allegory, fable, or moral tale, but given literary depth by quotations and allusions from the Bible and from English and Latin poets. Lady Mary's championship of moral virtues and of higher education for women is reminiscent of Steele, whom she knew and admired. She was also friendly with the pioneer feminist Mary Astell, twenty years her senior, whose *Proposal* for the foundation of a women's college and other pamphlets had greatly influenced Lady Mary's thinking.

Lady Mary denounced the excesses and stupidities of Society, the 'sensibility' then so much the mode. But her own character was capricious and quite unashamedly contradictory. She condemned Henry Fielding's novels and others of the time because 'They place a Merit in extravagant Passions, and encourage young People to hope for impossible Events, to draw them out of the Misery they chose to plunge themselves into, expecting Legacies from unknown Relations and generous Benefactors to distressed Virtue, as much out of Nature as fairy Treasures.' Yet when she was living in Italy and her daughter sent her a box of books, Lady Mary wrote that she 'fell on Fielding's works and was Fool enough to sit up all Night reading'. Of Samuel Richardson she said, 'I heartily despise him and eagerly read him.' *Clarissa* and *Pamela* were 'miserable Stuff' with a low style and absurd incidents, and would 'do more general Mischief than the Earl of Rochester's works'. And yet she confessed to weeping over *Clarissa* 'like any Milkmaid of sixteen over a sad Ballad'. Her mind and reason disapproved of sentiment, but her heart succumbed to it:

> 'All that Reflection and Experience can do is to mitigate, we can never extinguish our Passions. I call by that Name every Sentiment that is not founded upon Reason.'

It was the Age of Reason, but the human heart in all ages, at all ages, has reasons of its own. When Lady Mary was fifty, she left her husband and started upon a fresh pursuit of happiness in Italy with a young Italian writer and dilettante named Algarotti.

In the *Nonsense of Commonsense* Lady Mary Wortley Montagu hitched her political message to feminism. She reproached the majority of women for their selfish and frivolous influence, writing sarcastically, 'I am glad they can find, in the imaginary Empire of Beauty, a Consolation for being excluded every part of Government in the State . . . but with all Kindness for them, I am shock'd when I see their Influence prevail, in Opposition to Reason, Justice, and the Common Welfare of the Nation.' She attacked luxury in general, and more specifically fine clothes and jewels, rich eating and drinking, footmen, opera and quadrilles. She even condemned the acquisition of paintings and objêts d'art. As for Levées:

> 'Levées are really become such a Farce, that I wonder the ingenious Mr Hogarth has never thought of obliging the World with such a piece as a *modern levée*. I am convinced he would succeed as well as he has done in his *Modern Midnight's Conversational*. Because I am sure the Cringes and the Grins, and the fawning Countenance of a thoroughbred Levée-haunter would make as droll a Figure, as the idiot-face or Bedlamite posture of a drunken Sot or frolicsome Debauchee.'

This particular essay was thought to be so provocative that it was reprinted in part in the *London Magazine* for January 1738, with acknowledgements to the *Nonsense of Commonsense*.

Needless to say, Lady Mary did not practise the austerities she advocated. For all her intelligence, she was the most outrageous hypocrite. She wrote that the Lower Classes ought not to envy the Rich but ought to rejoice that they are spared their many cares. She begged the King to alleviate the suffering and oppression of the unfortunate labourer—but in her private letters called a belief in democracy 'silly Prejudice'. A cynic herself, she persistently attacked the cynicism of her time. She deplored that people no longer set much store by Reputation 'which was once a great restraint on Vice, even to those whose ill Dispositions incline them to the Practise of it.'—but now libel, slander, and gossip had become so rife that scandal was no longer feared and was therefore no longer a restraining influence against irresponsible behaviour. 'We see now frequently heaps of miserable Verses sold by the Help of initial Letters, which are sometimes ingeniously contrived to serve for several Names, that the Reader may apply as best suits his own ill Nature, and the Author escape a beating, by throwing the Application from one to another; and this Propagation of Scandal takes off the Fear of it'. Fourteen years after Lady Mary wrote that, John Cleland, author of the pornographic *Memoirs of a Woman of Pleasure* (better known as *Fanny Hill*), is said by Lady Mary's biographer, Robert Halsband, to have taken her as his model for a character in his next book. This was *Memoirs of a Coxcomb* (1751), in which his hero has an affair with a lascivious woman of fashion named Lady Bell Travers. Halsband asserts that 'the similarities between Lady Mary and Lady Bell

Travers are unmistakable. When Lady Mary had finished reading it she wrote on the flyleaf of her copy her initials and one word: *Instructif.* The most interesting thing about this anecdote is that Lady Mary should be openly in possession of a book by this notoriously licentious author.

Whether or not there was any foundation for the belief that Lady Bell Travers was a portrayal of Lady Mary, her policy when she was writing the *Nonsense of Commonsense* was that her publication should be completely pure. It should also be entirely free from gossip and scandal, indeed should fulminate against loose conduct and extravagant behaviour. It was not a policy that appealed to Lady Mary's printer, who saw no money in high morals. When the second number appeared, Lady Mary complained 'to my great surprise my Printer had thrown in a little Bawdy at the end of a Paragraph that no way led to any Idea of that sort'. She had written, 'Like a tender Mother who forces necessary Physick down the Throat of a be-loved Infant, tho' it squawls and struggles with all its Strength'; and to this the printer had added 'or like a Lover that, etc.'

> '"I'll assure you, Sir," said my Printer, in a Heat, "I have done all I could for the Service of your Paper; but it is a damn'd ministerial Thing, and the Hawkers refuse to sell it, and the Coffee-House will not take it in, and if you will rail at nobody, nor put in no feign'd Names that everybody may understand, all the Bawdy in the *Dunciad* will not carry it off."
>
> I interrupted the Printer by saying this was only intended to be a moral Paper.
>
> "A moral Paper," cried he, starting. "And how do you expect to get money by it?"
>
> "I do not purpose to get Money by it," said I. Upon which he turned from me with the air of compassionate Contempt, with which good-natured People look upon those they suppose *non compos mentis!*'

Some issues later, Lady Mary seems to have decided that politics, which were the original reason for her starting the *Nonsense of Common-sense*, were too immoral for her periodical. She wrote in No. VII, 14 Febru-ary 1738, which was reprinted in part in the *Gentleman's Magazine* . . . 'My Papers are only intended as short Essays of morality, without any touch of Politicks. I shall leave to the Authors of *Commonsense* the full Possession of their Puns and Ordures, both now and evermore.' She goes on to write of Sir Richard Steele and with what good taste he entertained his readers before he appeared attached to any party but that of virtue and good sense—that is, before Steele began his political pamphleteering which led to his expulsion from the House of Commons in 1714. Lady Mary says, 'That Gentleman had the glory of pleasing, without the Assistance either of Lewdness or Malice. I am willing to believe there yet remains a great Number of both Sexes still capable of being delighted with what is rational, rather than what is absurd and do not want any of those *Haut-Gouts* to relish a Paper. It is indeed a Proof of a very depraved Appetite, when the taste of Reading must be excited by coarse Raillery, or such wretched *double entendre* as can mean but one Thing.'

Nevertheless the printer was, it seems, only too right in his assessment of what it takes to sell a paper. The *Nonsense of Commonsense* ceased after the ninth issue, date 14 March 1738. Apart from Lady Mary's essays, it carried a few columns of news items, statistics, and stock reports, and these must have been supplied by a paid journalist. There was no revenue from advertising, as the paper carried none. From the fact that only two incomplete runs survive today, it is unlikely its circulation was wide. The printer was probably out of pocket by it. In any case, it is more than likely that Lady Mary herself tired of it, and found the time demanded in writing a weekly paper impossible to reconcile with the distractions of her social life. Also, hers was not a nature to enjoy anonymity for long. In her first issue, 16 December 1737, she had announced 'To be continued as long as the Author thinks fit, and the Publick likes it'. Probably she no longer thought fit—as we have seen, she seems to have turned against politics. On a batch of printed issues tied together she noted, 'All these wrote by me to serve an unhappy worthy Man'—by which she will have meant Walpole, who at that time was having difficulties and disappointments in his personal as well as his political life. The secret of the authorship of the *Nonsense of Commonsense* was maintained, but she had a writer's personal pride in her work. She kept the sixth of the printed essays, the one on feminism, noting upon it, 'Wrote by me. M.W.M.'

In the same year that Lady Mary Wortley Montagu discontinued her *Nonsense of Commonsense*, there arrived in London a lady who, although neither journalist nor editor, nor newspaper proprietor, cannot be ignored in this narrative, since she earned her living by her pen. It might be more accurate to say she kept herself alive by her pen, although not always out of debtors' prisons. Mrs Laetitia Pilkington (1712–50) was the diminutive wife of a Dublin clergyman who was a friend of Jonathan Swift. To oblige Swift, Matthew Pilkington was given the chaplaincy to the Lord Mayor of London by Alderman Barber, then the coming-in Mayor. This was the printer whose mistress was Mrs Mary Manley. Thus the Pilkingtons found themselves on the fringe of the publishing world. Laetitia had already had some success with a little published poetry, and she was delighted to find herself treated as a miniature lioness at literary parties. But back in Dublin again, scandal broke out, and Dean Swift was writing to Alderman Barber that 'He proved the falsest Rogue, and she the most profligate Whore in either Kingdom. She was taken in the fact by her own Husband.'

Of course, Swift had an instinctively tarnishing pen and his gossip must always be taken with a pinch of salt. But the Pilkingtons were undoubtedly in the divorce courts, and Laetitia found herself no longer the little darling of Dublin society. Ostracized and penniless, she set out for London. Her first, and almost last piece of good fortune was to get a poem published by Dodsley, on the strength of which Colley Cibber, the old Poet Laureate, engaged all the members of White's to subscribe to her efforts. In those days an unknown writer's only hope was to find a patron or someone influential enough to help him, or her, get published by subscription—that is, to collect sufficient people who would subscribe a guinea or two in advance to encourage a printer to publish the book or poem. Otherwise it was a case of hacking for the journals, or for the jobbing-printers, or possibly doing some ghosting for a man who wanted to attract attention as an author but lacked the talent to write. Again, a writer might come to some arrangement with a bookseller to work to his prescription—the prescription almost always being for a melodramatic tale, well larded with luscious rapes and murders. In the event, poor little Mrs Pilkington had to have recourse to all these methods of making money, except the last. And after being imprisoned for debt in the Marshalsea in 1742, she opened a shop in St James's for the sale of prints and pamphlets, advertising that she would write letters for a fee on any subject except the Law.

Laetitia Pilkington's memoirs appeared in 1748, two years before her death, and they give a vivid picture of how humble hack writers, male and female, went about earning a livelihood in the first half of the eighteenth century—devilling for other men, writing by the yard, odd-jobbing for publishers and printers, or selling their souls to the producers of scurrilous scandal sheets. Scribbling away for dear life, with the debtors' prison always just round the corner, Laetitia was fair game, as an unprotected woman, for any man who came along. Somehow she seems to have preserved her independence and her honour—spiritually, if not technically. In her memoirs she records that a Mr. Eyre called upon her at her lodgings; and when he went to bespeak the supper from the Devil Tavern at 10 p.m.—'no unreasonable Hour, as it was the Month of June'—she spent the interval giving thanks to the Almighty 'who had enabled me to live by his Gifts to me; for, sure I am that I could raise no Money by vile Means:

> By Heaven I had rather coin my Heart for Gold,
> And drop my Blood for Drachmas.'

Mr. Eyre ordered 'a slight but elegant Repast, with a flask of Champagne. We supped together with great pleasure . . . talked of History, Poetry, and every muse-like Theme; called all the mighty Dead before us, rejudged their Acts, commented on the works of Milton, Shakespeare, Spenser, and all the British classics.'

She was at great pains to represent all her evenings as chaste. Indeed, Mrs Pilkington emerges from her memoirs as an intellectual prig and a bit of a prude. Although Alderman Barber discontinued the acquaintance that he had enjoyed with Laetitia and her husband in the happier times when they were together and were the much petted protégés of Dean Swift, it is almost certain that Mrs Pilkington, even at her lowest ebb, will have considered herself a cut above Barber's mistress, Mrs Manley.

Chapter VI

THE 'FEMALE SPECTATOR' AND GOODWILL'S 'LADY'S MAGAZINE'

Mrs Eliza Haywood returns to the literary scene. Her Female Spectator; *its campaign against fashionable vice; its warnings on elopements; its correspondence column; its attitude to marriage and divorce. The* Parrot. *Mrs Haywood reverts to novel writing. The* Lady's Weekly Magazine. *Jasper Goodwill's* Ladies' Magazine; *its horror crime reporting and potted novels. The* Lady's Curiosity *and the* Young Lady. *John Newbury and his Juvenile Library.*

ﻬﻬﻬﻬﻬﻬﻬﻬﻬﻬﻬﻬﻬﻬﻬﻬﻬﻬﻬﻬﻬﻬﻬﻬﻬﻬﻬﻬﻬﻬﻬﻬﻬﻬﻬ

WHEN Mrs Eliza Haywood reappeared on the literary scene after an unaccountable gap of some sixteen years, it was as a very different character from the lively novelist and poet who had admitted in her *Female Dunciad* to 'little inadvertencies', and whose romances tended to have titles such as *Love in Excess*. She reappeared as editor of a monthly essay-paper called the *Female Spectator*, launched in 1744. This was not in the least like the *Female Tatler*, Mrs Manley's scurrilous political paper, and there was none of the 'coarse raillery, and wretched *double entendre* as can mean but one Thing' which Lady Mary Wortley Montagu had deplored in the publications of the day.

The *Female Spectator* was a monthly in much the same format as the *Spectator* of Addison and Steele, and like the *Spectator* at first consisted mainly of an essay. Introducing herself to her readers in her first issue as being 'far from young', Mrs Haywood (who was about fifty years old at the time) puts herself over as a reformed society sinner, 'wise in worldly Wisdom through first hand Experience':

'I have run through as many Scenes of Vanity and Folly as the greatest Coquet of them all—Dress, Equipage, and Flattery were the Idols of my Heart. My Life for some Years was a continual Round of what I then called Pleasure; and my whole Time engrossed by a Hurry of promiscuous Diversions . . . The Company I kept was not, indeed, always so well chosen as it might have been, for the sake of my own Interest and Reputation; but then it was general, and by Consequence furnished me, not only with the Knowledge of many Occurrences, which otherwise I had been ignorant of, but also enabled me, when the too great Vivacity of my Nature became temper'd with Reflection, to see into the secret Springs which gave Rise to the Actions I had either heard or been witness of . . . to judge of the various Passions of the Human Mind, and distinguish those imperceptible Degrees by which they become Masters of the Heart, and attain Dominion over Reason. With this Experience, added to a Genius tolerably extensive, and an Education more liberal than is ordinarily allowed to Persons of my Sex, I flatter'd myself that it might be in my Power to be in some measure both useful and entertaining to the Public.'

Mrs Haywood then introduces her editorial staff, who were more likely than not to have been imaginary. The first was a married lady, 'Whom I shall distinguish by the Name of Mira, a Lady descended from a Family to which Wit seems hereditary, married to a Gentleman every way worthy of so excellent a Wife, and with whom she lives in perfect Harmony.' The next was 'A Widow of Quality, who not having buried her Vivacity in the Tomb of her Lord, continues to make one in all the modish Diversions of the Times, so far, I mean, as she finds them consistent with Innocence and Honour; and as she is far from having the least Austerity in her Behaviour, nor is rigid to the Failings she is wholly free from herself, those of her Acquaintance, who had been less Circumspect, scruple not to make her the Confidante of Secrets they conceal from all the World beside.' In other words, she knew all the gossip and would not scruple to retail it in the *Female Tatler* for all the world to read. The third member of the staff provided contact with youth. She was 'the Daughter of a wealthy Merchant, charming as an Angel, but endued with so many Accomplishments, that to those who know her truly her Beauty is the least distinguished Part of her. This fine young Creature I shall call Euphrosine, since she has all the Cheerfulness and Sweetness ascribed to that Goddess.' Hardly the terms in which a modern editress would describe a young assistant. Contributions to the *Female Spectator* by staff members were to be anonymous —'They are to be considered only as several Members of one Body, of which I am the Mouth'.

Mrs Haywood next introduces her network of social spies:
'To secure an eternal Fund of Intelligence, Spies are placed not only in all the Places of Resort in and about this great Metropolis, but at Bath, Tunbridge, and the Spas, and Means found out to extend my Specula-

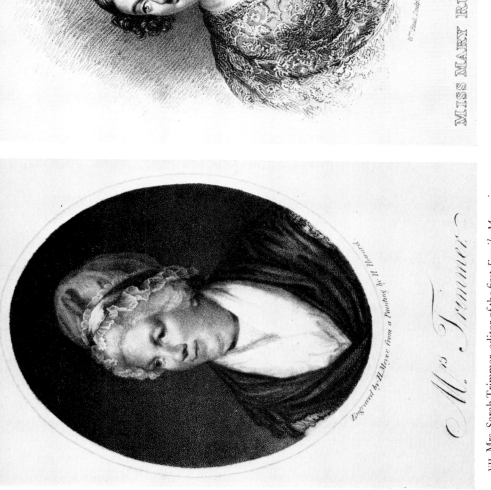

Engraved by H. Meyer from a Painting by H. Howard.

Mʳˢ Trimmer.

Wⁱⁱⁱ Bird Sculp Mʳ King Sᵗ Covent Garden.

MISS MARY RUSSELL MITFORD.

vii. Mrs. Sarah Trimmer, editor of the first *Family Magazine*
Miss Mary Russell Mitford, from an original painting by Miss Drummond, expressly engraved for *La Belle Assemblée*, June 1823

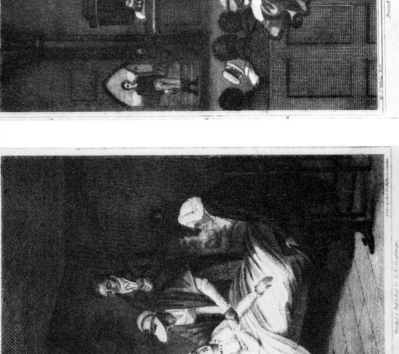

Eliza Amored survived by her friends.

Printed & Published by B.R. Goodman.

Mr Cunnington, on entering the Church, is struck with the beautiful appearance of Louisa Mildmant.

Printed & Published by B.R. Goodman.

W. White sculp.

viii. Illustration to a story entitled *Seduction*, Eliza dying in childbirth

Illustration to *The Gift of Filial Affection*; or *The Amiable Organist*. Both from the *Female Preceptor*, 1814.

tion even as far as France, Rome, Germany, and other foreign Parts so that nothing curious or worthy of Remark can escape me . . . simply by tumbling over a few Papers from my Emissaries, I have all the secrets of Europe, at least such of them as are proper for my Purpose, laid open at one View.'

Her readers are then told not to suspect any intentions to propagate scandal in the manner of that libellous scribbler, Mrs Manley:

'Although I shall bring real Fact on the Stage, I shall conceal the Actor's Name under such as will be conformable to their Characters; my Intention being only to expose Vice, not the Person. The sole Aim of the following Pages is to reform the Faulty and give an innocent Amusement to those who are not so, all possible Care will be taken to avoid everything that might serve as Food for the Venom of Malice and Ill-nature. Whoever, therefore, shall pretend to fix on any particular Person the Blame of Actions they may happen to find recorded here, or make what they call a Key to these Lubrications, must expect to see themselves treated in the next Publication with all the Severity so unfair a Proceeding merits.'

Thus did Mrs Haywood whet the appetite for libel and scandal, while at the same time declaring a crusade against the sins of Society. One must certainly allow that all the stories she includes in the *Female Spectator* carry the message that immorality does not pay. She exposes the dangers of masquerades in winter and of ridottos al fresco in summer; she deplores

'. . . such Definitions of that Passion as we generally find in Romances, Novels, and Plays. In most of those Writings the Authors seem to lay out all their Arts in rendering the Character most interesting, which most sets at Defiance all the Obligations, by the strict Observance of which Love can alone become a Virtue. They dress their Cupid up in Roses, call him the God of soft Desires and ever-springing Joys, yet at the same time give him the vindictive Fury and the Rage of Mars— show him impatient of Control and trampling over all the Ties of Duty, Friendship, or natural Affection, yet make the Motive sanctify the Crime. How fatal, how pernicious to a young and unexperienced Mind must be such Maxims, especially when dressed up in all the Pomp of Words! The Beauty of the Expression steals upon the Senses, and every Mischief, every Woe that Love occasions, appears a Charm.'

Clearly, Mrs Haywood would have made an admirable witness for the Crown in a prosecution for obscenity. She was not disposed to let literary merit excuse a tendency to corrupt. She deplored 'the Craving for Admiration prevalent among our young Ladies, some of whom are scarce entered their 'teens', and is distressed by 'the Love of company that makes our Ladies run galloping in Troops every evening to Masquerades, Balls and Assemblies in Winter, and in the Summer to Vauxhall, Ranelagh, Cuper's-Gardens, Mary le Bon, Sadler's Wells, both old and new, Goodman's Fields, and twenty other such Places, which in the Age of Luxury, serve as Decoys to draw the Thoughtless and Unwary together and, as it were, prepare the Way for other more vicious Excesses'.

At this period, those who belonged to the *beau monde* lived very much in the public eye. In those places of amusement cited by Mrs Haywood, men and women of fashion moved freely amongst the bourgeois man with his wife and daughters, and even rubbed shoulders with the *hoi polloi* who also frequented many of the same pleasure gardens. The fashionables behaved with little restraint or delicacy, and it is said that the ladies often emulated in riotous manners the gentlemen who accompanied them, sometimes even rivalling them in unashamed libertinism. Thus London was full of dangers for innocent girlhood, and the *Female Spectator* goes on to suggest that,

'. . . even worse Dangers lurk for the country-bred Girl who is never suffered to come to Town for fear their Faces should be spoiled by the Small Pox, or their Reputations ruined by the Beaux, and thus become an easier Prey to the Artifice of Mankind than those who have had an Education more at large. As they rarely stir beyond the Father's Pales, except to Church, the Parson, if he be a forward Man, and has Courage to throw a Love-Song or a Copy of Verses to Miss over the Wall, or flip it into her Hand in a Visit he pays the Family, has a rare Opportunity of making his Fortune; and it is well when it happens no worse: Many a Squire's Daughter has clambered over Hedge and Stile, to give a rampant Jump into the Arms of a young jolly Haymaker or Ploughman.'

But, although Mrs Haywood warned against reckless romance, she did not approve of arranged marriages:

'There are now no less than twenty-three Treaties of Marriage either concluded, or on the Carpet, between Persons of Condition, of which scarce the odd three afford the least Prospect of Felicity to the Parties concerned. Who sees Philmont and Daria together, without perceiving that nothing can be more adored by Philmont than Daria; nothing be more dear to Daria than Philmont? Do not the equally enamour'd Pair seem to shoot their very Souls to each other at every Glance?—Is Daria ever at the Opera, the Park, the Play without Philmont?—or does Philmont think any Company entertaining if Daria absent?—Yet Philmont is on the Point of Marriage with Emilia, and Daria has been long betroth'd to Belmont. Strange Chequer-work of Love and Destiny!'

Young gentlemen were almost as much chastised by Mrs Haywood's pen as young ladies. She lashed out at the 'Coxcombes and Finikins' of the *Beau Monde* and gave a list of the items on a bill for £38 9s 6d owed by a Cornet in the army to 'Rebecca Facemend', who has had to deliver up her Books on the Account of a Statute of Bankruptcy. As for the evil of gambling at cards, she vowed she could name a spot of ground within the liberties of Westminster 'which contains fourteen public Gaming-houses in the Compass of two hundred yards, all of which are every Night crowded with promiscuous Company of "the great Vulgar and the Small", as Congreve elegantly and justly calls all such Assemblies . . . at some of our great Chocolate-houses, many thousands of Acres are often swallowed up before Dinner . . . and the important Business of Whist which has become the Mode and, by being encouraged by Persons of Figure and Condition, render the lower Class of People (who are always fond of imitating their Superiors) ambitious, as it were, of being undone in such good Company'. She deplored that even sport was not free from gambling—'To hurl the Tennis-ball, or play a Match at Cricket were originally invented to try and preserve Strength and Activity, and to keep those of our Youth who were not born to meaner Labours, from Idleness and Effeminacy.'

Soon the *Female Spectator* had a correspondence column. There is a letter from a mother complaining that her daughter of fourteen 'thinks of nothing but going to the publick Breakfastings at Ranelagh with her Friends, and again in the Evening, and what she shall wear. Should she send her to a Relation in Cornwall, whose nearest Neighbour is twelve Miles distant, and whence, if she continues her rambling Humour, huge craggy Rocks on one Side and no less dreadful Mines on the other, will be her only Prospect?' The *Female Spectator* commiserated with the mother, but did not advise force, giving a cautionary tale of how a girl, closely confined by her parents, eloped with the first man who came her way by throwing letters out of her window.

A male correspondent complained of 'the immoderate Use of Tea',

'. . . a kind of Debauchery no less expensive and perhaps even more pernicious in its Consequences than those which the Men, who are not professed Rakes, are generally accused of. Taken to excess, Tea occasions Dejection of Spirits, and Flatulency which leads to the Drinkers having recourse to more animating Liquors. The most temperate and sober of the Sex find themselves obliged to drink Wine pretty freely after it, none of them nowadays pretend to entertain with the one without the other: the Bottle and Glass are as sure an Appendix to the Tea Table as the Slop Basin. Brandy and Rum and other Spiritous Liquors of a more exhilarating nature . . . their frequent use grow so familiar to the Palate that their intoxicating Qualities are no longer formidable . . . Vapours, Cholic, bad Digestion . . . Doctors' Fees, Apothecaries Bills, Bath, Tunbridge, the Spa.'

The *Female Spectator* replied rather tartly that she considered tea only harmful when 'the Affectations of some Tradesmen's Wives gives rise to the Ridiculous Behaviour our Correspondent described', and went on to observe that 'Excesses in all things are blameable . . . the Snuff-Box and Smelling Bottle are pretty Trinkets in a Lady's Pocket and are frequently necessary to supply a Pause in Conversation; but whatever Virtues they are possessed of are lost by a too confident and familiar Use'.

A rude letter came from a Gentleman signing himself 'Curioso Politico, White's Chocolate House, Nov. 9, 1744'. He challenged the *Female Spectator* to publish his letter verbatim, which she does:

'Did the Spies you boasted of in every Corner of *Europe* deceive the Trust you reposed in them, or did you only dream you had established such Intelligence. The latter I am afraid is most likely. Instead of the full and perfect Account of the most momentous Actions you made them hope, they find themselves for several months together entertained only with Home Amours, Reflections on Human Nature, the Passions, Morals, Inference and Warnings to your own Sex;—the most proper Province for you, I must own, but widely inconsistent with the Proposals of your first setting out. Are you not under the most terrible Apprehensions that, instead of the Woman of Experience, Observation, fine Understanding, and extensive Genius you would pass for, you should be taken for an idle, prating, gossiping old Woman, fit only to tell long Stories by the Fire-side for the Entertainment of little Children or Matrons, more antiquated than yourself? I have alleged no more against you than is the Sense of most of the Wits, as well the Men of Fashion I converse with.'

The *Female Spectator* replied in spirited fashion: 'Several of the topics he reproaches me for not having touched upon come not within the Province of a Female Spectator—such as Armies marching, Battles fought, Towns destroyed, Rivers crossed, and the like;—I should think it ill becomes me to take up my own, or Readers' Time, with such Accounts as are every Day to be found in the public Papers.' She continued with a flood of sarcasm, and finished,

'To check the enormous Growth of Luxury, to reform the Morals, and improve the Manners of an Age, by all confess'd degenerate and sunk, are the great Ends for which these Essays were chiefly intended: Many little Histories, it is true, are interspersed, but only to enforce *Precept* by Example. The *Female Spectator* is not altogether so indolent and insensitive to public Transactions as he imagines; and if he allows that *Virtue* is the surest Preservative of *Freedom*, he must allow that an Endeavour to improve the Morals of *Individuals* is the first step to be taken for raising up a *general* Ardor for maintaining and asserting those Privileges our Ancestors purchased for us with their best Blood.'

The correspondence column became the vehicle by which Mrs Haywood most pungently expressed her views on such subjects as jealousy in married life. 'As Mr Waller elegantly expresses it—

Our Passions gone, and Reason in the Throne,
Amazed we see the Mischief we have done.
After a tempest, when the Winds are laid,
The calm Sea wonders at the Wrecks it made.'

And also on separation and divorce—'When both Parties are equally determined to maintain their different Opinions, though at the expense of all that Love and Tenderness each has a right to expect of the other, and instead of living together in any Manner conformable to their Vows at the Altar, it is the Judgement of every member of our Club, that it is less Violation of the sacred Ceremony which joined their Hands, to separate entirely, than it is to continue in a State where to, Persons mutually dissatisfied, the most trifling Words or Action will be looked on as fresh Matter of provocation.' This was in reply to information that a letter signed Amonia inserted in the previous issue, deploring the conduct of her husband, 'had made some Noise in Town, and her husband, who it seems is a constant Reader of these Lubrications, is so much incensed against her for the public Complaint she makes of his Behaviour, that the Disagreement, which was before between them is now increased, even to a mutual Tendency towards Separation'.

The *Female Spectator* had her gentlemen admirers as well as critics. In Book XXII Mrs Haywood hinted that 'these Essays are now drawing towards a Period', and in Book XXIV, a letter dated Bartlet Square, 27 March 1746, comes from a gentleman who says 'Ladies—if such you are, for you must know I very much question whether you are feminine Gender or not—For God's sake what do you mean by intending to throw away your Pen, just at the time when its reputation is established—I am very certain you have not gone through half the Topics that have a Claim for your attention.' Mrs Haywood was not persuaded to continue, but compromised by saying

'. . . though we think it convenient to drop the Shape we have worn these last two Years we have a kind of narking Inclination to assume another in a short time . . . if so, Notice shall be given in the Public Papers . . . those who have testified their Approbation of the *Female Spectator* either by Subscriptions or Correspondence will not withdraw their Favour from the Authors, in whatever Character we shall next appear. Close as we endeavour to keep the Mystery of our little Cabal, some Gentlemen have at last found Means to make full Discovery of it. They will needs have us take up the Pen again and promise to furnish us with a variety of Topics as yet untouched on, with this Condition that we admit them as Members. We have not yet quite agreed on the preliminary of this League, but . . . we believe we shall not differ with them on Trifles, especially as one of them is the Husband of Mira.'

The *Female Spectator* was later collected in four volumes, similar in appearance to the bound *Spectators* of Addison and Steele. These ran into seven editions, the last edition appearing in 1771. The bound volumes had decorative title-pages and romantic engravings as frontispieces. Each was dedicated 'with the most profound duty and submission to a ducal lady:

'The Dutchess of Leeds, the Dutchess of Bedford, the Dutchess of Queens-
bury and Dover, and the Dutchess of Manchester'. The short quotations of
poetry which accompanied the introductory pages were in keeping with
the contents of the volumes:

Vol I.
> Ill Customs, by Degrees, to Habits rise,
> Ill Habits soon become exalted Vice. *Dryden.*

Vol II.
> Le Luxe et le Jeu sont deux grandes Sources de Misère
> Ce n'est pas la Naissance, les Biens, ou les grandes
> Emplois, qui vous rendront considerable dans le Monde,
> C'est la usage que vous en ferez. *L'Abbé de Bellegarde.*

Vol III.
> There is a Lust in Man no Charm can tame,
> Of loudly publishing his Neighbour's Shame;
> On Eagles Wings immortal Scandals fly,
> While virtuous Actions are but born to die. *Harv. Juv.*

Vol IV.
> Happy alone are those that can
> Govern the little Empire Man;
> Bridle their Passions and direct their Will,
> Thro' all the glittering Paths of charming Ill;
> Who in a fix'd unalterable State
> Smile at the doubtful Tide of Fate.
> And scorn alike her Friendship and her Hate. *Stepney.*

Mrs Haywood's industrious pen was not idle after she discontinued the
Female Spectator. In the same year, from 2 August until 4 October 1746,
there appeared nine numbers of a periodical that was very similar in format.
It was issued weekly as the *Parrot, with a Compendium of the Times by the
authors of the 'Female Spectator'*. It will be remembered that this was not the
first *Parrot*. There had been the one in 1728 discussed in the previous
chapter, which was conducted under the pseudonym of Mrs Penelope
Prattle, who was almost certainly Mrs Eliza Haywood herself.

After the demise of the second *Parrot*, Mrs Haywood reverted once more
to novel writing. Richardson's *Pamela* had appeared in 1740, followed by
Fielding's *Joseph Andrews* which started as a parody of *Pamela* but ended
in being an absorbing novel in its own right. These two authors had not

only created an entirely new reading public, but had raised the standard of the novel and shown that very considerable sales could be achieved by a book that appealed to people in all walks of life. It is noticeable that Eliza Haywood's novels during this second period of her output were more skilfully constructed and better written than her earlier romances, and this suggests that she was probably influenced by Richardson and Fielding. *Betsy Thoughtless* (1751) is crammed with excellently depicted characters, each chapter packed with incident and ending at a point in the plot that compels you to start reading the next. For example, at the end of Chapter XIII, when Mr Goodman discovered that his wife had been deceiving him, he ordered his servants to make up a bed for him in another part of the house and 'flung out of the room, saying, "Madam, perhaps we never more may meet between a pair of sheets!" Whether at that time he was determined to carry his resentment so far, or not, is uncertain; but what happened very shortly after left him no other part to take than that which he had threatened.' We have to start reading the next chapter to see what it was that happened shortly after.

Betsy Thoughtless was popular for a very long time, as also was Eliza Haywood's *Jenny and Jemmy Jessamy*, published in 1753. Sir Walter Scott refers to it at the close of *Old Mortality*, published in 1817, making an old lady praise *Jenny and Jemmy Jessamy* as being 'indeed pathos itself'. In the title of her last novel, published in 1756, Mrs Haywood brought forward once more her imaginary colleague on the *Female Spectator*. She called it *The Wife, by Mira, one of the authors of the Female Spectator*. One might conjecture from this that she looked back upon the *Female Spectator* as her greatest achievement and best-known work.

Other activities in periodical publishing at this time included the *Lady's Weekly Magazine*, issued under the direction of Mrs Penelope Pry on 19 February 1747. This issue is in the Bodleian Library, but no other can be traced. In her introduction to it, Mistress Pry promised to supply such incidents as might serve '. . . to fortify the Minds of those who are arrived to years of Maturity, and to obviate the Artifices and Designs upon the Young, the Credulous, and the Unwary'. There were to be notices of plays, balls, masquerades, music meetings, assemblies, and other parties of pleasure. Once every month a new song, set to music, was to be presented, and 'original Pieces of Poetry to heighten the Entertainment of some and to improve the rising Geniuses of others'. News from abroad would be

The LADIES MAGAZINE.

By *J A S P E R   G O O D W I L L*, of *Oxford*, Efq;

Numb. VI. From 𝔖𝔞𝔱𝔲𝔯𝔡𝔞𝔶, *Jan.* 25, to 𝔖𝔞𝔱𝔲𝔯𝔡𝔞𝔶, *Feb.* 8, 1752. VOL. III.

C O N T E N T S.

Hiftory of the Reign of his prefent Majefty King GEORGE the Secord 81

An Account of a NOVEL lately publifhed, intitled, AMELIA. By HENRY FIELDING, Efq; To which are added fome general Remarks 83

From the INSPECTOR 85

An Account of the Foundling Hofpital 86

ASEM and SALNED. An Eaftern Tale 88

A Collection of Advertifements from the Drury-Lane Journal

Verfes on Mrs. WOFFINGTON's Acting 91

Prologue to Mrs. Mary Midnight's Oratory ibid

Socrates on Death ibid

Verfes faid to be found in the Duke of BURGUNDY's Cradle 92

On a late Happy Marriage ibid

On the Report that a certain Courtezan got a Ten-Thoufand Pounds in the late Lottery ibid

Chronological Diary of Foreign and Domeftick Affairs 93

Particulars of the Order of the Funeral Proceffion of the late Prince of Orange ibid

Remarkable Paffage of one Mark Newby, from Culderftone in Yorkfhire 94

Story of a Ragman and his Afs ibid

Account of the barbarous Murder of one Albony, an Italian 95

Account from Dublin, of a Perfon's cutting off the Head of his Wife's Gallant ibid

Preferments, and Deaths, &c. 96

Bankrupts, and Stocks, &c. ibid

L O N D O N: Printed for the Proprietors, and fold by G. GRIFFITH, at the Corner of *Elliot's-Court* in the *Little Old-Bailey;* where all Letters (Poft paid) will be received; and by applying to him, by Letter or otherwife, all Perfons may be affured of being regularly ferved. *(Price Two-pence.)*

10. Contents list of the *Lady's Magazine* by Jasper Goodwill of Oxford Esq., No. VII, 25 January to 8 February, 1752

taken at first-hand from foreign prints, not from the secondary source of local publications, and whenever anything of a political nature was included, it would be presented by way of Dialogue, in an easy natural manner—in other words, it would be simply explained so that even women could understand it. Furthermore, Mistress Pry declared that no prospect of gain would ever tempt her to follow the mischievous custom of publishing 'scandalous Advertisements which tend to promote Vice, to encourage Debauchery and unwarranted Assignations, or such as are intended to wound and depreciate the Characters of particular Persons'. The opening number by no means lived up to all that was promised. Not that there were any scandalous announcements tending to promote vice, but simply because the contents were very dull. There was a poetical enigma, a dialogue on the 'Present Political History of the World', several dull items from Scotland, four dull columns on London affairs; then lists of births, deaths, promotions, casualties, and bankruptcies. It may have brightened up in later issues—on the other hand there remains no evidence to show whether it actually survived beyond the first one.

Two years later a much more exciting publication appeared, highly seasoned with horror reports upon criminal trials and executions. This tasty offering was issued as the *Ladies' Magazine, or Universal Entertainer*, by Jasper Goodwill, of Oxford, Esq., and was appropriately sold at the corner of Elliott's Court, Little Old Bailey. It was a fortnightly, averaging seventeen pages—good value for twopence. In his introduction Jasper Goodwill offered it as:

'. . . a most agreeable Amusement, either in the Parlour, the Shop, or the Compting-house, and a delightful Companion in Retirement; as it will contain an agreeable Variety of Subjects in the Circle of Wit, Gallantry, Love, History, Trade, Science and News; and will be a most innocent, diverting, and profitable Entertainment for young Masters and Misses, by giving them an Early View of the polite and busy World.'

The early view of the polite and busy world for young masters and misses included, once a month, fearful accounts of the sordid lives, trials, confessions, imprisonments and executions of notorious criminals. Titles of these pretty pieces included: 'Memoirs of the Wicked Life and Dying Words of John Collington'; 'An Account of Three Unhappy Women Executed at Tyburn'; 'The Remarkable and Atrocious Life of William Parsons'; 'The Trial of Mary Blandy for Poisoning her late Father'. There were also moral tales which warned of the dangers awaiting weak women, with titles such as 'The Treacherous Guardian' and 'Innocence Preserved'. There was a diary of events at home and abroad, play reviews, riddles, enigmas, and a lonely-heart column. For some time Goodwill ran a course of history by question and answer.

Altogether it was an astonishing twopence worth; but Goodwill was able to keep the price down by pirating a good deal of his material. He also had a splendid inspiration at one period for filling up his pages on the cheap. This was to publish an elaborate summary of Henry Fielding's *Amelia*. The plot was given in minute detail and spread over several numbers. This potted-novel idea was a very early forerunner of the 'novel in a nutshell' which early twentieth-century publishers found so popular— and the mid-eighteenth century readers of Jasper Goodwill's *Ladies' Magazine* were satisfactorily enthusiastic about the feature. Goodwill announced later that he had received letters from great numbers of female correspondents importuning him to insert 'such Novels as may at the same time divert and instruct'. His first choice for the diversion and instruction of these ladies was one of the novels of Mrs Aphra Behn, who in the previous century had delighted Restoration society with the licentious obscenity of her plays and novels. He printed fortnightly instalments of her *Oroonoko*, and filled out other issues with harmless essays purloined from the *Spectator*, and extracts from the *Whole Duty of Woman*. One of the arts of magazine editing was to filch as much material as possible from already published writing: there was no law of copyright, and authors had no redress for such pirating. Goodwill's *Ladies' Magazine* ran from 18 November 1749 until the issue of 10 November 1753, in which this notice appeared: 'The Publishers desire to acquaint the Public that Jasper Goodwill, Esquire, Author of this Work, having for some time been afflicted with a lingering Consumption, he gave up the Ghost last Monday; so that this Number concludes Volume Four and all his Lucubrations under the name of the *Ladies' Magazine*.'

In the year before Jasper Goodwill's death, another women's publication was issued by a male editor: the *Lady's Curiosity, or Weekly Apollo*, edited by Nestor Druid, Gentleman, and printed by C. Sympson at the Bible in Chancery Lane. This was more in the form of the earlier essay-papers, and most of the essays were on subjects to do with love and marriage: forced marriages, unhappy marriages, mercenary marriages, runaway marriages, every kind of marriage. An *avant-garde* note was struck by an essay on the 'Unreasonableness in Confining Courtship to Men'; and the paper was also advanced in carrying an occasional engraving. Nevertheless, it did not have the sensational content that had brought Jasper Goodwill's publication such success, and it is only known to have lasted thirteen numbers.

The *Young Lady by Euphrosine*, almost the last of the essay-paper type of publications, survived for less time still, appearing only seven times during 1756. 'Mistress Euphrosine's' simple hope was 'to improve or innocently entertain', and she seems to have been a bit of a prig. She declared herself to have come to despise 'the ridiculous Pursuits 'of her own sex, and desirous of substituting something of more decided worth. She rejoiced that her own youth had not been wasted on music, dancing, and Italian, but had been devoted to reading, reflection, and conversation with learned persons. She offered instruction in the proper employment of leisure, and advice concerning the prudence necessary in love. Then suddenly, in her seventh issue, she reported her inability to go on with the work because of an 'unhappy illness'.

Various clues suggest that Euphrosine may have been Eliza Haywood. It will be remembered that the youngest of Mrs Haywood's staff on the *Female Spectator* was named Euphrosine and that one suspected this staff—Euphrosine, Mira, and a Widow of Quality—to be imaginary. Mrs Haywood very likely wrote all the *Female Spectator* herself. It will also be remembered that her last novel, published in 1756, was called *The Wife, by Mira, one of the Authors of the Female Spectator*. She probably finished writing this novel the year before it was published, and may well have decided to launch a new periodical on the lines of the *Female Spectator*. The *Young Lady* ceased publication after its seventh issue because of Euphrosine's 'unhappy illness'; and Mrs Haywood died that same year. All the evidence suggests that the *Young Lady* killed off the gallant old lady, scribbling away till the last.

In 1750 Christopher Smart, poet and miscellaneous writer, joined with the bookseller Newbury to produce a publication called *The Midwife, or the Old Woman's Magazine, by Mary Midnight, with a Preface by Fernando Foot*. It was published in threepenny numbers and ran until 1753, afterwards being collected in three volumes. Its name belied its interest, for it was a humorous magazine, consisting of small pieces of prose and verse of a bawdy nature, decidedly too coarse for ladies. It did not come out under the imprint of Newbury, but of his stepson, Thomas Carnan, who published a rival almanack to the *Ladies' Diary* and later took over the retailing side of Newbury's business. Probably this was because the *Midwife* was not the kind of publication Newbury would wish his name to be associated with, for he was becoming widely known as a publisher of books for children. In 1765 and 1766 he published the famous *Goody Two Shoes* and *Giles Gingerbread*, also several other little books dedicated to 'all young Gentlemen and Ladies who are good or intend to be good'. They were tiny, Lilliputian books for children's amusement and instruction, and Newbury's Juvenile Library in St Paul's Churchyard was the great place for children to be taken to visit 'their old friend' Mr Newbury. His sixpenny publications splendidly bound in flowered and gilt paper, were more durable than the chap-books (simply folded and not stitched, rude in their execution and crude in their literary style) which were the staple literary diet of young people in the eighteenth century.

Boswell, in his London diary, wrote on 10 July 1763 of how he visited another publisher of children's books:

'I went to the old printing-office in Bow Churchyard kept by Dicey, whose family have kept it fourscore years. There are ushered into the world of literature *Jack and the Giants*, *The Seven Wise Men of Gotham*, and other story-books which in my dawning years amused me as much as *Rasselas* does now. I saw the whole scheme with a kind of pleasing romantic feeling to find myself really where all my old darlings were printed.'

Chapter VII
CIRCULATING LIBRARIES AND MID-CENTURY MAGAZINES

Libraries and popular novels. Fanny Hill. *Ralph Griffiths hires Oliver Goldsmith for his* Monthly Review. *Provincial libraries. Goldsmith's satire on library novels in the* Critical Review. *Frances Moore Brooke and her* Old Maid; *her dramatic criticism. Charlotte Lennox, novelist and editor of the* Lady's Museum. *Hugh Kelly and the* Court Magazine. *Chastity for women but not for men. Goldsmith's contributions to the* Bee *and the* Busy Body; *his editorship of the* Lady's Magazine. *Smollett's* British Magazine. *First serialization of a previously unpublished novel. Anna Williams and Dr Johnson.*

A BOOKSELLER named William Bathoe is generally credited with the origination of the circulating-library idea. Bathoe opened his library 'At the Blue Bible near Exeter Change in the Strand' in 1743. Another candidate is put forward by Henry Curwen in his *A History of Booksellers*, 1873. Curwen asserts that it was not Bathoe, but a bookseller named Wright, who founded the first circulating library in London at 132 Strand 'about 1730'. There was also the Reverend Samuel Fancourt, a dissenting minister, who is known to have set up, about 1740, the Universal Library in Crane Court, Fleet Street, announcing it as 'The Gentlemen and Ladies' Growing and Circulating Library, membership one guinea a year'. Maybe his were all dissenting books. Certainly his library would not have had novels on its shelves. In Edinburgh a circulating library was established by Allan Ramsay as early as 1726, but again it is unlikely to have handled fiction. The novels of that time were chiefly translations from the French or reprints of the more popular works of the Charles II period, imbued with Restoration bawdiness. There was Defoe, of course—not bawdy, but inclined to be coarse; and Mrs Manley, whose pen was far from polite. Her *Secret Memoirs* and *Power of Love* would not be allowed to defile any Edinburgh library, much less her *New Atlantis*.

By the time William Bathoe opened his library, the novels of Richardson and Fielding were beginning to provide fiction that was considered suitable even for young ladies; and, more important to the booksellers and librarians, these immensely popular novels had stimulated an appetite for reading among women of the middle class and even of the lower middle class, the wives and daughters of tradesmen and skilled artisans. By the mid-century many new novelists were beginning to cater for this appetite. Smollett's *The Adventures of Roderick Random* appeared in 1750, and Charlotte Lennox had a great success with her *Harriet Stuart*, published the same year. Mrs Haywood had got her second wind and was writing better novels than ever she did in her earlier period.

In 1749 John Cleland's notorious *Memoirs of a Woman of Pleasure*, more generally known as *Fanny Hill*, had been launched upon its long and chequered career. *Fanny Hill* would hardly have been circulated by any library. If she had been on the shelves, one can imagine with what guilty excitement she would have been taken out by the young James Boswell, who refers in his London diary of 1762 to having left a guinea security at Noble's circulating library. He certainly had a taste for fiction, because later on when he was confined to his apartment with 'the pox' he wrote, 'Noble also sends me from time to time a fresh supply of novels from his circulating library, so that I am very well provided with entertainment.' And he certainly got hold of *Fanny Hill* from somewhere, at some time, because on 31 March 1772, he wrote that he had met at Garrick's house 'old Cleland, in his youth the author of *The Woman of Pleasure*, that most licentious and inflaming book'.

The publisher of the book was Ralph Griffiths, a bookseller of Paternoster Row. John Nichols, in his *Literary Anecdotes*, says that Griffiths made a profit of some £10,000 from *Memoirs of a Woman of Pleasure*, having given Cleland twenty guineas for writing it at his, Griffiths's, suggestion. As well as being a publisher and bookseller, Griffiths was proprietor of the *Monthly Review*, which he founded in 1849. He engaged Oliver Goldsmith as a regular writer on the review, in return for board and lodging in his house and a miserably small salary. Mrs Griffiths shared her husband's business affairs and presided over editorial meetings. We do not know whether she was actively concerned with the publication of *A Woman of Pleasure*, but one likes to think she was. Goldsmith described her as being a large, capable, managing lady who wore a 'neat and elevated wire-winged cap'. He complained bitterly that his articles for the *Monthly Review* were altered by this managing lady and her husband, and afterwards described her in the *Critical Review* as 'a certain antiquated female critic of the *Monthly Review*'. Ralph Griffiths prospered exceedingly, as mean men

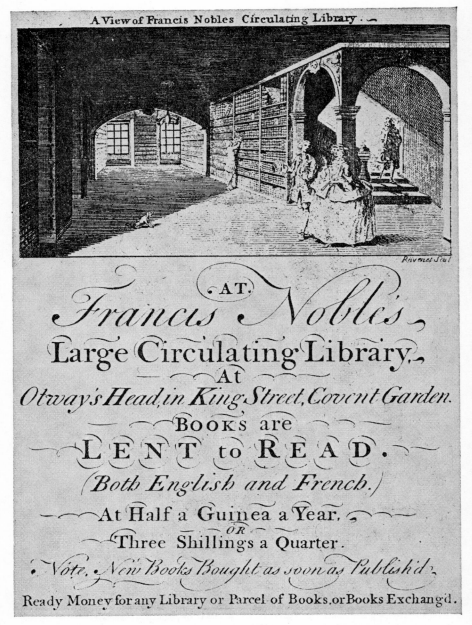

11. Trade card of Francis Noble's Circulating Library; from the collection of Sir Ambrose Heal (*British Museum*)

do, becoming one of the richest publishers of his day. At some point on the way up the social scale he became Doctor Griffiths, having, according to John Forster in his *Life of Goldsmith*, 'been awarded a diploma by some American university as obscure as himself'.

The circulating library idea spread to certain of the larger towns and cities. In 1745 the bookseller Nicholson of Cambridge was lending maps and lecture books to undergraduates—ten shillings a term for ten books. His library included the best editions of the classics, and standard works of English literature. In 1750 a Mr Hutton established a library in Birmingham, and in 1768 a Mr Priestly started one in Leeds. The *Annual Register* of 1761 said 'the reading female hires her novels from some Country Circulating Library, which consists of about a hundred volumes', and this was before William Lane of the Minerva Press started his nation-wide library operation.

Lane opened his Minerva Library in Leadenhall Street about 1770 (there is no record of the exact date), realizing it would be a most useful outlet for the light novels that were the principal productions of his press. When this was established he set about widening his market still further by establishing libraries in fashionable towns and watering places throughout the country. His enterprise was to have far-reaching effects both on the publishing trade and on the taste of novel readers, as will be seen in Chapter IX. But even before Lane's activities, circulating libraries were providing the chief outlet for women novelists, the chief encouragement for women to become novelists. Miss Lydia Melford in *Humphrey Clinker* (1771) wrote to her friend from Bath saying, 'We girls are allowed to accompany them to the booksellers' shops, which are charming places of resort where we read novels, plays, pamphlets, and newspapers, for so small a subscription as a crown a quarter.' A more intellectual type of reader was catered for by 'reading societies', very often in coffee-houses, where the subscribers were able to sit in the comfortable warmth of a blazing fire reading the books of their choice. In Dr Thomas Campbell's *Diary of a Visit to England* he writes on 21 March 1775, 'Strolled into the Chapter Coffee-house, Ave Mary Lane, which I had heard was remarkable for a large collection of books, and a reading society. I subscribed a shilling for the right of a year's reading, and found all the new publications I sought, and I believe what I am told that all the new books are laid in.'

In Smollett's *Critical Review* of August 1759, Oliver Goldsmith wrote a

12. Library labels in the collection of Dr John Johnson

satire on the popular novel of the day. His biographer John Forster, writing in 1848, referred to the 'unsparing yet not ill-natured satire with which he laughed at a form of novel which was then beginning to be popular; a foreshadowing of the insipidities of the Minerva Press; a kind of fashionable family novel with which the stately mother, and the boarding-school miss, were instructed to fortify themselves against the immoralities of Smollett and Fielding.' Goldsmith, for his satirical purpose, invented *Jemima and Louisa*, a tale in a series of letters professed to be written by a lady. In it he describes the fashionable novel:

'The female miss, it must be owned, has of late been tolerably fruitful. Novels written by ladies, poems, morality, essays and letters, all written by ladies, show that this beautiful sex are resolved to be, one way or another, the joyful mothers of children. Happy it is that the same conveyance which brings an heir to the family, shall at the same time produce a book to mend his manners, or teach him to make love, when ripe for the occasion. Yet let not the ladies carry off all the glories of the late productions ascribed to them; it is plain by the style, and a nameless somewhat in the manner, that pretty fellows, coffee-critics, and dirty shirted dunces, have sometimes a share in the achievement. We have detected so many of those imposters already, that in future we shall look on every publication that shall be ascribed to a lady as the work of one of this amphibious fraternity.'

He follows with the plot of a novel about two misses just out of boarding-school, written in letters, and ends his piece with:

'What need we tell *as how* the young lover runs mad, Miss is spirited away to France, at last returns; the sharper and his accomplices hang or drown themselves, her lover dies, and she, oh tragical! Keeps her chamber. However, to console us for this calamity there are two or three other very good matches struck up; a great deal of money, a great deal of beauty, a world of love, and days and nights as happy as the heart could desire; the old butt-end of a modern romance.'

If Goldsmith's suspicion was correct that most of the lady novelists were really men, it is ironical that in the eighteenth-century male novelists should pretend to be women, whereas in the nineteenth-century women novelists often felt themselves impelled to masquerade as men. The reason, of course, lies in the difference of the novels. A literary man would not want his name associated with 'the insipidies of the Minerva Press', although he might find it necessary to write romantic novels to enlarge his income; and a Victorian lady, if she wished to write a 'strong' novel, had in modesty to shield her identity under a masculine pseudonym, George Eliot and the Brontë sisters being the most famous examples. Even women journalists took men's names sometimes in order to write freely, uninhibited by what was considered proper for their sex. Mrs Thomson, when she published her *Recollections of Literary Characters* in 1854, wrote in her Foreword:

'These essays were originally published many years ago, some of them in *Bentley's Miscellany* and *Fraser's Magazine*. I wrote them under the appellation of "a middle-aged man" in order that, by better disguising myself, I might at that time express myself the more unreservedly.'

Although the mid-eighteenth century woman novelist and magazine contributor for the most part played safe with vapid moral tales and romances, there were some who qualified for higher rating. Frances Moore Brooke was referred to by John Duncombe in *The Feminead, or Female Genius* (1754) as 'a poetic maid, celebrated in Sonnet by Edwards in his *Canons of Criticism* and herself writing odes and beautifying the banks of the Thames by her presence at Sunbury, Chertsey, and thereabouts'. Later she became well known for her novels and plays, but the year after this panegyric appeared in *The Feminead* she launched a weekly periodical with the unromantic title of the *Old Maid, by Mary Singleton, Spinster*. This sold for twopence, and ran from 15 November 1755 until 10 April 1756. She took Samuel Johnson's *Rambler* as her model, declaring that she would abide by no particular plan but would write as caprice directed upon topics such as 'the fashions, plays, masquerades, the follies and vices of the sex'. She also wrote with original perception on literary topics, and her theatrical criticism was bold and trenchant. For example, she reprimanded the play-house for giving 'Tate's wretched alteration of *King Lear* the preference to Shakespeare's excellent original', and dared to scold Garrick, everyone's favourite actor and as such almost beyond criticism . . . 'Mr Garrick, who professes himself so warm an idolator of this incomparable poet, yet prefers the vile adulterated cup of Tate to the pure genius draught offered him by the master he avows to serve with such fervency of devotion'.

Frances Moore (as she was before her marriage) gave no explanation of her choice of the title of the *Old Maid* for her essay-paper; but in one of her over-elaborate allegories there is a sketch called 'A Vision of Marriage and Celibacy' in which she rejects the God of Marriage and comes down on the side of the Goddess of Celibacy—'in whose train Neglect, Contempt, and Derision are followed by Peace, Contentment, and a Youth, lovely as Morning, called Liberty'. Very soon after the appearance of this allegory, she gave up her liberty and her essay-paper to marry the Reverend John Brooke, rector of Colney in Norfolk. Women being what they are, rarely practising what they preach, it is no wonder that the cause of women's emancipation took so long to get off the ground. However, it must be allowed that Frances Moore Brooke contrived to continue her literary career after marriage. In spite of her *Old Maid* having been attacked by 'an obscure paper, "The Connoisseur", with extreme brutality', she had the whole issue of thirty-seven numbers reprinted in one volume; and in 1763 she published anonymously a novel called *A History of Lady Julia Mandeville* which went rapidly into four editions, and then two more in 1769 and 1773. There were other novels, one or two plays, and in 1783 a musical entertainment in two Acts called *Rosina* which had an unprecedented run. The opening number was a trio, 'When the Rosy Morn Appearing', that became a perennial favourite in concert programmes well into the twentieth century. How the Reverend John

Brooke reacted to his wife's literary and stage successes we do not know; but no doubt the money they earned made a very comfortable addition to his clerical stipend.

Charlotte Lennox, in contrast to Frances Moore Brooke, made her name as a novelist before producing a monthly periodical called the *Lady's Museum*, printed by the bookseller John Newbury. She was an Irish girl, born 1720, who came to England to stay with an aunt. On arriving in London she found that her aunt had died. In desperation she went on the stage, but found she had no talent at all for acting. In still greater desperation, and one step nearer destitution, she turned to writing. In this she found her métier; and her first novel, *Harriet Stuart*, won considerable acclaim. Dr Johnson thought very highly of it, and Charlotte became an accepted member of the literary circle which revolved around him. Boswell recounts that on 15 May 1784 Johnson told him: 'I dined yesterday at Mrs Garrick's with Mrs Carter, Miss Hannah More, and Miss Fanny Burney. Three such women are not to be found; I know not where I could find a fourth, except Mrs Lennox, who is superior to them all.'

Within two years the success of *Harriet Stuart* was repeated, even exceeded, by *The Female Quixote, or the Adventures of Arabella*. Henry Fielding declared that this novel 'entitled Mrs Lennox to rank as a woman of genius'. She translated from the French, and in 1758 published *The Philanderer, a Dramatic Pastoral*. Her *Lady's Museum* was issued in 1760 as a periodical 'Consisting of a Course of Female Education and Variety of other Particulars for the Information and Amusement of Ladies'.

In the first number Charlotte introduced herself as 'young, single, gay, and ambitious of pleasing', albeit with 'a strong passion for intellectual pleasures'. Yet her ideas upon the education of women were very conventional. In this issue she included a translation of a chapter from *The Studies Proper for Women*, in which young ladies were told to 'avoid all abstract learning, all thorny researches, which may blunt the finer edge of their wit and change the delicacy in which they excel into pendantic coarseness'. They were advised to select such learning as might suit 'the soft elegance of their form, add to their natural beauties and qualify them for the several duties of life'. These duties, it was implied, were marriage and childbirth. There also appeared in the *Lady's Museum* a translation of the Archbishop of Cambray's 'Treatise on the Education of Daughters', and a series of essays which recommended History and Natural Philosophy

117

as furnishing 'an agreeable kind of study calculated to banish languor from the sober amusements of the country and to repair the waste of intellect caused by the dissipations of the Town'. The wholesome use of leisure time was a frequently occurring theme. Yet it was by no means a dull compilation, for Charlotte's literary talents were very versatile. Her novel *Sophia* made its first appearance in the *Lady's Museum*, and also many of her own verses. The translations from the French of essays on the studies proper for women, were balanced by lighter essays on *Tatler* lines in a section called 'The Trifler'. There were also short tales, and a serialized feature called 'Philosophy for Ladies'. Each number published a song with music. It was not all her own work, for at some point she acquired a young collaborator, Hugh Kelly, also from Ireland.

Hugh Kelly was the son of a Dublin tavern-keeper, and went to London in 1760, when he was twenty-one. His ambition was to become a writer but, as the DNB puts it, he 'prudently announced himself as a staymaker'. It was not long before he was able to throw away the stays—by 1761 his 'smart style' obtained him a permanent post on a daily newspaper, the collaboration with Charlotte Lennox on the *Lady's Museum*, and the editorship of the *Court Magazine or Royal Chronicle*. The *Lady's Museum* ceased publication in February 1761. The *Court Magazine* became the *Court and City*, and then in 1764 the *Court, City and Country Magazine*. In 1765, under the pseudonym of 'Matilda Wentworth and Others', Kelly continued it as the *Court Miscellany or Lady's New Magazine*, which from 1770 was renamed the *Gentleman's and Lady's New Magazine*. The changes and mergers of magazines and their titles were just as frequent then as they are today.

Kelly, like Charlotte Lennox, had very versatile talents. He later wrote two comedies. One of these, *False Delicacy*, when printed had the remarkable sale of 10,000 copies in one season. His *A Word to the Wise* was produced in 1770, but, according to Boswell, 'Kelly being a writer for ministry in one of the newspapers, it fell a sacrifice to popular fury and, in the playhouse phrase, was *damned*.' After his early death in 1777, the proprietor of Covent Garden, had it put on for one night for the benefit of Kelly's widow and children, and for this performance Dr Johnson wrote a Prologue in verse.

In 1767 Hugh Kelly had been appointed by Newbury to be editor of the *Public Ledger*. Also in that year he published a novel called *Memoirs of a Magdalen or, the History of Louisa Mildmay* in which the hero, Sir Robert

Harold, writes of a personal problem to the correspondence column of a magazine. His dilemma, upon which the plot of the novel hangs, is that before the day fixed for his marriage he had overcome his betrothed's resistance to his too passionate embraces and anticipated their wedding night. He still loves her, but doubts whether he dare marry so frail a woman and thereby risk sullying the sacred name of wife: 'I have succeeded, fatally succeeded, with this amiable wretch, and both of us must bid adieu to happiness for ever.' He fears, since she has yielded to him before marriage, that 'with so quick an appetite' she will soon lose her fastidiousness and accept other lovers after marriage. However, all ends happily. She convinces him by a severe course of penance over a long period that he can safely marry her. At no point is it ever suggested that Sir Robert Harold's own conduct in the pre-marital incident was in any way dishonourable or that he was to blame for despoiling the innocence of 'this amiable wretch'. The novel is an excellent example of contemporary attitudes towards the different standards of morality expected in men and in women, and of the paramount importance attached to chastity (for girls only) before marriage. One must allow, of course, for a certain amount of romantic exaggeration in fiction. In another novel of the period, a bride who had allowed her future husband to anticipate their marriage flees to a nunnery—not in revulsion from the beast in man, but to save *him* from *her* 'polluted embraces'.

Oliver Goldsmith, in spite of his satirical attacks upon feminine taste in light reading, was himself contributing to a ladies' monthly and to two other periodicals which, although they were not exclusively produced for women, benefited greatly from the new class of reading females. The names of these two magazines were the *Bee* and the *Busy Body*. The first issue of the *Bee* was on 6 October 1759, and it was published weekly by Wilkie at 3d. Its editor was Eustace Budgell, a relative of Addison who had contributed to the *Tatler* and the *Spectator*. The *Bee* consisted of a collection of essays of which Goldsmith wrote anonymously all those of any distinction. It only lasted for eight numbers; but later, when Goldsmith became well known for more important work, his pieces for the *Bee* were reprinted in innumerable publications. They were admired as ingenious and amusing, and were a source of profit to many people, but not to their author. They were also collected and republished by Dodsley in December of the same year they appeared in the *Bee*; and several of the

THE
LADY's MAGAZINE,

For APRIL, 1763.

The Life of Edward Seymour.

 DWARD SEYMOUR, earl of Hertford, who was afterwards invested with the dignity of Protector, died upon a scaffold; and, as he had been instrumental in bringing his brother to the block, the providence which made him expiate his crime upon it, must be allowed to be entirely just. His brother's blood cried for vengeance against him; and it will appear, by the sequel, that it did not cry in vain.

We shall say nothing of his family in this place, as we have spoken of it in the former article. Being brother to Jane Seymour, with whom Henry VIII. married immediately after the death of Anne Bullen, he was soon after created lord Seymour, and viscount Beauchamp, and then earl of Hertford. From that time, he always held a distinguished rank at court, as well during the queen his sister's life, as after her death. Henry VIII. expressed all along a great esteem for him, and employed him in several military expeditions, in which he acquitted himself in such a manner as gained him more and more the regard of his master.

VOL. IV.   3 F   At

13. The *Lady's Magazine* edited by Oliver Goldsmith; first page from the issue of April 1763

best were included in the volume of Goldsmith's essays published in 1765.

Only three days after the first issue of the *Bee* came the first issue of the *Busy Body*, a thrice-weekly periodical published by Pottinger at 2d, which came out every Tuesday, Thursday, and Saturday. Again this was a collection of essays, although longer ones than in the *Bee*. One of Goldsmith's best known contributions was 'On the Clubs of London', afterwards republished in his *Essays*. The *Busy Body* lasted for only twelve numbers. That was, in fact, four more numbers than the *Bee*, whose publishers had meanwhile launched a monthly which was to continue over the next four years, until 1763, and with which Goldsmith became closely concerned. It was named the *Lady's Magazine*. It was not, as will be remembered, the first of that name. Nor yet was it to be the last. The first had appeared from 1738 until 1739; the second was the one run by Jasper Goodwill of Oxford, Esq., which ran from 1749 until 1753. Goldsmith's was the third, and seven years after it disappeared from the publishing scene, in 1770, there appeared the fourth *Lady's Magazine*. This was sub-titled *or Entertaining Companion for the Fair Sex*; and it continued, with slight alterations to the sub-title, until it was incorporated with the *Lady's Museum* in 1832. For the nine years from 1786 until 1795 there was a rival publication running concurrently under the title of the *New Lady's Magazine*, edited by the Rev. Mr Charles Stanhope.

Cheerfully ignoring everything that had gone before, the proprietors of the *Lady's Magazine* of 1759–63 introduced it as *the first Miscellany expressly appropriated to the Fair Sex*. It was also introduced as being under the management of a female editor named the Honourable Mrs Caroline A. Stanhope. Goldsmith's biographer, James Prior, is suspicious of this lady: 'The disguise of sex is so thinly preserved as to be penetrated in every page.' No doubt Mr Prior, writing in 1837, held the contemporary view of the inefficiency and fragility of female abilities, and we may suspect him of a certain bias. On the other hand it is possible that the Rev. Mr Charles Stanhope, who later conducted the *New Lady's Magazine*, may have had something to do with it. Again, since there is an interval of twenty-seven years between the launching of the two publications, it could have been his mother. Since she cannot be traced in any book of reference, the authenticity of the Hon. Mrs Caroline A. Stanhope must remain a matter of surmise. The issue of December 1759 carries a full page steel engraving entitled *Habit of a Lady in 1759*, which puts this *Lady's Magazine* amongst the earliest, if not making it *the* earliest monthly magazine to carry such a

14. A very early uncoloured costume engraving from the *Lady's Magazine* of December 1759, entitled 'Habit of a Lady in 1759'

fashion engraving. The accompanying text is headlined *Of the fashionable Dress of Ladies* and asserts that Mrs Stanhope is a lady; and yet perhaps we may suspect her of protesting too much:

> 'It is at the request of a correspondent, in the behalf of herself and acquaintance, and from a sense that many others at a distance from London wish to have information on the head, that we enter on a subject of this frivolous importance. Our readers of the other sex will hold us cheap for this; and some of our grave friends perhaps will blush: but they are to remember that Mrs Stanhope, however much they are pleased to think of her in her high character of Writer of a Magazine, is yet a women; and, as such, does not blush to own that, after the principles of decency and virtue, she thinks the arrangement of a set of good trimmings, one of the most important things in the universe.'

That last sentence could well have come from the sarcastic pen of a man. Mrs Stanhope, if Mrs Stanhope she was, goes on to say:

> 'I have engaged the ingenious Mr Walker to execute a design of a Lady in a perfectly genteel undress; and for the assistance of those in the country who, as they have not opportunities of seeing the originals, may dress by that figure, I shall endeavour to accommodate to it certain plain instructions.'

There were no more fashion plates in this first volume, although there were three other engravings of different subjects, including one of the actress Mrs Cibber in the character of Imoinda in Aphra Behn's *Oroonoko*, a dramatized version of the novel. There were also pages of songs set to music each month.

James Prior doubts that Goldsmith's share in the *Lady's Magazine* amounted to much in the first year, but says that a year after it appeared he had become its editor. This may or may not have been so. What is certain is that the Honourable (or mythical) Mrs Stanhope continued to be nominally editor, addressed to as such by correspondents, until the final issue of the magazine in December 1763. But of course Goldsmith may have been masquerading as Mrs Stanhope—it would appeal to his rather quirky sense of humour. Thomas English of the *Annual Register* refers to him as editor, saying that Goldsmith furnished the magazine at first with only a few poetical pieces, but that when he was editor his prose contributions were considerable—in fact he wrote a large part of its contents. His serialized

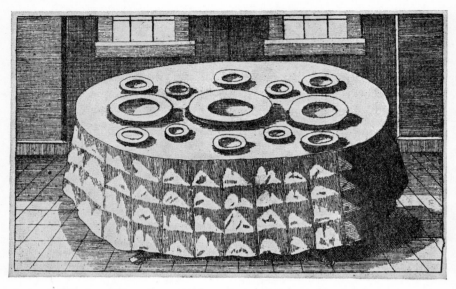

15. Woodcut illustrating cookery column of the *Lady's Magazine*, 1763: 'Model of a Table for about fourteen Persons, furnished with a Number of great and small Dishes properly ranged.'

life of Voltaire was the first paper in every issue until the magazine's conclusion in November 1763. Then there were his 'Chinese Letters'. Other contributions included his paper on popular preaching and some thoughts on the English poets. John Forster, in his biography of Goldsmith, says that he retired from the editorship at the close of a year, that is in 1761, when he had raised its circulation to 3,300—'if Mr Wilkie's advertisements are to be believed'. Unfortunately Forster does not say what the circulation was when Goldsmith began his editorship. An advertisement in the *Lady's Magazine* for August 1762 stated that in three years above 120,000 numbers had been sold, or more than 3,300 per month. Presumably this figure was averaged out over the three years.

Meanwhile the novelist Tobias Smollett had become associated with the bookseller John Newbury of St Paul's Churchyard and in 1760 became editor of the *British Magazine* in which Newbury had an interest. Smollett asked Goldsmith to become a regular contributor to this magazine. Newbury also started a daily newspaper on 12 January 1760, called the *Public Ledger*, edited by Griffith Jones; and it was said that the immediate popularity of the paper was due to contributions by Goldsmith. He sent in light, entertaining sketches twice a week, for which he was paid £100 a year—good pay, considering the purchasing power of a guinea then. Dr Johnson was contributing in a similar way to Newbury's *Universal Chronicle*, a weekly newspaper begun in April 1758, in which *The Idler* first appeared. But Johnson, unlike Goldsmith, was said to have received a share of the profits of the paper for writing *The Idler*; and when collected into volumes, two-thirds of the profit went to him, one-third to Newbury.

Smollett's *British Magazine* was launched at a time when there was an extraordinary number of new periodicals coming upon the publishing scene—not one of which was destined for a long life. Announced almost at the same time as the *British Magazine*, there was the *Imperial*, the *Public*, the *Weekly*, and the *Royal Female*. This last, which only lasted from March to December 1760, was edited by Robert Lloyd, and from July to December contained the *Meddler*. There were already the *Lady's Magazine*, the *Gentleman's Magazine*, the *Universal*, the *London*, and the *Grand Magazine of Universal Intelligence*. Then, surpassing them all in the splendour of its name, came the *Grand Magazine of Magazines*. With so many already in the field, it is no wonder that Smollett felt his *British Magazine* must be introduced in an important manner and his own part in it, as an established author of some note, made clear. The first number appeared on 1 January 1760, with a fulsome dedication to Mr Pitt, who was then the idol of the nation. The second number came out with this announcement:

BY THE KING'S AUTHORITY

Dr Smollett having represented to his Majesty that he has been at great labour and expense in writing original pieces himself, and engaging other gentlemen to write original pieces to be published in the *British Magazine or Monthly Repository for Gentlemen and Ladies*, his Majesty was pleased to signify his approbation of the said work by granting his royal licence to the said Dr Smollett: and this Day is published, price 6d, embellished with three curious Copper-Plates, Number II of

THE BRITISH MAGAZINE

or

MONTHLY REPOSITORY FOR GENTLEMEN AND LADIES

by T. Smollett, M.D. and Others.

Printed for H. Payne at Dryden's Head in Paternoster-row; and sold of all Booksellers in Great Britain and Ireland. Of whom may be had No. I.

What really gave the magazine its immediate impetus was that Smollett had a new novel in hand and had the then original idea of publishing a chapter in each issue. His first novel *The Adventures of Roderick Random* (1748) had been a best seller. *Peregrine Pickle* (1751) had been almost equally popular. Now, month by month, *The Adventures of Sir Launcelot Greaves* appeared in the *British Magazine* and assured it a faithful readership for the two years the novel serialization lasted. It was a brilliant idea, both for circulation raising, and circulation holding; and it was an idea quickly taken up by Charlotte Lennox, editor of the *Lady's Museum* and also a novelist. At that time her novels were probably as popular as Smollett's, and almost certainly they were more highly esteemed in literary circles, the circles where the opinions of her admirer, Dr Johnson, were of great influence. It was Charlotte Lennox's third novel, *Sophia*, that made its first appearance, before being published in book form, month by month in the *Lady's Museum*.

Goldsmith's contributions to the *British Magazine* consisted of his usual magazine wares: essays, stories, oriental tales, some of which he republished later in his volume of *Essays*. The story called 'The History of Miss Stanton' was almost certainly by him, as it has the first germ of *The Vicar of Wakefield* in it, and some of it is very much in the spirit of *The Deserted Village*. Smollett, who was involved with a multiplicity of literary projects—histories, novels, criticism—was never an essayist, and it is thought that his serialized novel and some general overseeing amounted to as much as he could spare time to give to the *British Magazine*. Andrews has it in his *History of British Journalism* that John Huddlestone Wynne was really the editor—the man who in 1770 became involved in the publication of the *Lady's Magazine* of that date.

Prodigal writer that he was, Goldsmith was pirated in the most outrageous fashion. There was scarcely a periodical publication of his day without several of Goldsmith's essays or sketches reprinted from other sources, nearly always unacknowledged. A particularly flagrant freebooter was the *Imperial Magazine*, which was started in January 1760 at the same time, and in rivalry with, the *British Magazine* with which Goldsmith was so much engaged. The very first number of the *Imperial Magazine* included two of Goldsmith's papers from the *Bee* as original essays: Goldsmith was in the ironical position of having to compete with his own work, from which the pirates were benefiting gratis.

At one time Goldsmith promised to contribute to a volume of Miscellanies collected by Miss Anna Williams who, like the editresses of the 'Annuals' sixty years later, impressed all her friends and acquaintances to contribute, including Mrs Thrale. Dr Johnson provided the most important pieces in her *Miscellany*, but it is not certain that Goldsmith ever kept his promise. He was very pressed in all senses of the word. Anna Williams became blind at an early age, but contrived to continue her literary activities. Dr Johnson did not meet her until after her sight had gone. He befriended her in many ways, and invited her to live in his house, with her own apartments. Always, before he went to bed, he took tea with her and recounted the doings of his day.

One way and another the sixties were an interesting decade in periodical publishing for women. Particularly interesting was the trend for publications to be planned to cater for both sexes, including both in the title. The *Universal Museum, or Gentleman and Lady's Polite Magazine of History, Politicks, and Literature* ran from 1762 until 1770; and in 1763 there appeared the second *Country Magazine*. Its sub-title was: *Calculated for the Gentleman, the Farmer, and his Wife*. The gentleman's wife did not come into its calculation. Country gentlemen and farmers had common interests and common meeting-grounds; their wives also would have had some common interests—but no common meeting grounds. The Women's Institutes were a feature of country life still very far in the future.

Chapter VIII

THE 'LADY'S MAGAZINE' AND THE BLUE STOCKINGS

Introductory address and contents of the Lady's Magazine *of 1770. Vogue for oriental tales. Mercenary marriages and runaway romances; female intelligence defended. Elizabeth Carter and Dr Johnson. Mrs Montagu and Fanny Burney. The Blue Stockings and Boswell. Hannah More and her literary earnings. The Blue Stocking code compared with the moral convictions of contemporary novelists and magazine writers. Epistolary serials; satires on Court characters.*

ᘿᘿ

I T is a common characteristic of all magazine proprietors to announce their new publications as having arrived to fill a long-felt want, and to claim for them features that have never before been offered. The *Lady's Magazine or Entertaining Companion for the Fair Sex*, launched in August 1770, was no exception. Where it was exceptional was in that it really did break new ground and find a formula so satisfying to its readers that it continued successfully for nearly eighty years. It was a monthly, price 6d, and the proprietor was a Mr Coote, although his name was not given on the title-page, nor that of the editor, whose introductory address to his readers began:

ADDRESS TO THE FAIR SEX

'As your Sex is in this age more employed in reading than it was in the last, it is sometimes surprising that no periodical production should at present exist calculated for your particular amusement, and designed to improve as well as delight.'

This was treating Hugh Kelly's *Court Miscellany, or Ladies' New Magazine* with a fine disregard. Truth to tell it did fold the following year, whether or not through the competition of the *Lady's Magazine* we do not know. But it had lasted six years, which was longer than most of the mid-century magazines. *The Address to the Fair Sex* continued:

'The subjects we shall treat of are those that may tend to render your minds not less amiable than your persons. But as external appearance is

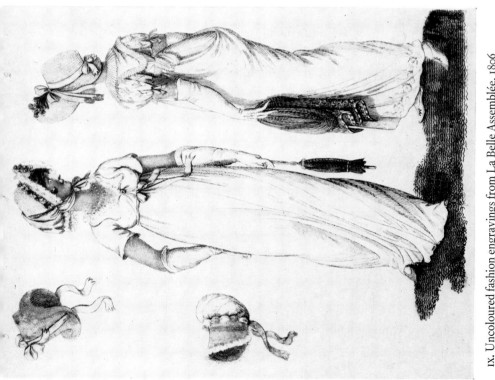

IX. Uncoloured fashion engravings from La Belle Assemblée, 1806

LA BELLE ASSEMBLÉE,

OR,

𝔅ell's

COURT AND FASHIONABLE

MAGAZINE,

FOR APRIL, 1807.

x. 'Fashionable Party at the Frascati in Paris'; engraved from a popular
French print expressly for La Belle Assemblée, April 1807.

the first inlet to the treasures of the heart, and the advantages of dress, though they cannot communicate beauty, may at least make it more conspicuous, it is intended to present the Sex with most elegant patterns for the tambour, embroidery, or every kind of needlework; and, as the fluctuations of fashions retard their progress into the country, we shall by engravings inform our distant readers with every innovation that is made in the female dress. As this is a branch of information entirely new, we shall endeavour to render it more worthy of female attention, by an assiduity which shall admit of no abatement. . . . In this we consult not only the embellishment but likewise the profit of our patronesses. They will find in this Magazine, price only sixpence, among variety of other Copper-plates a Pattern that would cost them double the money at the Haberdasher.'

The *Lady's Magazine* was not wrong in boasting that no previous publication had included fashions in dress; but it was exaggerating its own coverage of the subject. The elegant pull-out patterns on thrice-folded tissue paper were not of dresses, but simple embroidery patterns for embellishing aprons, handkerchiefs, gentlemen's ruffles and waistcoats. The engraved fashion plates were very few and far between. As in Mrs Stanhope's *Lady's Magazine* of 1759, there was only one in the first year. It was entitled 'A Lady in Full Dress' and there was an essay upon 'The Present Fashionable Dress for Ladies' which warned against vulgar display: 'As in literature a forced parade of knowledge constitutes pedantry, so in dress the extremes of fashion, instead of being ornamental are ridiculous.' After this essay there followed two columns of notes on the current vogue, drawing attention to the engraving as 'a perfect model for the present mode of every woman of *taste*'. But this was not a regular monthly feature: it was ten years before there was a monthly article on dress, and ten more before there were regular fashion notes from London and Paris. The uncoloured fashion engravings were still only occasional, and the 'elegant patterns' of 'curious sprigs' and other floral elegancies for embroidery continued until the end of the century. The Introductory Address promised:

'interesting Stories, Novels, Tales, Romances, intended to confirm Chastity and recommend Virtue will be inserted every month . . . and a Lady of some eminence in the literary world has promised to enrich our collection with a sentimental Journey, during her progress through

THE

Lady's Magazine,

OR

ENTERTAINING COMPANION

for the

FAIR SEX,

Appropriated solely to their

USE and AMUSEMENT.

Vol. XXIII. for the YEAR 1792.

===

LONDON.

Printed for G.G.J. and J. ROBINSON,

Nº 25, Pater-noster Row.

16. Title page to bound volume of the *Lady's Magazine*, Vol. XXIII, 1792

this Kingdom; and as she intends, after she has completed her tour of this Island, to extend her travels through the Continent, we doubt not, but her Article will be as entertaining to the imagination, as it will be instructive to the understanding.'

This serial named *A Sentimental Journey* was one of the editorial promises which was fulfilled. Starting in the first issue with 'The Stage Coach', the series is clearly inspired by Sterne's *Sentimental Journey*; but it has much merit of its own, being well written, amusing, and full of shrewdly observed incident and intriguing information. Another regular feature was an inset on a threefold page of the words and music of a song set by Mr Hudson. Sometimes it was set to existing verses, sometimes to 'A New Song' first published in the *Lady's Magazine*. It will be remembered that the words and music of currently successful songs were featured in the *Gentleman's Journal* of eighty years earlier.

Apart from the features already mentioned, the Contents of the first issue of the *Lady's Magazine* were:

'Happiness the Effect of Misfortune—A Real History
Friendship—An Allegory
The Tailor's Dream—An Oriental Tale
Letters to the Editor of the Lady's Magazine
Comfort for the Afflicted
The Blind Husband
The Counsel of Feridown to his Children—An Oriental Fable
Origin of the Convent of Montserrat—from Baretti's *Journey to Genoa*
An Account of the English Nunnery at Lisbon—also from Baretti
The Contented Hermit
The Effects of Avarice—An Oriental Tale
Superstition, ghosts and spectres, the Folly of believing Tales of
    Apparitions
Three pages of Verse
Foreign News, Home News, American News (from Boston, with an
    extract of a letter from New York)
Promotions in the Church
Births, Marriages, Deaths, Bankruptcies.'

Each issue carried a copper-plate engraving, sometimes illustrating a story, sometimes a theatrical scene from a current play; or it might be a view of a city, or simply a romantic picture telling its own story; very occasionally it was a fashion plate.

All in all, the *Lady's Magazine* gave a good bill of fare for sixpence. Francis Place wrote rather disparagingly in his notebooks (1825–30) that it was successful *because* it was only sixpence, and aimed at the lower middle class. Yet editorially it was very alive. Each month it introduced new features. In the second number, for instance, it was announced: 'As the French language is almost universally spoken, and as it is deemed a necessary accomplishment for ladies, it is requested by several of our friends that we would appropriate about one page of our Magazine to a little tale or essay in that language. We therefore give a tale from an elegant book just published in France entitled *Mélanges de Litérature Orientale*.' One doubts that the editor of a magazine aimed at the lower middle class today would consider including stories in the French language.

Oriental tales were at this time having a great vogue, and there were no less than three in the first issue of the *Lady's Magazine*. The public appetite for everything oriental continued until the influence of 'Gothic' novels began, towards the end of the century, to have its effect on the fiction in magazines. Horace Walpole published *The Castle of Otranto—A Gothic Story* anonymously in 1764; but the first of its avowed imitators did not appear until 1777. This was Clara Reeve's *Old English Baron*, in which the author's preface says; 'It is written upon the same plan as *The Castle of Otranto* with a design to unite the most attractive and interesting circumstances of the ancient romance and modern novel.' Following Clara Reeve, there came a host of minor Gothic novelists, and the height of the vogue was reached with Mrs Ann Radcliffe's powerful *Mysteries of Udolpho* (1794) and M. G. Lewis's erotic best-seller *The Monk*, published in 1795, which was considered even more horrific.

Although Smollett in his *British Magazine* and Charlotte Lennox in the *Lady's Museum* were the first to serialize complete novels in instalments before publishing in book form, the *Lady's Magazine* pioneered the idea of publishing extracts from books about to be published—a feature that is today a great standby of Sunday newspapers. In its second issue there were two extracts from Mallett's *Northern Antiquities—On the State of Matrimony among the ancient Northern Nations*. Anything about matrimony was then, as now, sure-fire magazine material. In this same issue, a letter to the editor from a male correspondent lamented his not being able to marry 'my lovely Lelage' because of her parents' objection:

'I am in love, deeply absorbed . . . a mutual affection possesses both our bosoms . . . yet her father will not grant her to me because I want the sum of £1,000 more to add to my little stock. We oft propose a thousand schemes of elopements, but the terrors of filial disobedience, and the doubts and fears of little, lovely *Lelage*, interpose with such discouraging symptoms, that when we have raised a pleasing ideal fabrick, it tumbles to the ground, and blasts our love-sick hopes.'

The doubts and fears of little, lovely Lelage, were no doubt agitated by her reading of women's magazines. As it was at the beginning of the century, so too in the second half; their message was that elopements always ended in desertion, that girls who defied their parents were set for inevitable, irretrievable ruin. Even replying to this love-lorn letter, the *Lady's Magazine* gave no suggestion of sympathy to the idea of elopement, although it deplored the father's mercenary attitude. Magazines have always been on the side of romance and true love (while emphasizing that true love is the marriage of true minds); but they always counselled caution. And at this point in social history they restricted their crusading to demand the same code for men as for women and a less mercenary approach by parents. They condemned arranged marriages, but never condoned runaway romances. Replying to the lover of little Lelage, the editor (who in this letter reveals himself to be a man) wrote:

'Alas! Parents, would ye but be advised by a man, who has whisked through the giddy circles of pride and vanity, ye would first consider what constitutes happiness in marriage, before the *last* necessary ingredient—money. What are the miserable consequences of such unnatural unions where money is the sole consideration? What made the amiable Lady P— renounce her spousal bed? What made the Lady Sarah Bunberry guilty of A—y? What made the Duchess of Graftoun have recourse to F—ca t—n? And what could allure Lady Grosvenus from conjugal fidelity, but incongruous, unnatural, and ill-consulted wedlocks?'

And in another issue (May 1771) he wrote on the same subject:

'The marriage ceremony is serious, is an awful one, and ought not to be trifled with. Trifled with! It is shamefully profaned, when the contracting parties join their hands with a mutual consciousness of being totally averse to the engagements which they devoutly promise to fulfil'.

The *Lady's Magazine* was also a stout defender of women's equality in intelligence, and inserted this letter from a male correspondent in order hotly to deny his assumptions:

> 'It will not be denied that there are many women of rank and fortune who have an extensive education as 'tis possible for men to have; and some women of this stamp have wrote, but their performances have chiefly consisted of plays, romances, novels, letters, etc., and none I ever heard of wrote in more studious and elaborate literature.'

Here the editor interjected, citing the Blue Stockings: 'the author is under a mistake, as he will own, if he only recollects the names of Madame Dacier, and Miss Carter, etc.' The letter then continued:

> 'There are many arts too harsh for female capacity, absolutely, and in fact indispensably necessary for society, as navigation (which proceeds from astronomy) and the rest of the mathematicks, even arithmetick (to enter deeply into it) and these, I apprehend, are without the female sphere.'

The editor might well have drawn his correspondent's attention to the *Ladies' Diary*, founded 1704 and still flourishing, in which abstruse mathematical problems were the main feature—not just 'arithmetick entered deeply into', but geometry and algebra. Also astronomy, even if the ladies did not proceed from it to navigation.

Elizabeth Carter (1717–1806) whom he cites, was the most learned of all the Blue Stockings. Her father taught her Latin, Greek and Hebrew, and a Huguenot refugee taught her French. She taught herself Italian, Spanish, German, Arabic, and Portuguese, studied astronomy and the geography of ancient history. When she was only sixteen years old she was contributing verse to the *Gentleman's Magazine*, and before she was twenty-two she had published a small collection of poems. There followed her annotated translation of Crousaz's attack on Pope's *Essay on Man*. An obituary notice in *La Belle Assemblée* of February 1806 says of Mrs Carter that she wrote 'the beautiful "Ode to Wisdom" which was originally introduced to the public in Richardson's celebrated novel *Clarissa*'. For her translation of Epictetus, which was published by subscription, she was reputed to have earned the astounding sum of £1,000. What translator now could hope for an equivalent reward in the money values of today? While working on Epictetus she was preparing her youngest brother for the University of Cambridge. Yet her learning brought her as much censure as praise. It was unwomanly. Dr Johnson, however, insisted that she had plenty of domestic virtues—'My old friend, Mrs Carter, could make a pudding as well as translate Epictetus from the Greek and work a handkerchief as well as compose a poem'. In a letter to Edward Cave of the *Gentleman's Magazine* in 1738 he said, 'I have composed a Greek Epigram to Eliza, and think she ought to be celebrated in as many different languages as Louis le Grand.'

Always these scholarly women were on the defensive, as were their friends on their behalf, since skill at making puddings and working handkerchiefs was considered more praiseworthy in a woman than all the learning in the world. And indeed Mrs Carter, although she never married (the Mrs was a courtesy title she acquired in middle life) was by no means a scholarly recluse spurning the pleasures of social life. She learned the spinet and the German flute, loved dancing when she was young, enjoyed a rubber of whist all her life, and was an enthusiastic gardener. After the death of her clergyman father's second wife, she bought a house at Deal and lived with him there for half of each year, spending the other half in London and on visits to friends. She died in Clarges Street in her eighty-ninth year. The house at Deal is a modest professional gentleman's residence with a low-walled front garden, little more than a hundred yards from the sea front but well protected from the gales. It is now the Carter House Hotel, and bears a plaque which honours Mrs Carter for her learning, not for her puddings. It reads: *Mrs Elizabeth Carter, the Celebrated Scholar and Author, lived in this house from 1762 until deceased. Royalty and Society visited her here.*

Dr Johnson called Mrs Elizabeth Montagu 'Queen of the Blues', and Walpole remarked that she had 'the air and manners of a woman accustomed to be distinguished'. It was at her elegant house in Portman Square that the Blue Stockings most often met. Her especial ability was not so much scholarship as administration, and in spite of her participation in the literary life of London she was an efficient and active manager of her husband's big collieries which were a twelve-day coach journey from London. Fanny Burney became one of the group after the startling success of her *Evelina*, published in 1778 when she was twenty-six years old; and it was the patronage and influence of Mrs Delaney that were to blame when

Miss Burney, after repeating the success of *Evelina* four years later with *Cecilia*, accepted the appointment of Second Mistress of the Robes to Queen Charlotte, instead of developing her position as an author. A position at Court was, after all, more socially secure. And although everybody agreed that her writing had great esprit, she had her detractors. As Leigh Hunt wrote later, 'Miss Burney surprised the reading world with her entertaining but somewhat vulgar novels'.

The Blue Stockings were by no means exclusively feminine. In fact the stockings that gave their name to this society of intellectual ladies adorned masculine legs. Boswell describes in his *Life of Dr Johnson* on 23 April 1781, how it all started:

'About this time it was much the fashion for several ladies to have evening assemblies, where the fair sex might participate in conversation with literary and ingenious men, animated by a desire to please. These societies were denominated *Blue-stocking Clubs*, the origin of which title being little known, it may be worth while to relate it. One of the most eminent members of those societies when they first commenced was Mr Stillingfleet (Benjamin Stillingfleet, author of tracts relating to natural history, etc.) whose dress was remarkably grave, and in particular it was observed, that he wore blue stockings. Such was the excellence of his conversation, that his absence was felt as so great a loss, that it used to be said, "We can do nothing without the *bluestockings*"; and thus by degrees the title was established. Johnson was prevailed with to come sometimes into these circles, and did not think himself too grave even for the lively Miss Monckton (now Countess of Cork), who used to have the finest *bit of blue* at the house of her mother, Lady Galway.'

Boswell himself who, as we know from his London diary, enjoyed the society of women for other purposes than elegant conversation, was always enchanted to be among the Blue Stockings. 'We were all in fine spirits', he recorded of an evening at Mrs Garrick's house in the Adelphi when Hannah More, Mrs Carter, Sir Joshua Reynolds, Dr Burney, and Dr Johnson were there, 'and I whispered to Mrs Boscawen, "I believe this is as much as can be made of life."' On another occasion in such cordial company (this time preceded by a convivial dinner) he writes of 'wandering about in a kind of pleasant distraction'.

The zenith of the Blue Stocking salons was during the years 1770 to

1785; and it was in the mid-seventies that Hannah More was introduced to Mrs Montagu, then quite an elderly woman, as were most of the more distinguished members of the group. They gave a generous welcome to this outstandingly intelligent young woman, whose quick wit was combined with a reforming spirit and *avant-garde* feminist ideals in sympathy with theirs. She was their sort. During the seventies Hannah published plays and ballads and essays on education; and her poems 'Bas Bleu', 'Sensibility', 'Florio', and 'Bishop Bonner's Ghost' gave the Blue Stockings prestigious publicity beyond their own immediate circle. The classical pseudonyms that veiled contemporary personalities in these poems aroused the curiosity of the Court and the *beau monde*. Hannah was, in fact, doing more elegantly what Mrs Manley and Mrs Haywood had done so scandalously and libellously more than fifty years earlier. But unlike those much vilified ladies, Hannah More was extravagantly praised by literary society.

In 1777 Hannah More's tragedy *Percy*, to which David Garrick wrote both the prologue and epilogue, was performed at Covent Garden with Garrick playing the principal part. It earned her £600. Hannah was a dear friend of the Garricks, and during 1775 had lived at their house in the Adelphi and their villa at Hampton for many months. They gave her a separate room in which she could study quietly and receive friends privately. She also contributed to Dr Johnson's *Rambler* (as did two other Blue Stockings, Mrs Chapone and Mrs Catherine Talbot). Later Hannah More's *Strictures* upon the education of girls had widespread influence. She and her four sisters had started a private school for girls in Bristol which became well known for its unusually high standard of education—unusual, that is, for those days. Hannah was not concerned in its management for long, leaving it to her sisters while she led a more glamorous life in literary London. Much later, after the publication of her *Cheap Repository Tracts* (see Chapter XII), she retired to the Mendips, where she instituted a school for cottager's children in her village, later starting schools in ten other villages in the surrounding country.

Of all the Blue Stockings, Hannah More was the one with the most published work to her credit. Her only novel, *Coelebs in Search of a Wife* appeared in 1808 and went through twelve editions within a year. Her share in the profit was said to have been more than £2,000. She died a very rich woman, thanks entirely to her writing, for her parents had not been well off. In contrast, most of the other Blue Stockings were women of reasonable private wealth, and they did not write for money. They wrote lengthy, elegant letters, mainly to each other, producing between them an enormous quantity of correspondence. And it is from these letters that we can best learn what the Blue Stockings stood for. They deplored the idle extravagance of fashion. They discredited romance and passion, but at the same time condemned marriage by barter, declaring it a crime. They held exalted opinions about friendship as being the finest emotion of human nature, the surest, safest foundation for marriage. And—most important because most revolutionary—they believed there should be 'one moral standard' for men and women. In fact their convictions were exactly opposite to those held by the writers of romantic novels and magazine fiction. Eliza Haywood, for instance, whatever she may have suffered at men's hands, and despite her 'little inadvertencies', was entirely conventional in condoning the moral standard of the early and mid-eighteenth century; that is, one code for women, another for men. She accepted that a woman who broke the code must expect to suffer irretrievably, whereas a man could always be forgiven and his indiscretions forgotten—unless, of course, they resulted in his *financial* ruin. Even a later novelist and dramatist, Elizabeth Inchbald (1753–1821), whose famous *A Simple Story* (1791) is regarded as one of the earliest examples of a 'novel of passion' and is thought to some extent to have inspired *Jane Eyre*, did not challenge the code. When the husband of her heroine returns from a two-year absence abroad and discovers that she has had a brief affair during his absence, he utterly repudiates not only her but also the child of their marriage, his own daughter, and vows never to see either of them again. She pines away and dies. The daughter finds eventual happiness.

In April 1771 the *Lady's Magazine* introduced their first serial story, which continued many months: 'Memoirs of a Young Lady of Family, Written by Herself, and addressed to a Female Friend'. This followed the always popular form of epistolary novels that had begun before the beginning of the century with the elegant Familiar Letters, became universally popular with Richardson's *Pamela* in 1740, and reached its widest readership of all with Fanny Burney's *Evelina* in 1777. It was a form which was a natural for serialization, and we find it being used again in the *Lady's Magazine* ten years later for a fascinating series of letters under the title of 'The History of Augustus Pembroke and Miss Woodley'. The magazine had the best of both worlds by declaring itself from its very first issue to be against the prevailing morals of high society, and then exposing the evils in revealing sketches which must have been irresistible reading for those of their subscribers who led dull respectable lives. There were delicious glimpses of the behaviour of their superiors in Society with whom 'the fear of not appearing *Bon Ton* carries more horror and distress with it than the fear of offending their maker'. The editor observes acidly that 'until virtue becomes fashionable, our modern set of fine gentlemen, will continue to pursue follies and debaucheries of every sort more from fashion and example than from any real inclination on the one hand, or pleasure they can afford them on the other'.

In April 1771 the magazine began a series called *The Court Mirrour* in which,

> 'It is proposed to represent the real portraits of the most celebrated toasts of St James's, with their *genuine features*, and their *real complexions*. We shall, with infinite pleasure, dwell upon the virtues and perfections of the aimiable part of the Sex, who shine in such a conspicuous point of view . . . At the same time we shall not suppress the likenesses of those ladies, whose ridiculous, or vicious pursuits, should be held forth to themselves to reclaim their conducts, and serve as a warning to others, to shun those paths which have led them to just satire and public reprehension. And we can assure our fair readers, the *Court Mirrour* will be as frequently held up to the fops, petit-maîtres, bucks, fox-hunters, gamesters, fortune-hunters, and every species of ridiculous male characters within the purlieus of St James's, without sparing either *Maccaroni* or *Dilettante.*'

The editor then invited readers to send in any examples of the sins of society which had come within their own knowledge; and although he had earlier said he would suppress the likenesses of those whose behaviour was to be exposed, he now invites his readers to recognize them, 'As a specimen of our future plan, we shall lay before our readers two exalted and well-known characters within the courtly circle, whose features will immediately strike the most cursory observer'. The first of these so recognizable profiles was entitled 'A Female Court Living Character—Dolabella':

Dolabella is of an ancient and noble family, upon which she greatly piques herself. She married a man of inferior rank to herself, for whom

THE

Lady's Magazine;

OR,

Entertaining Companion for the FAIR SEX, appropriated solely to their Use and Amusement.

For MAY, 1792.

This NUMBER contains,

1 The Forest of Alstone. A Tale. 227
2 True Piety, Virtue, and Human Happiness considered, 229
3 Account of Dunstable Priory, Oxfordshire, 231
4 A plagiarism detected, 232
5 Gonzalo de Cordova. An Heroic Romance. 233
6 Alexis; or, the Cottage in the Woods, 238
7 Anecdote, 245
8 Account of the new Comedy called The Fugitive, 246
9 The Rival Princes, 248
10 Spanish Etiquette, 249
11 Extract from the Comedy of A Day in Turkey, 250
12 Virtue not consequent on Birth, 254
13 Anecdote, 255
14 On the peculiar Province of Genius, 256
15 A Vision, 257
16 A Guardian's Advice to a young Gentleman, 259
17 Description of the Houses and Furniture of the Athenians, 260
18 Anecdote of Garrick and Lord Orrery, 262
19 On assuming Airs of Consequence, 264
20 On the Danger of misplacing Confidence, 265
21 Enigmatical Lists, 268
22 Poetry.— Prologue to the Fugitive. —Epilogue to the same.—Prologue spoken at the French School near Soho.—Songs in the Comedy called A Day in Turkey.—The Negroe's Complaint.—Answers to Rebuses. — A Rebus.—Charade.— Enigma. 269—272.
23 Foreign News, 273
24 Home News, 276
25 Births, 279
26 Marriages, ibid.
27 Deaths, 280

This Number is embellished with the following Copper-Plates, viz.

1. A new fancy Pattern for working in Colours.—2. An interesting Scene in Alexis; or, the Cottage in the Woods.—3. A View of Dunstable Priory, Oxfordshire. —And, 4. Jonathan, a Song in the Oratorio of Saul, the Music by Mr. Handel.

LONDON, Printed for G. G. J. and J. Robinson, No. 25. Paternoster Row, where Favours from Correspondent will be received.

17. Contents page of the *Lady's Magazine*, May 1792

she has obtained titles and distinctions. He is a man of gallantry and she fails not to make reprisals for his conduct, upon every handsome fellow with whom she dares trust her person and her secrets; which, tho' she thinks inviolably kept, afford conversation for half the scandalous card parties in town. *Pleasure and dissipation* is her motto. She professes herself a patroness of the arts, and her levées are constantly attended by painters, sculptors, and musicians; but as the last captivate her most, she bestows her greatest favours and attentions upon them, and to this musical *gusto* we may trace the late *harmonic meetings* which have made so much noise (harmonious and discordant) within and without the walls of Carlisle-house. Her equipages are the most splendid, her retinue the most numerous, and her person the most conspicuous of any at St James's, where she eclipses ambassadors, and outshines all our female nobility, except in youth and beauty. She was a mother at twenty, and is now a girl at fifty; but she is in her second bloom, and will long be a public evergreen.

Dolabella has her parallel in 'A Male Court Living Character—Lord Dapperwit':

'Lord Dapperwit is a member of the Dilettanti. He has made the tour of Europe, and understands sculpture, pictures, architecture and music (in his own opinion) as well as any man in Europe. He has all the terms at his fingertips and *frequently* applies them properly; he would no more forgo an auction at Christies, or an harmonic meeting, than he would miss a pool at quadrille with Lady Sansprendre of a Sunday evening. His lordship subscribes to every book of sculpture and architecture that is published, and the artists pronounce him the greatest patron of the age. He has lately paid £1,480 for a *copy* of a Reubens worth £3. But his lordship is still a Dilettante.'

How close these sketches were to actual living characters it is impossible for us to gauge. But they give a glimpse, if a distorted one, of the manners and morals of the Court and Society at that time; and no doubt subscribers to the *Lady's Magazine*, even if they could not identify the living models of the character sketches, enjoyed speculating about them and pretending that they knew which referred to whom. It was a feature that will have ensured that the magazine was talked about, a splendid circulation builder. The journalist's maxim that 'names make news' holds good, even when readers can only speculate about the identity of pseudonyms.

Chapter IX

PUBLISHING PLAGIARISM: NOVELS AS DRUGS

Wheble's pirate Lady's Magazine. *The Rev. Mr Charles Stanhope's* New Lady's Magazine. *Reader participation. Improprieties and plagiarism by contributors rebuked. Economical management. Old Bailey reports. William Lane's circulating libraries. Novels as time-killing drugs. The* Novelist's Magazine. *Carnan's* Ladies' and Gentlemen's Diary *edited from the Royal Military Academy. Tytler's* Gentleman's and Lady's Magazine *edited from a debtor's prison.*

꿍ꂅꀦ

THE immediate success of the *Lady's Magazine* led to defection amongst those associated with it. The traitor was a bookseller named Wheble, who seems to have been concerned in the editorial direction as well as in sales and distribution. Wheble conceived the idea of bringing out a magazine of his own under the same title and deceiving the public into thinking they were buying the genuine *Lady's Magazine*. A report of this attempt was given in an editorial in the twelfth issue of the *Lady's Magazine*, that of July 1771:

'*To the ladies*

'The Authors and Proprietors of The Lady's Magazine gladly seize every opportunity of acknowledging their obligations to their fair Patronesses, and the Public, for the generous Encouragement they have afforded this Work, and for their discernment and Justice in discouraging the malignant Attempts of a desperate *Adventurer*. From the legal Determination on Monday July 8, 1771, in the court of King's-Bench, Guildhall, the Ladies can no longer hesitate in deciding which is the genuine Work, and will therefore please to order the *Original Lady's Magazine* published by Robinson & Roberts.

'The Judge declared from the Bench in his Summing-up ". . . and that WHEBLE had been guilty of a Fraud, not only in publishing a Pamphlet under a false signature, and endeavouring to impose it on the Public as a Continuation of a genuine Work, published by Robinson & Roberts, but also in pretending that the real Magazine, purchased by the Plain-

THE
NEW LADY'S MAGAZINE;
Or, Polite, Entertaining, and Fashionable
COMPANION FOR THE FAIR SEX:
A Work Entirely Devoted to Their Use and Amusement.

AND CONTAINING

More in Quantity, and a much greater Variety of New, Original, and Select Pieces (in Prose and Verse) on the most curious, useful, and entertaining Subjects, than are to be found in any old Rival and inferior Publication of the Kind whatever.

For MAY, 1789.

[Embellished with, 1. SHEEP-SHEERING, a beautiful Print, engraved by RAVENHILL.— 2. Monthly NOSEGAY of FLOWERS for JUNE.—3. A New PATTERN for a SHAWL. —And, (4.) The ECHO, a NEW SONG, Set to MUSIC.]

THIS ELEGANT FEMALE MISCELLANY CONTAINS

Notes to Correspondents - - - 226
History of Louisa Leeson; or the Triumph of Virtue, and Punishment of Vice, continued - - - - 227
Abdulselam and Chelnissa, a Turkish Novel, concluded - - - 233
The Adventures of a Shilling, continued 239
Diary of a Lady of Fashion in London; or a Sketch of High Life - - 241
A select Collection of Letters by the Right Hon. Lady Mary Wortley Montague, continued - - - - 243
The Sisters, a Tale - - - - 247
Philadelphia, a Novel, continued - 249
The Monthly Nosegay - - - 252
Anecdotes of the late celebrated Mr. John Henderson - - - - ibid.
The Echo, a New Song, set to Music 256
The History of Miss Clara Davenport, continued - - - - 258
The Theatre, No. XIII. - - - 261
Metaphorical Description of the First of May - - - - - 262
Enigmatical Solutions and Questions ibid.
Entertaining Anecdotes - - - 265

POETICAL ESSAYS.
Sheep-Sheering - - - - 266
A Matrimoniad - - - - ibid.
Sonnet to Spring - - - - 268
Advice to the Fair - - - - ibid.

On Women - - - - - 269
The Shepherd's Resolve - - - ibid.
Mary's Dream, or Johnny's Ghost - ibid.
Stanzas inscribed to the amiable Miss Anna White - - - - ibid.
On Spring; addressed to the Ladies - 270
The Thanksgiving Day - - - 271
Morning - - - - - 272
Night, a Sonnet - - - - ibid.
A Song - - - - - ibid.
The Female Advocate, by W. Hamilton Reid - - - - - ibid.
To Love - - - - - ibid.
Jealousy - - - - - ibid.
Foreign News - - - - 273
Insurrection at Paris - - - ibid.
Death of the Ottoman Emperor - - 274
Home News - - - - 275
Trial of the Rights of the Citizens of London - - - - ibid.
Account of an Earthquake - - 276
Sentence of the Law for giving a Challenge ibid.
The Queen's Letter to the King of Prussia - - - - - 277
Particulars of a Duel between Lieut. Northey and Lieut. Gordon - - 278
Promotion - - - - - 279
Births, Marriages, and Deaths - ibid.
Advertisement of Barnard's New History of England - - - - 280

The Whole Published under the immediate Inspection of

THE REV. MR. CHARLES STANHOPE,
Author of the NEW POLITE TUTORESS, or LADY'S BEST INSTRUCTOR.

LONDON:
Printed, by Royal Authority, for ALEX. HOGG, at the KING'S ARMS, No. 16, Paternoster-Row (by whom the Communications of ingenious Persons—Post Paid—will be received, and immediately transmitted to the Editor); and sold by all Booksellers, Stationers, and News-Carriers in Town and Country.

[To be continued MONTHLY.—Price only Six-pence.]

18. Contents page of the Rev. Mr Charles Stanhope's *New Lady's Magazine*, May 1789

tifs, was surreptitious and an Imposter upon the Public; and, besides, that Wheble's Behaviour was highly treacherous to the original Proprietor, Mr Coote, to whom he could be considered in no other light than as a Servant or Agent."'

Wheble must in fact have been more than 'a servant or agent' since it was he, according to the DNB who appointed John Huddlestone Wynne to the editorship of the *Lady's Magazine*. John Nichols, in his *Literary Anecdotes*, writes of Huddlestone Wynne as editor of the *Lady's Magazine*; and Andrews, who calls him 'this pushing genius' says he also edited the *British Magazine*. It is possible he took over from Smollett. When Huddlestone Wynne started writing for the papers he assumed the name of George Osborne, Esq., and was the 'Mother Osborne' of Sir Robert Walpole's time. He edited the *Gazetteer* for some months and was employed as a compositor on the *General Evening Post*, for which he was also required to contribute 'a short article of poetry every day'—a contract which Andrews says 'he frequently performed under trying circumstances'. Huddlestone Wynne's son admitted that it was 'impossible for a man of his ardent imagination to avoid on every occasion sacrificing too freely at the shrine of Bacchus'. On one of these Bacchic occasions he was run over by a hackney coach, as a result of which he was lame for the last ten years of his life. During the eighteenth century there were many journalists who sacrificed themselves on the shrine of Bacchus. The life of authors, poets, and miscellaneous writers of any kind, however talented, was a battle for survival, a fight against debts and disasters. To enjoy it they had to be resilient characters with something of a devil-may-care spirit.

Although that first attempt at setting up a rival to the *Lady's Magazine* was effectively scuppered, fifteen years later another adventurer sailed in. This time it was a clerical buccaneer named the Rev. Mr Charles Stanhope, and he called his publication the *New Lady's Magazine; or Polite & Entertaining Companion for the Fair Sex,* published under the immediate inspection of the Rev. Mr C. Stanhope. He adopted exactly the same title as the original magazine, simply adding *New*. Perhaps the Reverend gentleman benefited from more divine guidance than that other pirate Wheble, for his publication ran successfully in rivalry with the original *Lady's Magazine* throughout nine years, from 1786 to 1795. He seems to have been a quite shameless braggart, for his title-page claimed that his magazine contained:

'more in Quantity, and a much greater Variety of New, Original, and Select Pieces (in Prose and Verse) on every curious, useful, and entertaining Subject, than are to be found in any other Publication of the Kind whatever'.

In the second issue, that of March 1786, the page opposite the title-page had this:

'The *rapid Sale* of the *First Number* having already carried *two large Impressions* and the *Demand* for this New Lady's Magazine *still increasing* in all *Parts of Europe*, Notice is hereby given, that *This Day is Published*, a *Third Edition* (*Revised and Corrected*) of Number 1, Price only 6d.'

A further paragraph in very small type read:

'We were sensible the *extensive* Sale of the New Lady's Magazine would materially affect those who are interested in any *old Publication* of the Kind, and raise an Alarm which their own Negligence and Mismanagement have been the just Occasion of. We have accordingly met with a very strong Opposition from a certain Quarter, but the Ladies are no longer to be trifled with. Such unfair Conduct as Mr R.'s we were obliged to expose, and his Demerits being tried before a Female Tribunal, the Ladies declared against his tyrannical Behaviour, and left off the old and imperfect Publication, in Favour of our New, Complete, Elegant, and Improved *Lady's Magazine*.'

Mr R. must have been Mr Robinson or Mr Roberts, and one feels for him under this bludgeoning attack. What did his unfair Conduct and Tyrannical Behaviour to his readers amount to? We do not know. But it certainly seems unfair conduct on the part of the Rev. Mr Charles Stanhope to have in his first issues a serial called 'A New Sentimental Journey through England'—a direct crib of the *Lady's Magazine*'s 'Sentimental Journey' series. Other features included an essay 'On the Present Mode of Female Education' ('It is not incumbent on the fair-sex to acquire the knowledge of Bacon, the oratory of a Demosthenes, or the grammatical pronunciation of a Johnson') and *The Female Rambler* who noted that 'there is a pleasure that results even from the prattle of a pretty woman, though without meaning'. Another essay is 'On the State of Matrimony in South Britain':

'If you see a gentleman and lady in the same coach, in profound silence,

The Bay of WEYMOUTH, *in Dorsetshire.*

19. Engraving from the *New Lady's Magazine* of 1789, accompanying article on Weymouth as 'a place of the most fashionable resort, in consequence of their Majesties' visit to His Royal Highness the Duke of Gloucester'.

the one looking out at one side, the other at the other side, never imagine they mean any harm to one another; they are already honestly married.'

The magazine also published a cookery column, and items of general interest—for example, a report of a rat being suckled by a cat. History was provided by such contributions as 'An Accurate and Complete History of Capt. Cook's First Voyage Round the World', and literature by reprinting the English Prize Oration at Oxford. There were poems, book reviews, and regular reports on Foreign and Home affairs, enigmas and rebuses. An enigmatical list was given of Old Maids in D-t-d, and of Bachelors of Barnstable, Devon, with a view to getting them together—or simply to sneer? And another enigmatical list featured 'Ladies' Names at Eastland Boarding School, Greenwich'—perhaps the Editor's daughter was a pupil. There were warnings against the Male Danger: the Rake, the treacherous Fop, the Seducer—with painful anecdotes. There was a monthly song composed by Mr Hook, elegant patterns for embroidery and cloth work, some health and beauty notes and the magazine was embellished with:

1. A most elegant plate, containing a variety of Ladies fashionable Head Dresses for the present Year.
2. A fine Portrait of Mrs Jordan in the Character of a Country Girl.
3. A beautiful Representation of Miss Brunto as Euphrasia in the Grecian Daughter; these two admirable portraits finely engraved by Thornton.

A fulsome little piece about Queen Caroline ended with a cut at the 'Dolabella' type described in the original *Lady's Magazine*'s attack on the morals and manners of the Court: 'As comparisons are odious it would be invidious to draw parallels between Her Majesty and some of the Court Ladies. Suffice it to say, that such of them as act contrary to the rules of virtue and decorum have ever met with her disapprobation.'

The issue of July 1786 announced the commencement of 'Six Numbers each containing two Sets of various original Patterns executed in real Paper Filigree, by Charles Stuart, 5s 3d each.' Paper filigree work was a craze with middle-class ladies at this time—a way of filling in time during the endless leisure they felt it essential to have in order to show they were gentlewomen. It was no longer considered appropriate for gentlewomen to occupy themselves with household duties. The November issue of this year gave an 'Historical Account of the Origin and Progress of Paper

Filigree-Work', followed by a description of its contemporary manifestation:

> 'Filigree work, as now revived by modern artists, consists of narrow slips of paper, either crimped or plain, of various colours with gilt edges, which are artfully bolted or joined together in such a manner as to form an embellishment suited to any particular work of fancy which the female artist may think proper to ornament.'

A very female hobby.

The fact that the *New Lady's Magazine* was able to run in rivalry with the original *Lady's Magazine* for nine years, with very similar contents, is proof of the expansion of the market for feminine reading matter, and the widening scope of women's interests—after all, the magazines offered much more than paper filigree and embroidery patterns. It was in the Rev. Charles Stanhope's magazine that George Crabbe poured out much of his most sentimental verse. His father, who lived in Aldeburgh, was a subscriber to the magazine. Such regular male readership in country places indicates general interest, not exclusively feminine, in the contents. That it should have been the original magazine that outlived its rival, continuing triumphantly for a further fifty years after the Rev. Charles Stanhope's publication went under, may have been partly due to the strength of what would now be called 'reader participation'. The 'Letters to the Editor' column and advice to readers on personal problems will have given its subscribers a sense of belonging. Women living in country districts had few social contacts outside their family and immediate circle of acquaintances within carriage distance. In winter time their isolation could seem endless. The *Lady's Magazine*, arriving each month, would give them a feeling of friendship with other women, all over the country, who had the same problems and preoccupations as they themselves. Even the contributors to the magazine were corresponded with through its columns. The overriding reason for this was almost certainly to save postage; but at the same time it will have given readers the sensation of being acquainted with the people whose literary work they read. They would get to know something of their shortcomings, and of their relations, cordial or strained, with the editor. Acknowledgments of the receipt of manuscripts, apologies for delay in printing them or for holding them over, and also rejections, with reasons, were all given on this editor's page, which was on the inside cover of the magazine.

It seems to have been the serial writers who gave the most trouble. There were repeated requests for them to send continuations to their stories: 'The author of "The Treacherous Husband" will excuse us if we remind him that he promised us a continuation of his piece, and at the same time add that we are *forced* to this by the united clamours of at least fifty of our fair correspondents'—an editorial exaggeration, one suspects. 'Though a disagreeable task, we cannot help calling upon authors whose pieces are unfinished, to wind up their bottoms; as we have received several complaints on that subject.' 'The continuation of "L'Histoire d'Emile" is received but came too late for publication.'

If a contributor had a good excuse for being late, the editor was ready to publish this too, and so exonerate her from clamant readers' reproaches: The translator of 'Harlequin Sauvage', for example, could not only expect their sympathy, but call for their assistance. The reason she gave for being unable to finish her serial was that 'the original was burnt when she was obliged to fly with no other clothing than her shift. She has applied to all the French booksellers in London for a copy, but can get none, and if any of the patronesses of this magazine can procure her one, promises to return it within a day, and translate it.' The Editor every now and then praised punctual contributors, no doubt as encouragement to others. Dr Cook, who supplied the Medical Corner, is warmly complimented for being always on time: 'The punctuality of his favours notwithstanding his advanced age is deemed highly commendable.'

Some contributors had to be reprimanded for improprieties: 'We desire Gulielmus . . . to revise his piece, as in its present dress it is not quite fit to be introduced into the company of ladies.' And a great many contributors seemed to be guilty of plagiarism. 'The riddle of T.B.-H. is copied from an old magazine published by Wheble, and we have suspicions that the "Essay on Charity" submitted by the same author falls under the same predicament?' Wheble again. Obviously the *Lady's Magazine* would spurn to print a piece that had appeared in any publication of his. Sometimes the plagiarism is spotted by a reader, and the editor swings into action: 'The advertisement we have received from a correspondent of a literary fraud by a person who has imposed on us, in arrogating the productions of another person, gives us concern, and should raise a blush in the imposter.' On the other hand, in some cases the editor defended his regular contributors with indignation: 'We are sorry to intimate that we have received a letter this month signed "Justus" wherein Constantia

Maria is treated with uncommon rigour, is branded with the stigma of Plagiarist, and as such a discredit to our Magazine'—but the editor feels she was being unjustly accused: 'Knowing her real character, real name, and distinguished abilities' he was printing this information so that '. . . she may take an opportunity of refuting the charge, and we doubt not that she may'. One cannot help feeling it would have been kinder to have written to Constantia Maria privately, but one gets the impression that the management's policy was to avoid postal expenses whatever happened. At least this regular contributor was being defended—whereas there was no defence of a poet who was already under a cloud: 'The "Verses to a Lady at Caermarthen" and "A Declaration of love" come from a hand that has already deceived us and cannot be inserted until their originality is properly authenticated.'

These plagiarists could have been motivated sheerly by the hope of glory, because it seems there was no payment for contributions to the *Lady's Magazine*. One rejected contributor even suggests that people pay to have their work accepted, but the editors indignantly deny this. Yet in one issue they make a point of having published 'Censor's' pieces *gratis*, as though it were more usual to demand payment for the honour of having one's work appear in the magazine. It is not really surprising that they were able to hold the price at 6d—after all, a not insignificant sum in those days. With no contributions to pay for, with acknowledgments being given through the columns of the magazine and all other correspondence conducted by the same method, expenses must have been minimal. They did not even return rejected manuscripts. Moreover, they must have had quite a considerable advertising revenue once the magazine was well established. By 1780 there were publishers' advertisements on the covers; and in September 1781 an important four-page inset supplement advertising the Medicated Baths in Panton-Square, Hay-Market, erected by R. Dominiceti, M.D., which included four testimonials from delighted bathers. This establishment was for both sexes: 'Ladies are attended by women well experienced in Bathing, and the Gentlemen by Men, equally qualified.' All the testimonials were from men.

The price, as Francis Place asserted, may have had something to do with the success of the *Lady's Magazine*, but its continued supremacy over all rivals must certainly have been due to it really giving the ladies what they wanted. Its formula was the formula that magazine editors were to follow for nearly two centuries: a little instruction, a little fashion,

THE HAWTHORN BOWER.

Set to Mufic by an eminent MASTER.

The Words by Mr. CUNNINGHAM.

Andante.

Pa—lo—mon in the hawthorn bower, With fond im—patience lay; He counted ev'—ry anxious hour That ftretch'd the te—dious day. The. ro—fy

20. First page of a song in the *New Lady's Magazine*, September 1789

beauty, health, cookery; some free offers such as the embroidery patterns and music sheets of songs; a good serial story, some shorter romantic tales, some charming romantic pictures; a little sentimental verse. And, of course, the answers to readers' letters, the heart-throb column. It also had some features that modern magazines do not have. It carried announcements of births, marriages and deaths. A column of bankruptcies was dropped early in its history. It also had some Home News and a little Foreign News— from Constantinople, Cadiz, Ostend, St Petersburg, Hanover, Florence, Paris, The Hague, Brussels, Smyrna. In those days of slow communications, a monthly magazine could give its readers foreign news that *was* news to them, while comment on Home Affairs did not have to be immediately after an event.

The magazine also included occasional reports from the Law Courts. The editor may have remembered that accounts of criminals and their lurid lives had been an extremely popular feature in Jasper Goodwill's *Lady's Magazine* of the early 1750s. Certainly the choice of trials reported in this later *Lady's Magazine* seems to have been made on the basis of maximum horror content. In the issue of July 1781, for example, there was 'A concise Account of the Trial at the Old Bailey on June 29th of Mr H. G. De La Motte', who was tried on a charge of High Treason for collecting evidence for the purposes of furnishing our Enemies:

151

Engraved for the Lady's Magazine.

Charlotte Bateman,
A Tale.

21. Illustration to a romantic tale in the *Lady's Magazine*, November 1782

'The jury, after short deliberation, pronounced the prisoner guilty, and sentence was immediately passed on him, To be hanged by the Neck, but not till dead, then to be cut down, and his Bowels taken out and burnt before his Face, his Head to be taken off, his body cut into four quarters, and to be at his Majesty's disposal. The Prisoner received the awful Doom with great composure.'

Thus the *Lady's Magazine* catered for many tastes, offering their fair readers strong meat at times. It seems a little ironical, in view of this unexpurgated Old Bailey report, that a contributor should have been asked to revise his piece as 'not being quite fit to be introduced into the Company of Ladies'. But then it was the innocence of ladies that had to be protected, and easy morals were seen as the danger. No one was squeamish then about violence, blood and butchery. No doubt the editors gauged their readers accurately by offering them, under cover of the respectability of the Law Courts, something more sensational than moral tales and sentimental verse.

It was at about the time when the *Lady's Magazine* was founded that the owner of the Minerva Press, William Lane, started his first circulating library as an outlet for the novels he was publishing. The majority of books on the Minerva list were romances written for women and by women; the libraries would ensure that even more women would become addicted to novel reading. Indeed, the feminine appetite for light fiction was becoming insatiable. More women, in more classes of society, were acquiring the reading habit. The availability of novels in circulating libraries was itself an incentive for girls to learn to read. Even domestic servants (a very numerous class) were becoming novel readers. Their hours on duty were inhumanly long, but there were spells during the days and nights in which being on duty simply meant being on call. Some of the endless, idle hours could be filled with novel reading, when the footmen were not around to flirt with. As a book critic of the *Edinburgh Review* in November 1783 wrote, novels were 'time-killing drugs'. And no doubt most of them could be classed as housemaid's choices. Rees and Britton wrote of 'the variety of books, called novels, which the Minerva Press was continually producing and distributing to all the circulating libraries in the country. From £10 to £20 were the sums usually paid to authors for these novels of three volumes. The Colburns and Bentleys drove this trash out of the market.'

In households where there were magazines coming in each month, they

Engrav'd for the Lady's Magazine.

The Happy Escape.

22. Illustration to a romantic tale in the *Lady's Magazine*, March
1782

provided another incentive to learn how to read. The 1770s saw a positive spate of women's publications, and the reason none of them except the *Lady's Magazine* saw the decade out was probably because of incompetent management and inefficient editorship, not lack of demand. The *Sentimental Magazine, or General Assemblage of Science, Taste, etc.* was launched in 1773 and lasted until the December issue of 1775. This was no mere sugary assemblage of romantic waffle as its title seems to imply. The word sentimental had not by then acquired the meaning of indulgence in emotion. It meant 'characterized by refined and elevated feeling'. But the next publication to appear, in 1775, had no elevated ambitions. It simply offered the favourite topic that never failed—and still never fails—to attract women readers. It was called the *Matrimonial Magazine, or Monthly Anecdotes of Love and Marriage*. Then in 1776 someone had the idea of a bi-lingual publication and brought out the *Gentleman & Lady's Magazine in French & English*. Or, to give its Gallic title: *Le Magazine du Monde Politique, Galant et Littéraire*. This brave attempt at a cultural periodical only lasted for three numbers. It was followed by two more short-lived magazines: the *Magazine à la Mode or Fashionable Miscellany*, 1777; and the *Gentleman's & Lady's Museum*, 1777 to 1778. Then the appetite for fiction, nothing but fiction, was fed by the bookseller James Harrison with his *Novelists Magazine*.

Harrison may not have been the originator of the idea of dividing up already published books into small portions and issuing them periodically in numbers; but his *Novelists' Magazine* spread the idea widely. It published in instalments many of the larger and currently most popular novels at that time. Instalments came out weekly, printed in octavo, in double columns, stitched up, and priced at 6d each. One of the attractions was that Harrison included engraved 'embellishments', selecting young artists of already acknowledged merit, many of whom afterwards became well known. They included Stothard, R. Corbould, Smirke, and Burney; and the engravings were executed by many of the most talented engravers of the day, including Heath, Sharpe, Grignion, Milton, and Neagle. At one time 12,000 copies of each number of the *Novelists' Magazine* were sold weekly, and it continued from 1780 until 1888, totalling in all twenty-three volumes. Its success encouraged Harrison to publish during 1786 and 1787, with embellishments by the same artists, a *New Novelists' Magazine, or Entertaining Library of Pleasing and Instructive Histories, Adventures, Tales, Romances, etc.* The difference was that, instead of serializing long novels, it published short stories. And Harrison followed this up with a publication called the *British Classics*, which reprinted extracts from the *Spectator*, *Tatler*, *Guardian*, *Connoisseur*, and other quality periodicals.

Harrison's subsequent periodical publishing included the *Pocket Magazine, or Elegant Repository of Useful and Polite Literature* (1794) and in the following year the *Lady's New and Elegant Pocket Magazine or Polite and Entertaining Companion for the Fair Sex*. These little magazines were published monthly and carried work of high quality, both in illustration and text. For the most part the embellishments were portraits, but there was a series of small engraved views from drawings by J. M. W. Turner, who was later to become the most famous English landscape painter. Writers who contributed included the two Miss Porters and their brother, the poet, artist, and traveller; also R. A. Davenport, who sometimes acted as editor.

During the 1770s there was a controversy in the world of almanac publishing. In December 1775 Thomas Carnan, stepson of John Newbury the bookseller, brought out for the following year a *Lady's & Gentleman's Diary or Royal Almanack*, in direct competition with the *Ladies' Diary* founded at the beginning of the century and still as popular as ever. Carnan had taken over John Newbury's bookselling business in St Paul's Churchyard when Newbury died in 1767. He had the idea that the Stationers' Company, publishers of the original *Ladies' Diary* which was now edited by Charles Hutton, FRS, Professor of Mathematics at the Royal Military Academy, had no legal title to the monopoly of almanacs as they claimed. To test the situation Carnan began to publish almanacs of his own. Charles Knight has a typical Charles Knight version of the affair in his *Shadows of the Old Bookseller*. He writes: 'The Stationers' Company, having anathematized Carnan as the base publisher of counterfeit almanacs, sent him to prison on a summary process, as regularly as he issued his annual commodities. So he always kept a clean shirt in his pocket, that he might make a decent appearance before the magistrate and the keeper of Newgate.' The Stationers' Company did in fact bring an action against Carnan after he brought out his first issue, but their claim was disallowed by the Court of Common Pleas, so Carnan was able to continue with his *Lady's & Gentleman's Diary or Royal Almanack*. He chose Reuben Burrow to be editor.

Burrow was a mathematician who a little before this, about 1774, had been appointed 'mathematical teacher in the drawing-room at the Tower', where there was then a training school for artillery officers, afterwards merged in the Royal Military Academy, Woolwich. As with the original *Ladies' Diary*, part of Carnan's publication was devoted to mathematical problems, these being set by Reuben Burrow and various contributors, including a Samuel Rogers who was possibly, but not probably, the poet. In 1780 the word 'Gentleman' was dropped from the title; and in the following year Burrow, who had ceaselessly quarrelled with his rival Hutton on the *Ladies' Diary* and with the Royal Military Academy, seems to have abandoned his editorship or been requested to give it up by the proprietors. From then on he eked out his living by taking private pupils in mathematics and doing a little work for various publishers. Carnan's *Lady's Diary* continued until 1786.

The debtor's prison at Holyrood is an even more unexpected place in which to produce a lady's magazine than the Royal Military Academy; but for some months during 1772 James Tytler published the *Gentleman & Lady's Magazine* while imprisoned there. He used a press of his own construction, on which he also printed a volume of essays. James Tytler, described by the DNB as a 'literary hack and scientific dabbler', must have found it difficult while in prison to provide the kind of material about the fashionable world that gentlemen and lady magazine readers expected. But not so difficult as it seems to us now. Quite fashionable people could find themselves in the Fleet or the King's Bench prison, 'temples of idleness, debauchery, and vice' though they were. You could be imprisoned for debts of less than a guinea before 'costs' were added to them. If you had rich and influential friends they could arrange for your imprisonment to be less unpleasant—better food, more drink, a room to yourself. One could have visitors without restriction, hold parties and carouse as in a tavern. The painter Benjamin Robert Haydon was twice in the King's Bench Prison. He made sketches for paintings there, and described the scene to S. C. Hall: 'Baronets and bankers; authors and merchants; painters and poets; dandies of rank in silk and velvet; dandies of no rank in rags and tatters; idiotism and insanity; poverty and affliction; all mingled there in indiscriminate merriment, with a spiked wall twenty feet high above their heads.'

James Tytler survived his sojourn in the Holyrood debtor's prison, even though his magazine did not. Later he started another, calling it the *Weekly Mirror* (1780), but it lasted very little longer. Then in 1786 he launched a weekly paper in Edinburgh called the *Observer*—not the English *Observer*, which was founded five years later. In 1784 he made a balloon ascent at Comely Gardens in a fire balloon of his own construction, and claimed to be 'the first person in Great Britain to navigate the air'. A man of parts—perhaps too many. He might have had more success as a literary man had he not been such a 'scientific dabbler'.

Chapter X

POCKET BOOKS, SEASIDE LIBRARIES, AND WOMEN DRAMATISTS

Harrison Ainsworth on ladies' pocket books. Lane's Ladies' Museum. *The* Lady's
Daily Companion. *The Austens in Kent. Lane's monthly* Novelist. *Minerva
Libraries in seaside towns. Mrs Radcliffe and her* Mysteries of Udolpho.
The vogue for Gothic fiction. Jane Austen satirizes it in Northanger Abbey.
Elizabeth Inchbald's A Simple Story *; her plays and dramatic criticism.* Lovers'
Vows. *Other women dramatists: Hannah More; Mrs Cowley; Mrs Robinson.*

WILLIAM LANE of the Minerva Press, whose main publishing
interest was in the fertile field of romantic novels, also brought
out various annual publications. His *Ladies' Museum, or Complete Pocket Memorandum Book* was the first of these. It was published in
December 1773 for 1774, with the notice that it was to be continued annually. But there does not seem to have been another issue until 1805. There
were then eight more in intermittent years, the last one being the issue
published in December 1819 for 1820. There had been a very similar
production in 1769 called the *Ladies' Complete Pocket Book*, and there may
well have been many others. Harrison Ainsworth, in his introduction to
the first *Keepsake* (1828) wrote about the pocket-books 'of the time of our
grandmothers'. He compared them with the tiny pocket-books of the time
he was writing, which was a period when fashion did not allow women
to have pockets in their dresses. Instead they carried little reticules. His
grandmother's pockets, in contrast, were of tremendous size, positive
panniers:

> '. . . but everything was on a large, warm, household scale in those
> days. We remember a series of pocket-books in a great drawer, that, in
> addition to their natural size, seemed all to have grown corpulent in
> consequence of being fed with receipts and copies of verses, and cuttings out of newspapers. The hook of the clasp had got from eyelet to
> eyelet, till it could unbuckle no further. These books, in the printed
> part, contained acrostics and rebuses, household receipts for various
> purposes, and a list of public events. There was love, politics, and eating.'

POCKET-BOOKS AND KEEPSAKES.

23. Heading to Harrison Ainsworth's introduction to
the first *Keepsake*

Since William Lane's *Ladies' Museum* was very small, bound in leather, and about the same size as a prayer-book, only slimmer, pocket-books must have grown fat soon afterwards and then reduced again in the 1820s when, to fit the dress of the time, they were as Harrison Ainsworth wrote 'all for compression and minuteness'. His description of them could almost apply to the *Ladies' Museum*:

'They endeavour to contain the greatest quantity of matter in the smallest compass; to which end the little nonpareil types now in use are of great service. A person may now have the old Pocket-book and old Almanack, and the old Tablets (in the shape of leaves of vellum) all confined in a Lilliputian book no thicker than a penny's worth of gingerbread. The diffusion of literature has carried off the verses and stories from pocket-books of this description, now called Souvenirs, Atlases, and Pocket Remembrancers; and as the smallness of the type enables them to afford a great addition of letter press, there have come up, by degrees, all those lovely lists of lords and commons, and household officers, and battle array of Army and Navy, which form the sole literature of many an aspiring youth in employment, and many a lieutenant's sister on a rainy Sunday. . . . Afterwards come the bankers, with each his pleasing address; and lastly, the hackney-coach fares, so very useful, that everybody resolves to lug them out and convict the coachmen on the spot; which he never does, because he knows it will be to no purpose.'

The *Ladies' Museum*, although so miniscule, contained all the ingredients that had become essential to a woman's publication. It was embellished with 'An elegant view of the late Royal Review at Portsmouth, from a drawing taken on the spot'; and also with an engraving of 'A Lady in the genteelest full Dress'—in fact, a fashion plate. Its other contents were:

1. An Address to the Ladies of Great Britain from the Editor
2. Useful Lessons for the Conduct of female Life (Virtue, Learning, Industry), with the moral:
    'Virtue itself needs no defence,
    The surest Guard is Innocence'
3. New and elegant Bills of Fare for every Season of the Year
4. One-hundred-and-eight pages ruled for a Memorandum-book on an approved plan (for owner to enter up her engagements, accounts, etc.)
5. Twenty-four of the most approved Country-dances, with directions for dancing in time
6. The favourite new Songs—sung at Ranelagh, Vauxhall, etc.
7. Select pieces of Poetry
8. Maxims and reflections for the Conduct of female Life
9. Historical anecdotes in honour of the Fair Sex
10. Alcanor and Doristuis. A Tale
11. Conjugal Felicity and The exemplary Wife, or Virtue rewarded at Last: A Tale
12. Description of a Fribble
13. Select thoughts on Conservation
14. Character of a good Wife
15. Useful receipts in Cooking, Confectionery, etc. (These included: To Roast a Haunch of Venison, To Dress Ortalans, To Fry Oysters, To Roast an Eel, To Florendine a Kidney of Veal, To Boil a Turbot, and Beef à la Mode)
16. Rates of Hackney Coachmen, Chairmen, Watermen, etc.
17. A table of Expenses
18. Necessary Tables for Marketing, etc.

These contents were very similar to another little pocket-book of which there are six editions at Jane Austen's house at Chawton: the *Lady's Daily Companion* for the years 1788, 1789, 1791, 1792, 1799, and 1800. The owner of them, who made daily entries in the diary part, was Caroline Pym-Hales, daughter of Sir Thomas Pym-Hales, Member of Parliament for Dover. Born in 1772, she married the Hon. William Gore in 1798, and died in 1852. Her *Lady's Daily Companion* of 1791 and 1792 contain frequent reference to the Austen family. Jane Austen's brother Edward, who had been adopted as heir to their landed cousin Mr Thomas Knight of Godmersham Park in Kent and Chawton, Hampshire, was engaged to marry Elizabeth, daughter of Sir Brook Bridges of Goodnestone Place, the big house of a neighbouring village. Mrs Austen was evidently staying at Goodnestone House at the time of this entry in Caroline Pym-Hales's pocket-book: *Feb. 7, 1791,* 'Went to Adisham Church and Cath and Harriet walked from there to Goodnestone and found all the family at home, and Mrs Austen there.' By November the wedding is drawing near: *Nov. 27th, 1791,* 'We all went to Adisham Church except Mrs Chanay, and afterwards us four went in the coach to Goodenstone and then walked with them to see the improvements which were made there as Mr Austen and Elizabeth are to live there.' They were to live in a small house in the village until Mrs Knight, by then widowed, retired to Deal and the young couple took over Godmersham Park, Edward also taking the surname of Knight. Then the final entry: *Dec. 27th, 1791,* 'Sophia and Elizabeth Bridges were both married this morning at Goodnestone, the former to Mr W. Deedes and the latter to Mr Austen. I hope they will be very happy.'

The *Lady's Daily Companion* was printed in Canterbury by Simmons and Kirkly, Price one shilling; and apart from its blank pages for the diarist's entries, the contents for the edition of 1788 were:

1. Poetical Address to the Ladies
2. Description of Frontispiece
3. Description of the latest Fashions
4. Country Dances
5. Description of Mrs Palmer's new Theatre in Wellcose Square
6. Table of Kings and Queens, etc.
7. Extensive Marketing Tables
8. Ruled pages for Memorandum, etc.

9. Rates for Hackney Coachmen, Chairmen, and Watermen agreed by the last Act of Parliament
10. Original Poetry
11. New Songs sung at Vauxhall in 1787
12. Forms of Complimentary Cards
13. Answers to the last Year's Enigmas
14. New Enigmas for 1788

The 1789 edition had all these things, and in addition three copper-plates, one of which was a fashion plate: 'Lady in Full Dress of 1788, and Four of the Most Fashionable Head Dresses'. Also an account of new fashions in Paris in September and October 1788. Although this fashion report would seem to be three months out of date, the pocket-book was published in December for the following year so that there is not so much time-lag as there appears. And of course fashions did not change so swiftly then as now. Modes that were the *dernier cri* in Paris in September 1788 would be considered avant-garde in London in January 1789—altogether *too* avant-garde for country districts. In Jane Austen's letter to her sister Cassandra of 8 January 1801, she refers to having met Mrs Powlett at a dinner party who was 'at once expensively and nakedly dress'd'—she was wearing the post-revolutionary fashions of Paris which not surprisingly caused a sensation in rural Hampshire. The *Lady's Daily Companion* for 1799 was 'enriched with twenty-four beautiful descriptive vignettes, designed by Stothard and finely engraved by Angus, selected from Goldsmith's celebrated poems "The Traveller" and "The Deserted Village"'. There was also a list of Penny Post Offices, and of Mail Coaches, 'with their Rents and the Inns they go from'. A page for each week of the year was provided for the owner of the pocket-book to make entries of household accounts.

In July 1791 William Lane began a shilling monthly called the *Novelist, or Amusing Companion*, which was advertised the previous month in the *Star*. The prospectus, bearing the motto 'We cull the choicest', promised that each number would contain 'eighty pages and upwards of Tales, Histories, Adventures, Anecdotes, from the best modern publications'; and in addition 'a Variety of Originals and some of the best Translations from the French'. Mr Lane was evidently economically filling a large part of his magazine by 'culling the choicest' from contemporary works, no doubt without payment or acknowledgment. However, it was to be 'embellished with beautiful engravings', which were always expensive. By the second number, August 1791, he had changed the title to the *Polite Repository, or Amusing Companion*; and at the end of the year the monthly parts were bound in one complete volume, price seven shillings, or in two volumes, half-bound, at three shillings and sixpence each. These volumes were intended to 'answer both as a genteel present for the New Year, and also as an annual entertaining companion for the Circulating Libraries'. Similar bound volumes are thought to have been issued at the end of 1792, but no copies can be traced. After the turn of the century, the Minerva Press issued various ladies' miscellanies. The *Ladies' Museum* came out for the years 1806, 1808, 1809, 1810, 1813, 1815, 1816, 1817, and 1820. The *Ladies' Companion* was issued for 1806, and the *Ladies' New and Elegant Pocket Book* for 1812, 1815, 1819; the *Ladies' Mirror or Mental Companion* published intermittently since at least 1785, appeared in 1800, with later issues in 1810, 1814, 1816, 1817, 1818.

Pocket-books and periodicals were, however, only a very small part of William Lane's publishing activities. His major operations were in the publication of novels and their distribution all over the country through his circulating libraries. When he first set up as a publisher, circulating libraries were already a well-established idea—the early beginnings were related in Chapter VII. They had opened up a new market for books, most particularly for novels, and the book trade as a whole had benefited. The bookseller Lackington wrote in his *Memoirs*, 'I have been informed that when circulating libraries were first opened the booksellers were much alarmed, and their rapid increase added to their fears, had led them to think that the sale of books would be much diminished.' But he then goes on to say that, far from being diminished, sales had been greatly promoted because the cheap supply of books had given whole families a taste for reading, with the result that 'thousands of books are purchased every year, by such as have borrowed them from the libraries and after reading, approving of them, and becoming purchasers.' According to Mrs Griffeth in *Genuine Letters of Henry and Frances* (1766–70), the booksellers declared that out of an edition of one thousand copies 'the Circulating Libraries . . . take off 400'. Thomas Bellamy, a miscellaneous writer who founded the *Monthly Mirror, Reflecting Men and Manners* (1795–1810) was one of the many people who established circulating libraries towards the end of the century.

All authorities are agreed in giving William Lane the credit for taking

THE

Old English Baron:

A

GOTHIC STORY.

SHEFFIELD
Printed by C. & W. Thompson
Albion Office
And Sold by Longman, Hurst & Co. & B. Crosby & Co.
LONDON.

24. Title page to Clara Reeve's *Old English Baron* (1777); edition circa 1816

Engraved for the Lady's Magazine.

The Rivals.

25. Illustration to a moral tale in the *Lady's Magazine*, October 1782

circulating libraries to every big town, and in particular to every seaside resort, large or small. Credit, perhaps, is the wrong word: many people regarded the circulating libraries as being as dangerous for young ladies as pornography for young gentlemen. 'Madam,' said Sir Anthony Absolute in *The Rivals* (1775), 'a circulating library in a town is as an evergreen tree of diabolical knowledge. It blossoms through the year. And depend on it, Mrs Malaprop, that they who are so fond of handling the leaves will long for the fruit at last.' But the frequency with which they were denounced is an indication of their success. William Lane persuaded shopkeepers of all kinds, all over the country, to give over a few of their shelves to the formation of a lending library; not only booksellers and bookbinders, but engravers and picture-framers, grocers, jewellers, confectioners, tobacconists, perfumers, ironmongers, all manner of shopkeepers might also become librarians. In an advertisement in *The Correspondent* he offered to supply anyone who wished to embark on a circulating library with a stock of books from his warehouse, and his prospectus of 1791 repeated the offer. Those who wished to engage in 'an employ both respectable and lucrative' were informed that a library containing from 100 to 5,000 volumes could be had at a few days' notice, along with a catalogue for the subscriber, and full instructions 'how to plan, systemize, and conduct' the library. Fanny Burney writes, 29 May 1779, of a milliner and library-woman at Brighton. An 'Agent to the Imperial Fire & Life Office' in Cambridge was also the proprietor of a library. But the larger libraries in London were owned by booksellers who did not as a rule follow any other trade, although they were usually ticket-selling agents for the theatres.

Lane did not pay his authors very much, and he himself waxed exceedingly rich on the proceeds of their labours. Samuel Rogers could 'well remember the splendid carriage in which he used to ride, and the footman with their cockades and gold-headed canes'. A forerunner, indeed, of the socialite publishing tycoons of today. It was in the seaside towns and spas, where visitors had nothing whatever to do and the idle days were endless, that the libraries were most rewarding. When the hero of one of the Minerva Press novels, *Frederic & Caroline* (1800), strolls into a circulating library at Margate 'furnished from the Minerva' the author comments: 'Where, in these enlightened days, is there a bathing-place without such a receptacle of literary knowledge?' *Literary knowledge* was not what most people would call the books in these libraries, but then it was a Minerva Press author writing, and she no doubt wished to flatter her publisher. In

26. Library label from the collection of Dr John Johnson

Charles Dickens's sketch of *Our English Watering-places* he writes of the library attached to the Assembly Rooms where 'the leaves of the romances (were) reduced to a condition very like curl paper. This is the library for the Minerva Press. If you want that kind of reading, come to our watering-place.' Charles Lamb referred to the Minerva libraries as supplying 'These scanty intellectual viands of the whole female reading public', and declared that the Minerva Press became a synonym for works 'completely expurgated of all the higher qualities of the mind'. On the other hand, Leigh Hunt put in a good word for a Minerva Library in his autobiography:

'I had subscribed while at school to William Lane's famous circulating library in Leadenhall Street, and I have continued to be such a glutton of novels ever since, that, except where they repel me at the outset with excessive words, I can read their three volume enormities to this day without skipping a syllable . . . I think the authors wonderfully clever people, particularly those who write most; and I should like the most contemptuous of their critics to try their hands at doing something half as engaging.'

Leigh Hunt gave his favourite authors at this time as being Fielding,

Smollett, Voltaire, Charlotte Smith, Bage, Augustus La Fontaine, and Mrs Radcliffe.

Mrs Ann Radcliffe was the wife of the proprietor of the *English Chronicle*. She published *The Sicilian Romance* in 1790 and *Romance of the Forest* in 1791; then *The Mysteries of Udolpho*, published in 1794, brought her fame— and £500. Her next novel, *The Italian*, made £800. She became the most widely read of all the 'Gothic' novelists whose original inspiration came from Horace Walpole's *The Castle of Otranto*. Indeed, the Gothic-romantic vogue in literature was known as Radcliffian mania. The mania gradually pervaded women's magazines, and by the end of the century Gothic stories had entirely superseded the previously so popular oriental tales. There was a strong Germanic flavour to the Gothic movement, a Wagnerian wallowing in predestined doom, a piling up of horror and laying on of suspense. Nature became awesome, craggy, dark with impending disasters. Pine forests were rent with flashes of forked lighting. Ruined monasteries were the setting for strange ceremonies by moonlight. Sliding panels led to underground passages where lanterns were inexplicably dashed out of trembling hands. There were oak chests containing blood-stained garments, supernatural apparitions, tapestries that seemed to move, white faces at turret windows.

Yet the Radcliffian mania should not be allowed to overshadow Mrs Radcliffe's undoubted talent as a writer. Her characters, even today, are real and recognizable, although they weep more and rant more than would be natural now. Her depiction of minor characters is quite brilliant. In *The Mysteries of Udolpho* there is the excitable lady's maid, Annette, who will not stop chattering of her own affairs at moments of crisis; and also the old housekeeper Dorothée at the Chateau de Blanc. Dorothée, speaking of the young marchioness who died so mysteriously when she herself was a young maid at the Chateau says, 'We all loved her well, and I shall always grieve for her. Time runs round!—it is now many years since she died; but I remember everything that happened then, as if it was but yesterday. Many things that have passed of late years are gone quite from my memory, while those so long ago I can see as if in a glass.' But what most influenced other writers was Mrs Radcliffe's power to create an atmosphere, her sensitivity to the effect of scenery on a mood, to the effect of the weather, or of the time of day, on a vulnerable human spirit. This power was emphasized by a critic writing in 1863, Julia Kavanagh in her *English-women of Letters*:

'It is not only by her works that Mrs Radcliffe must be judged; it is by her power over the minds of her contemporaries and her successors. None of those who have followed her in the regions of romance has escaped her influence. Critics, poets, have felt it. To her Hazlitt acknowledged that he owed his love of moonlit night, autumn leaves, and decaying ruins. Strange power that could thus rule, thus awaken, fictitious tastes, likings and feelings.'

The influence of this strange power on a young girl's imagination is the theme of Jane Austen's *Northanger Abbey*, written in 1798 but not published until 1818 when the Gothic vogue was waning in favour of historical romances in the Waverley manner. Jane Austen mocks Mrs Radcliffe and her imitators, but she mocks with affection, not derision. Her heroine Catherine Morland says to Henry Tilney:

"But you never read novels, I dare say?"

"Why not?"

"Because they are not clever enough for you. Gentlemen read better books."

"The person, be it gentleman or lady, who has not pleasure in a good novel must be intolerably stupid. I have read all Mrs Radcliffe's works, and most of them with great pleasure. The *Mysteries of Udolpho*, when I had once begun it, I could not lay down again; I remember finishing it in two days, my hair standing on end the whole time."

At the end of *Northanger Abbey* Catherine realized that all her embarrassments and griefs could be traced to the influence of the novels she had been reading: 'Charming as were Mrs Radcliffe's works, and charming even as were the works of her imitators, it was not in them that human nature, at least in the midland counties of England, was to be looked for. Of the Alps and Pyrenees, with their pine forests and their vices, they might give a faithful delineation; and Italy and Switzerland, and the South of France might be as fruitful of horrors as they were represented.'

But there were other books in the major city libraries besides Gothic novels and 'the insipidies of the Minerva Press'. The catalogue of Lane's Leadenhall Library included all the great names of the eighteenth century: Johnson, Goldsmith, Gibbon, Addison, Richardson, Smollett, Sterne; also the poets, travel writers, historians. And although one of the most popular novels of the last decade was undoubtedly romantic, it was not at all Gothic and was very much better written than the general run of fiction at

Engraved for the Lady's Magazine.

Unexpected Surprise

27. Illustration to a 'gothic' tale in the *Lady's Magazine*, June 1782

that time. This was *A Simple Story* by Elizabeth Inchbald, published in 1791, which went into a second edition in the same year. She had received only £200 for the copyright of the book, but it brought her fame as an author and commissions to write for the reviews: Prince Hoare enrolled her as a contributor to the *Artist, a collection of essays relative to painting, etc. etc.*; and she wrote articles for the *Edinburgh Review*. She was already a successful dramatist. For her first farce she received 100 guineas; and then *Such Things Are*, produced in 1787, brought her in £900. But Leigh Hunt said 'her novels, which were written in a style to endure, were her chief merits'; and Mrs Gore, the very successful writer of Society novels of the Regency period, makes one of her characters speak of 'the exquisite *Simple Story* of Mrs Inchbald . . . In the whole range of romance, I know not a more pathetic transition than from Miss Milner's wedding-day to her death bed, from her innocent youth to her guilty maturity, as hazarded in that interesting work.'

Elizabeth Inchbald's career, which began by running away from home to go on the London stage, was itself full of drama. Towards the end of her life she was so famous that the publisher Phillips of St Paul's Churchyard offered her £1,000 for her memoirs without seeing the manuscript. Some people were of the opinion that her chief claim to fame lay in the prefaces she wrote to Longman's edition of *The British Theatre* in twenty-five volumes, of which she was the editor. In her criticism of Thomas Holcroft's *The Deserted Daughter* she compares her own anxiety over the morals of stage productions with the actual state of moral behaviour in the society around her, which she finds worse than in even the most objectionable play and every bit as depraved as that of the Restoration:

'But when by degrees, the fashionable world shall have become so philosophic in love, and concerning all the rights of wedlock, that scarce any event in gallantry shall create embarrassment on the score of refined sentiments, the resource of an author in his profession will be then nearly destroyed. For scrupulous purity of character, and refinement in sensations, are the delightful origin of all those passions, those powerful impulses of the mind, on which the works of imagination are chiefly founded. As *The Deserted Daughter* has not been written many years, the readers of fashion will possibly be surprised that the wife of Mordaunt should feel the slightest concern on the account of her husband's former or present excesses, in the character of a libertine lover.'

Elizabeth Inchbald's own best-known dramatic work was a play called *Lovers' Vows* which she adapted from an English translation of the German of Kotzebue's *Love Child*, sometimes called *Natural Son*. She admitted to having toned down the 'forward and unequivocal manner' in which the original heroine had announced her affection for her lover. This she considered would have been 'revolting to an English audience'. In Jane Austen's house at Chawton there is a playbill of a Winchester theatre announcing *Lovers' Vows* by Elizabeth Inchbald. This does not necessarily mean that the Austen family actually went to see the play in Winchester; but it was Mrs Inchbald's version of *Lovers' Vows* that Jane Austen chose for the amateur theatricals in *Mansfield Park*—the theatricals that were brought to such an abrupt conclusion when Sir Thomas Bertram arrived home unexpectedly from the West Indies and found his family rehearsing, to his outraged disapproval. And we do know that Jane had seen another Kotzebue play in Bath. In a letter to Cassandra on 19 June 1799, she wrote: 'The play on Saturday is, I hope, to conclude our gaieties here.' She did not say what the play was to be; but Jean Freeman in her *Jane Austen in Bath* quotes a theatre review in the *Bath Herald & Register* for 29 June 1799:

> 'The *Romance of Bluebeard* was preceded by Kotzebue's admirable drama of *The Birthday Day*. If the German author has justly drawn down censure for the immorality of his productions for the stage—this may be accepted as his *amende honorable*—it is certainly throughout unexceptionally calculated to promote the best interests of virtue, and the purest principles of benevolence, and though written much in the style of Sterne, it possesses humour without a single broad Shandyism.'

Whoever translated *The Birthday Day* into English may have had the same ideas as Elizabeth Inchbald about what would be 'revolting to an English audience', and watered down the original accordingly. Alas that we should not have Jane Austen's comments upon the production.

Other women dramatists of the second half of the eighteenth century included Hannah More, whose *Percy* was extravagantly admired. Her next play was *The Fatal Falsehood*. This was attacked in the *Saint James's Chronicle* by Mrs Cowley, who accused Miss More of producing a plagiarism of her tragedy *Albina*. Miss More wrote a 'temperate reply' (but surely not very tactful) denying knowledge of the very existence of such a tragedy as *Albina*.

Mrs Cowley's best-known play was *The Belle's Stratagem*. It was first produced at Covent Garden in 1780, and Mrs Inchbald had a part in this production—her first appearance on the London stage. It was patronized by the Queen, and when published dedicated by permission to Her Majesty. At the same time it was recorded as being 'not unproductive of pecuniary emolument'. Mrs Cowley's first play had earned her 800 guineas, and *The Belle's Stratagem* brought in considerably more money, as well as flattering critical esteem. The financial success is interesting, since Mrs Cowley's original incentive to write plays was purely pecuniary. The story goes that she was in a box at Drury-Lane at the presentation of *The School for Wives* and asked one of the party she was with 'What emolument is the author likely to derive from his piece?' The reply was 'About £500'. This very considerable sum made such an impression on Mrs Cowley that she sat down the next morning and before dinner had produced the first act of *The Runaway*. The comedy was completely finished in a fortnight, and sent anonymously to David Garrick. When it was put on it received such applause that it was played for several nights in succession, and was the first to introduce the practice of 'running plays'.

Many other plays followed, 'the extreme facility of Mrs Cowley's pen is not less remarkable than the strength and variety of its powers' wrote one critic. She also wrote verse, and in one of her poems, 'The Scottish Village', generously does honour to the female genius of Mrs Barbauld, Miss Burney, and Miss Seward. In spite of all this heady success, Mrs Cowley seems to have led a blameless family life. In *Public Characters of 1801–2* we find the anonymous male author expressing surprise that a woman writer, and connected with the stage at that, can be so untarnished:

'In the different characters of daughter, wife, and mother, the conduct of our fair author has been most exemplary. There is nothing about her that indicates the writer; her manners are lively and unassuming. The general tenor of her life has been by no means *theatrical*; at the Playhouses she is very seldom seen; and her life has been so strictly domestic, with no intercourse with the Theatres beyond what was necessary for the production of her Plays; it has also prevented the accumulation of materials for a more busy biography; perhaps, however, the very circumstance of want of incident is the highest praise; for to be public as a GENIUS, and private as a WOMAN, is to wear laurels gracefully veiled.'

Very different was the account this same writer had to give of Mrs Robinson. Mary Robinson (née Darby) was born in Bristol in 1760 and for a short time attended the famous school run by Hannah More's sisters. But her father lost a considerable fortune and at an early age she was removed from the care of the Misses More (who were expensive) to a seminary near London. At fifteen she married Mr Robinson, then a student in Lincoln's Inn. There is no record of this having been an elopement from the seminary, but the student lawyer seems to have been just the type for an irresponsible escapade. He was certainly in no position to support a wife; and 'having imprudently offended a near relation on whom he depended for a considerable fortune', pecuniary difficulties induced Mrs Robinson to make the stage her profession. Jane Williams, in her *Literary Women of England*, says briefly of Mrs Robinson that 'in the character of Shakespeare's Perdita her extraordinary beauty rendered her at once famous and infamous', and leaves it at that. The *Ladies' Monthly Museum* of January 1801 has a portrait engraving of Mrs Robinson and in the text says, 'In the character of "Perdita" she attracted the notice of a very distinguished Personage, and quitted the stage. Our remarks will now be confined to Mrs Robinson's literary pursuits, which publicly commenced in 1778.' But the author of *Public Characters* tells more. He relates that

> 'as Perdita she attracted the notice of an illustrious character, and after a long series of such attentions from such a lover as, we apprehend, few hearts could resist, whether we consider his rank, his figure, or his accomplishments, she quitted her profession in favour of one so armed at all points to captivate and conquer. This attachment lasted little longer than a year; and Mrs Robinson was left to the poignant regrets of her own mind, with no other solaces than the actual comforts arising from £500 per annum.'

He tells us everything except the name of the lover 'so armed at all points to captivate and conquer'; but no doubt at the time he was writing (1801) it was not difficult for any reader to conjecture this correctly considering 'his rank, his figure, his accomplishments'.

Mrs Robinson hid her shame on the continent for nearly five years, and on her return in 1788 set herself to literary labours . . . poems, a satire on *Modern Manners*, a tragedy called *The Sicilian Lover*, a pamphlet named *Vindication of the Queen of France*, published anonymously, and another called *Thoughts on the Condition of Women, and the Injustice of Mental Sub-*

ordination, which a contemporary critic called 'sensible and generous'. She followed this up with a considerable number of two- and three-volume novels; and under the signature of Laura Maria wrote for the magazines in the style of the Della Crusan rhymers. Later she took Sappho as her pseudonym, and was much criticized for this, even though literary tribunals had honoured her with the title of 'The British Sappho'. The *Public Characters* writer, despite his generally prim approach to women, comes down on the side of Sappho—'daring to place her on the Sapphic throne even with a Smith and a Seward'.

Sappho or no Sappho, she died in poverty in a cottage at Englefield Green in 1800 at the age of forty. Poverty ? What happened to that handsome £500 a year maintenance from her aristocratic lover ?—a very comfortable income in those days. Her literary remains were posthumously published for the benefit of her only child, a daughter. Whether this was the daughter of the improvident law student who was her husband, or of the illustrious seducer, we do not know. It is possible, of course that the child was the proof of some subsequent attachment, and this would account for the termination of the £500 a year.

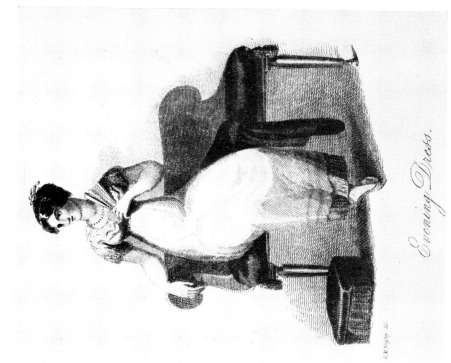

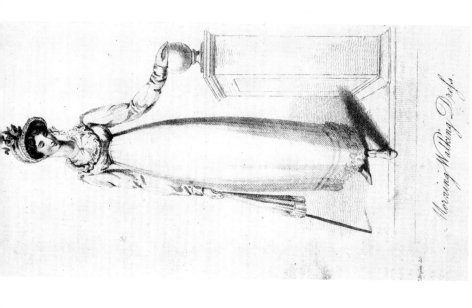

XI. Two hand-coloured aquatints in the *Lady's Magazine*, March and June 1816.

XII. Marguerite, Countess of Blessington; after the watercolour by A. E. Chalon

Chapter XI

JOHN BELL, MARY WELLS, AND MRS JOHNSON

John Bell: typefounder, printer, publisher, bookseller. The Life of George Anne Bellamy. *Charlotte Smith, her poetry and novels.* The Morning Post. *Bell's British Library. Visits of the Prince of Wales.* The World, or Fashionable Gazette. *Edward Topham, editor; the Rev. Charles Este, gossip writer. Mary Wells, actress; her connection with the* World. *The stage and literature as professions for women. Mrs Johnson founds the first Sunday newspaper.* Bell's *Weekly Messenger; contemporary advertising.*

ᘛᘚ

JOHN BELL was one of the most conspicuous figures in the publishing world at the end of the eighteenth century and during the first three decades of the nineteenth century. He was bookseller, printer, publisher, typefounder, and journalist, and he also ran a circulating library. He was the first printer to discard the long f (s) from his fount of type.

John Bell's career as a bookseller began in 1769 when he was twenty-four years old, and he became noted for backing unusual and daring publications. Charles Knight wrote about him as 'the mischievous spirit, the very Puck of booksellers'. One of Bell's best-sellers was *Apology for the Life of George Anne Bellamy, written by Herself*, in six volumes, the first of which appeared in 1785. George Anne Bellamy was an actress, born in 1731, who was said to be 'mistress to half the aristocracy of England'. John Bell advertised her book as a work that would disclose the hitherto unsuspected secrets of every well-known man-about-town. It can be re-garded as an early forerunner of the libellous memoirs of Harriette Wilson, which were published in 1825 by Stockdale. The DNB is defeated by Miss Bellamy's career off the stage, and simply records, 'Her private adventures cannot be followed'.

Bell's less sensational publications included the *Wanderings of Warwick* by Charlotte Smith, a very different character from George Anne Bellamy. Charlotte was a brave woman of gentle upbringing, who wrote poetry and novels to support herself and her numerous children through a long series of misfortunes and calamitous lawsuits over family money. At one time she spent many months in prison, keeping her husband company. Her first literary effort was a thin quarto volume of poems of a pastoral nature, called *Elegiac Sonnets*. Pastorals, shepherds and shepherdesses were in vogue, and the little volume was an immediate success, running swiftly into a second edition. Her first novel *Emmeline*, was followed within a year by *Ethelinde*, and then three more novels between 1791 and 1793. In a biographical sketch of Charlotte Smith in *Public Characters of 1800–1*, the anonymous author has a passage which describes with compassion the attitude of society towards any woman who wrote for her own livelihood, or to support her family:

'The penalties and discouragements attending the profession of an author fall upon women with a double weight; to the curiosity of the idle and the envy of the malicious their sex affords a peculiar incitement: arraigned, not merely as writers, but as *women*, their characters, their conduct, even their personal endowments become the subjects of severe inquisition; from the common allowances claimed by the species, literary women appear alone to be exempted: in detecting their errors and exposing their foibles, malignant ingenuity is active and unwearied—vain would be the hope to shield themselves from detraction, by the severest prudence, or the most entire seclusion: wanton malice, in the failure of facts, amply supplies materials for defamation, while, from the anguish of wounded delicacy, the gratification of demons seems to be extracted. Besides her sharing as a literary woman this general and most unjust persecution, Mrs Smith individually created enemies by the zeal and perseverance with which she endeavoured to obtain justice for her children, of men who hated her in proportion as they had injured her.'

John Bell's first newspaper enterprise was the *Morning Post* which was launched in 1772 by a syndicate of twelve men. The syndicate included the founders of Christies and Tattersalls, and the other members had varying commercial interests. The idea was that if they could run their own newspaper they could secure better positions for their own advertisements at much less cost than in other newspapers. John Bell, with his knowledge of printing and publishing, was the principal proprietor for nearly fifteen years. The first editor was Henry Bute, a dissolute young clergyman whose brawling had earned him the nickname of 'The Fighting Parson'. The readers they aimed to secure were the fashionables or would-be fashionables of London who were avid for scandal, gossip, and titillation. One of the best circulation-building ideas was in the very first number: the offer for sale of a complete list of the names and addresses of 'those ladies of the Town to be found at home in or near Piccadilly'. Inevitably, as was bound to happen sooner or later, Bute was imprisoned for libel, the suit being brought by the Duke of Richmond. After that, the *Morning Post* became a whip for the Treasury to beat the Prince of Wales, but changed over to the Prince's side when he offered the manager of the newspaper a thousand guineas and £350 a year to keep Mrs Fitzherbert out of his columns. Understandably, from then on it became regarded as a paid mouthpiece of Carlton House, and would have had no place in the history of women's reading had it not been bought by Daniel Stuart in 1795 and turned into an entirely different kind of newspaper: 'cheerfully entertaining, not entirely filled with ferocious politics', a respectable paper that ladies could read as well as gentlemen. Stuart engaged writers of literary ability, amongst them Charles Lamb, who became a regular contributor at 6d a paragraph, and it is from his pen that we get the flavour of the 'cheerfully entertaining' topics, including dress, that pleased the ladies:

'The chat of the day—scandal, but, above all, dress—furnished the material . . . A fashion of flesh, or rather pink-coloured hose for the ladies, luckily coming up at the jucture when we were on our probation for the place of Chief Jester to S's Paper, established our reputation in that line. Then there was the collateral topic of ankles. When an occasion to a truly chaste writer like myself, of touching that nice brink, and yet never tumbling over it, of seemingly ever approximating to something "not quite proper"; while, like a skilful posture-master, balancing betwixt decorums and their opposites, he keeps the line from which a hair's breadth deviation is destruction . . .'

The *Morning Post* had certainly become a different paper from the one which published its list of the ladies of the Town.

John Bell's library began as a centre for the distribution of French literature and about 1780 became known as the British Library. His special *Collection de Petits Formats* was advertised as being available *chez John Bell, Imprimeur-Libraire, à la Librairie Britannique dans le Strand*, and his Subscription Library was advertised as including 'English publications, and every sort of publication which shall appear in Paris from this day

1st January 1787'. In Fanny Burney's diary there is this entry: 'Friday se'night my mother accompanied by my father to Streatham on a visit to Mrs Thrale for four or five days. We invited Edward to drink tea with us, and upon the plan of a *frolic* we determined upon going to Bell's circulating library at which my father subscribes for new books.' Clearly, if Dr Burney were a subscriber, this circulating library dealt in books of a more learned quality than William Lane's so popular libraries. Nevertheless, it is pleasing to imagine that some of the French books were of a kind that the learned doctor would never dream of reading (or at least being seen reading) in English editions. Bell's library was situated conveniently near Covent Garden. Leith Hunt says in his *Autobiography*, 'Unfortunately for Mr Bell he had as great a taste for neat wines and ankles as for pretty books.' The Prince of Wales, who had the same tastes, often dropped in to look at the new books and refresh himself with Bell's alcoholic hospitality. Andrews described Bell as 'a man of meagre education but great taste, not only gross and sensual in the matter of wine and women, but refined in regard to literature and art', and went on to say that 'after having lost a lot of money by his costly production of *Bell's British Theatre*, he put the finishing stroke to his fortunes by inviting the Prince of Wales to an entertainment at his house . . . he was thenceforward the victim of duns and lawyers, the quarry of writ-servers and bailiffs'.

Bell's most famous newspaper enterprise was the *World, or Fashionable Gazette*, which ran from 1787 to 1794. Bell knew the fashionable world, and had a flair for interpreting the taste of the *bon ton*. His associate in this publication was Captain Edward Topham, a gentleman of means, who took on the editorship. Fashionable was used in the sense of smart Society, not of dress, for this was not a publication expressly for women. Rather the reverse, indeed, since it was the correspondence of Humphries and Mendoza, two boxers who challenged each other through the *World*, which raised the paper's circulation to a very profitable peak. It seems to have reached, from its first number, the most exalted places in fashionable society. No fewer than 3,000 copies were sold of the first issue, 'and a further thousand printed to accommodate the orders of the Court at Windsor'.

As much credit for the success of 'this elegant sheet' must be given to Topham as to Bell. For Captain Edward Topham was a man of birth, who had commanded a troop of Guards, and with his social connections he was able to pioneer a new kind of Society journalism written 'by gentlemen for gentlemen'. He brought into the *World* a third associate, the Reverend

Charles Este, an 'Old Westminster' who was one of the royal chaplains, a man of science and of great mental and personal activity. Most of the paper was, in fact, written by Este, whom the printer never saw, but who during the day was 'everywhere that a gentleman of taste could be'. Each night he forwarded to the publishers 'the harvest of a quiet eye upon fashionable folk and their doings'. It is interesting that this pioneer of gentlemanly gossip-writing should have been a clergyman, as was one of the pioneers of periodical plagiarism, the Reverend Charles Stanhope. *Public Characters of 1805* says of the *World*:

> 'With the exception of the *Anti-Jacobin*, no public print ever went upon the same ground; not depending so much on the immediate occurrence or scandal of the day, as upon the style of writing and the pleasantries that appeared there. In truth, some of the most ingenious men contributed towards it; and when the names of Merry, Jerningham, Andrews, Mrs Cowley, Mrs Robinson, Jekyll, and Sheridan are mentioned as having frequently appeared in this print, the remark will not be doubted. The poetry of the *World* was afterwards collected into four volumes; Merry and Mrs Cowley were the Della Crusca and Anna Matilda who were so long admired, and who, during the whole writing of those very beautiful poems, were perfectly unknown to each other.'

The Mrs Robinson and Mrs Cowley mentioned as contributors were the successful playwrights discussed in the previous chapter.

It was alleged that one of Topham's principal reasons for being concerned with the *World* was to use it as a vehicle to help the careers of his stage friends, most particularly that of Mary Wells, a Drury Lane actress who was his mistress. A contemporary of this famous beauty declared that she 'had submitted four children to Topham before entering into stern matrimony with him'; but the DNB does not allow her to have achieved matrimony with Topham at all. Her father died in a madhouse when she was small, her mother kept a tavern frequented by actors, and her first marriage was to an actor named Wells, who deserted her almost immediately. At one period her salary at Covent Garden was as much as £10 a week but 'the chances of a brilliant career were neutralized by irregularities'.

Some of her irregularities after the long association with Captain Topham ceased must have landed her in low water, for it was in the Fleet Prison she married her second husband, Joseph Sumbel; and in 1811 she published *Memoirs of the Life of Mrs Sumbel, late Wells, of the Theatres Royal Drury Lane, Covent Garden and Haymarket, written by herself.* These memoirs rambled rather incoherently and a great part of them were occupied with details of her travels in search of her children, who refused to know her. 'Drunkenness', says the DNB, 'seems to have supervened on madness.' But in the days of her beauty and of her affair with Topham, she was a glamorous creature. The romance is said to have started when Mrs Wells, through the medium of a friend, asked him to write her an epilogue for a benefit performance. The author of *Public Characters* recounted with delicacy the way in which the affair came about:

> 'The reading and instructing her in the delivery of this epilogue produced interviews which the company of a woman so beautiful must always make dangerous. There are, as Sterne says, "certain chords, and vibrations, and notes that are correspondent in the human feelings, which frequent interviews awaken into harmony". In return for the greatest gift a man can receive, the heart of a most beautiful woman, Topham devised every method to become serviceable to her interests and dramatic character and advance the reputation of her he loved. It has been said more than metaphorically, that "love first created the *World*".'

During the period that Mary Wells was Topham's mistress, the *World* was full of praises for her performances. But the actress seems to have given as much to the paper as she received. She assisted in its production and contributed many vivacious and entertaining essays. From her *Memoirs* it appears that she was a frequent intermediary between the editor and the publisher, that is between Edward Topham and John Bell. In spite of her reconciliatory efforts, the two men eventually quarrelled irrevocably, and Topham withdrew the contract for printing the *World* from Bell, continuing the paper for five more years alone. Maybe John Bell considered Topham published too many puffs for his stage friends—although this would not, in those days, have been considered particularly reprehensible. As Leigh Hunt says, 'It was the custom at that time for editors of papers to be intimate with actors and dramatists. They were often proprietors as well as editors; and, in that case, it was not expected that they should escape the usual intercourse, or wish to do so.' Elizabeth Inchbald, who was a friend of Mary Wells, also contributed to the *World*, using the pseudonym of 'The Muse'.

28. The first Sunday newspaper, published by Mrs E. Johnson

It is very noticeable how often in the eighteenth-century actresses became writers. It took courage to act, and it took courage to write. A woman could only succeed in either career if she were possessed of exceptional determination and endurance. She also needed exceptional optimism to carry her through the inevitable reverses of fortune and merciless bludgeonings of fate. Since the stage and literature were the only two paid professions open to women with creative talents, if one failed her she had no choice but to attempt the other. Often it was necessary for one to supplement the other in order to avoid resorting to the profession that required no talent.

Many intelligent women whose talents were more practical than creative helped their husbands actively in business affairs, or courageously carried on the family business when widowed. And there were women who built up their own successful business ventures from the start. As far as we know there was no man helping Mrs E. Johnson when in 1779 she founded the first Sunday newspaper ever produced, the *British Gazette and Sunday Monitor*. And this was especially enterprising since it was an entirely new departure in publishing. There could have been no estimating the possible market for it, if any. What is more, it was illegal to sell anything but milk and mackerel on a Sunday, and people hawking newspapers were subject to a fine. This does not seem to have deterred Mrs Johnson—after all, with a little ingenuity (and the female mind tends to be more ingenious than the male when it comes to law-breaking) there is usually some way of doing an illegal thing in a perfectly legal way. But what might surely have made Mrs Johnson doubtful of success was that the public already had a choice of no less than seventeen different newspapers published in London every week. Seven of these came out every week-day morning, eight came out three times a week, one twice weekly, the other only once a week.

However, what the citizens hungered after and could not be given too much of was, according to Andrews, 'political gossip, conjectures, guesses, anticipations, pure inventions—all supposed to be genuine until contradicted next day . . . crumbs of information which had been dropped from the great man's table, picked up by his footmen, and spiced for the news collector'. Mrs Johnson's *British Gazette and Sunday Monitor*, price 3½d, had all the usual features of a daily newspaper, including a section for Home and Foreign Affairs; but it also ran an epitome of the week's spiciest news from the dailies, sometimes acknowledged, sometimes not. The very latest news was printed in a Postscript on the back page—we should now call it 'Stop Press'. In the first column of the front page, the place usually reserved for the theatres by the contemporary dailies, Mrs E. Johnson placed her one concession to the Sabbath: a feature headlined 'For the *Sunday Monitor*', and comprising some kind of sermon or religious instruction. From the start she seems to have been successful in attracting advertisers. No doubt they felt that her readers would have more leisure to read about their products and proposals than the readers of week-day newspapers.

In her 'Proprietress's Address' for the New Year 1781, Mrs Johnson 'thanks the Public for the very great and general support she has experienced in this, the *Original Sunday Newspaper*, and also takes this opportunity to inform the public that *four thousand papers* are published every Sunday morning in the Cities of London, Westminster, etc., which circumstance must give a most pleasing sensation to all advertising customers'. She was probably exaggerating her circulation figure a bit, but certainly the newspaper continued to prosper and Mrs Johnson remained at the helm for eighteen years. In 1798 a certain S. Johnson succeeded to the direction. It is reasonable to suppose he was her son. At any rate he made no change in the style, matter, typography, nor in the address of the newspaper office. But in 1805 the title was changed to *Johnson's Sunday Monitor and British Gazette (and London Recorder)*;

29. Initial letter heading the first column of Mrs Johnson's *British Gazette and Sunday Monitor*

and in 1812 Draper Brewman, a member of a well-known family in the newspaper business, acquired the property. In 1814 Draper Brewman sold out to John Stokes, who simplified the title to a briefer, more modern style: the *Sunday Monitor and London Recorder*.

The success of Mrs Johnson's pioneer Sunday newspaper was observed by John Bell who at that time was at one of his periodical low ebbs financially. He assessed the new market she had opened up and decided there was room for a rival Sunday publication. He got others interested in the project and in 1796 launched *Bell's Weekly Messenger*, which was printed on Saturday for delivery 'at the Sunday Breakfast Table of every Person who wishes to be informed and amused', thus probably getting it in earlier than Mrs Johnson's paper. Andrews has it that John Bell 'picked up a strange, loose, clever sort of character for his first editor—one Boldini, who had been a teacher of languages in some of the first families, an opera-house poet, and a thorough adventurer, although a man of unquestionable ability'. Leigh Hunt described Boldini as 'A Person who looked the epitome of squalid authorship. He was wretchedly dressed and dirty, and the rain, as he took his hat off, came from it as from a spout.' But he also said, 'He wrote a good idiomatic style, and was a man of abilities.' Later Boldini was suspected of being a spy, was deported under the Aliens Act and became a reader of English newspapers for Bonaparte. His intimacy with some of the influential families of England, through teaching their children, was supposed to have been of use to the French government. Andrews says, 'The last his old friends heard of him he had started a carriage and was dashing about Paris with the equipage of a nobleman.'

185

Bell's Weekly Messenger flourished, either because of Boldini's 'unquestionable ability' or in spite of his questionable character. And from 1799 an extra edition was printed on Mondays containing the market prices for the day. It became much esteemed for its country politics and accounts of country town markets. What is more, it flourished without the help of advertising revenue. John Bell had announced at the start that his Sunday paper would include no advertisements 'in view of his intention to secure the widest possible family circulation'—an intention that would have given a modern magazine proprietor every hope of securing a great deal of advertising. But most of the advertising of the day was not considered suitable for feminine eyes to light upon, and Bell was anxious that 'Female delicacy should not be invaded by the ribaldry which too often disgraces most contemporaries'. This nicety may seem quite out of character with his own happy-go-lucky personal conduct, but it illustrates how wives and daughters were shielded within the domestic circle from the outside world of men, mistresses, and the stage.

Scrupulous niceties, for once, seem to have led to success, including success abroad. In the 7 November 1802 issue of *Bell's Weekly Messenger* there was an announcement that it was 'the only newspaper printed in England which is at present permitted to be received in any part of France'. Perhaps Boldini was already in Paris and still had a stake in the *Messenger*. By the next year, copies printed exceeded 6,000 per issue; and a special number for Nelson's funeral sold 14,405 copies. In 1822 *Bell's Weekly Messenger* claimed to be distributing not less than 10,000 copies a week. It seems to have been profitable for everyone except Bell, who, as Leigh Hunt put it, 'was one of those men whose temperament and turn for enjoyment throw a sort of grace over whatsoever they do, standing them instead of everything but prudence, and sometimes even supplying them with the consolations which imprudence has forfeited'. An attractive, loveable man, John Bell—he can be seen as the willing sport of fate. His most famous periodical, *La Belle Assemblée* (founded 1806) comes into Chapter XIV. It was a landmark in the history of magazine production, and justified C. H. Timperley's tribute to John Bell in his *Dictionary of Printers and Printing*: 'He had an instinctive perception of what was beautiful in every possible combination of the arts'.

Chapter XII

EDUCATING 'THE POOR' AND FAMILY MAGAZINES

Mrs Sarah Trimmer. Sunday schools and charity schools. The first Family
Magazine. *Hannah More and her* Cheap Repository Tracts. *Attitudes towards
educating 'the poor'. Religion at a low ebb. Absentee clergymen and buck
parsons. Sewing instruction for the poor. Pre-Victorian household magazines.
The* Female Preceptor. *Seduction in prose and verse for the rationally devout.
Avant garde exponents of wider education for women. Reactionary beliefs
about wifely duties.*

A CONTEMPORARY of Mrs Johnson and John Bell who must undoubtedly have considered their Sunday newspapers sinful, was
Mrs Sarah Trimmer. Mrs Trimmer (1741–1810) was herself a
publishing pioneer, but in a very different field from that of Mrs Johnson.
She was the instigator and editor of the first family magazine. Family magazines of varying degrees of domesticity, combined with features of a moralizing character and with a general pervasion of prudery and Christianity,
were to become an increasingly dominant department of periodical publishing for women in the nineteenth century. But this department did not
exist in the eighteenth century before Mrs Trimmer's good offices.

Good offices, indeed, were Mrs Trimmer's speciality, pious sentiments
her forte. Her father was a Mr Joshua Kirby of Ipswich who, a contemporary writer in a woman's magazine tells us, 'had the honour of teaching
Perspective to the King, then to the Prince of Wales, and afterwards to
Her Majesty'. Later this maestro of perspective became Clerk of the
Works at Kew Palace, and it was then that his dutiful daughter Sarah met
her future husband. Sarah had been educated in the usual female accomplishments at a boarding-school in Ipswich kept by Mrs Justinier—'a
woman of elegant manners and refined sentiments who had in early life
moved in a circle of fashion; but an imprudent marriage had cut her off
from her family connections, and obliged her, in order to procure a respectable maintenance, to undertake the education of young ladies'. These
'imprudent marriages' occur again and again in the eighteenth century as

having been the initial impetus for women having to earn money. It is therefore not surprising, since they happened so often in real life, that imprudent marriages feature so frequently in the novels and magazine fiction of the period—nearly always with the message that the world is by no means well lost for love.

In Mr Trimmer, Sarah evidently met her perfect mate. He was 'a man of an agreeable person, pleasing manners, and exemplary virtues, about two years older than herself. In the course of their union she had twelve children, six sons and six daughters.' After about twenty years of matrimony and childbirth, she was encouraged by the publication of Mrs Barbauld's *Easy Lessons for Children* to emulate that publication, and even go one better. In 1780 she published *An easy Introduction to the Knowledge of Nature*, sternly followed in 1782 by *A Sacred History, selected from the Scriptures, with Annotations and Reflections, adapted to the Comprehension of Young Persons*. In 1786 came *The Oeconomy of Charity*, a treatise on the formation and management of Sunday schools. There were at that time the old-established parochial charity schools, originally instigated by the Society for Promoting Christian Knowledge which was founded in 1696; also a few schools endowed or supported by private individuals. Otherwise there was no provision for the education of the poor.

Robert Raikes of Gloucester is generally credited with starting the Sunday school idea in 1780, his connections with the Press (he was proprietor of the *Gloucester Journal*) enabling him to spread the cause and arouse sympathy with his efforts. The *Gentleman's Magazine* gave his scheme a great deal of editorial support, and in 1785 Raikes and some other philanthropists started the 'Society for Promoting Sunday Schools'. But in fact there had been people running Sunday schools before. Hannah Ball, a Wesleyan Methodist, kept a Sunday school at High Wycombe from 1769 until her death in 1792; and even earlier, about 1763, the Reverend Theophilus Lindsey and Mrs Catherine Cappe had gatherings of the same kind at Catterick. Mrs Trimmer's treatise of 1786 became the textbook or manual for all those who had by her time established Sunday schools attached to their church in towns and villages all over the country. The schools were popular with parents because they not only taught religion but also reading and writing. Furthermore it was a mercy, praise be to the Almighty, to be able to pack the children out of the house and off to school on Sunday afternoons.

The indefatigable Mrs Trimmer also wrote various history books and scripture books, and her published works included a *Charity School Spelling Book, Family Sermons, Teacher's Assistant*. One dreads to think of her feelings regarding Mrs Johnson's Sunday newspaper, so different from the Trimmer works in content, despite its front-page religious column. It was 'to counteract the pernicious tendency of immoral books which have circulated of late years among the poorer classes of people to the obstruction of their improvement in religion and morals' that, in 1788, Mrs Trimmer launched the *Family Magazine*. She described it as 'a book of instruction and amusement for cottagers and servants, containing various matters which have a tendency to improve and lead the mind to religion and virtue'. Clearly the instruction overshadowed the amusement, if any. It is true there was a story in each number, but these stories were called *Instructive Tales*.

The background for the tales was a country village. The Squire, Mr Andrews, and his Lady, were endowed with an extremely tender regard for their poor neighbours, and were commendably desirous of contributing to their welfare and happiness. The character of Mrs Andrews was, at the time the *Family Magazine* was appearing, suspected to be intended to resemble the benevolent author. The *Instructive Tales* formed the principal part of the magazine, and they were designed to convey to the lower orders many improving lessons. They were also intended to guide their superiors in the proper manner of treating the poor in order to correct many of the faults peculiar to their humble station in life. Other subjects calculated to improve were introduced. Each number included a sermon, which was usually abridged from the works of some learned Divine of the Church of England; also descriptions of foreign countries so written, with revolutionary France in mind, as to make the lower orders appreciate the comforts and advantages of their own blessed island, peculiarly favoured by the Deity, and render them contented with its government and laws.

The *Family Magazine* only lasted a year. Priced at 3s a copy, it was far and away too expensive for humble readers. Mrs Trimmer must surely have hoped that the Lady Bountifuls of the village would buy the magazine to circulate amongst their cottagers. In any case, its format was too ambitious to pay its way. Mrs Trimmer was an unremittingly busy woman, but in no sense a businesswoman. Also, one may surmise, the magazine was a little before its time. The Poor were not readily prepared to be preached to by their betters before Queen Victoria came to the throne. They had neither much leisure in which to read, nor light to read by, in their dark cottages. Nor indeed, could many of them read, if it came to that, even though their

30. Hannah More

children might be benefiting from the instruction of charity schools and Sunday schools. In those cottages which the *Family Magazine* did reach, it was likely to have been the children who read its contents out loud to the parents rather than the other way round. Some parents, however, themselves attended Sunday schools for the opportunity of instruction in reading and writing.

Hannah More had much the same interests at heart as Sarah Trimmer, but a less tactless, more acceptable way of setting about furthering those interests. She believed, as educational reformers before her had believed, that to teach the Poor to read without providing them with 'safe' books was not conducive to religious or moral reform. But she was realistic enough to see that it was necessary to provide reading material that would attract them by its presentation rather than repulse them. It was a brilliant and perceptive idea to adopt for her *Cheap Repository Tracts* the format of the stories and ballads for community singing supplied by the chap-books and broad-sheets that were sold in the streets by hawkers and pedlars. She even had them illustrated with the same kind of crude but lively woodcuts. The reading matter was to be 'a variety of things somewhere between verse papers and hymns, for it is vain to write what people will not read. These verses are made to attack gross immorality or dishonest practice and by trying to make them a little amusing in the manner as well as ornamental in the appearance, we may in time bring them to still higher things.' She herself investigated the material sold by hawkers and pedlars, and made a large collection of *sans-culotte* literature, sold for a penny. Most of these broadsheets were coarse, salacious stuff, many of them glamorized the life of sponging on society and sharp practice; some of them were saturated with superstition. But even more disturbing to Miss More were the Jacobin imprints—alluring novels, stories, and songs published by 'The School of Paine'—which were hung up for sale outside shops and in doorways inviting the certain corruption of any young person who had a few pennies to spare. Tom Paine's *Age of Reason* was one of the immoral books against which law cases were instituted by the Proclamation Society, founded by Wilberforce in 1787, later called the Society for the Suppression of Vice and Immorality.

Of the one hundred and fourteen *Cheap Repository Tracts* published in the years 1795 to 1798, Hannah More herself wrote at least fifty—in clear, very simple language. In some of them her endeavour was to counteract the pervasion of those political principles which the French Revolution had made so fashionable—a pervasion which, starting with the intellectuals, was now seeping down to the lower levels of society. One of the tracts in this particular series was entitled *Village Politics*, and achieved a very wide circulation. In other series her sisters, the schoolmistresses of Bristol, contributed seven tracts. Mrs Chapone of the Blue Stockings sent a contribution entitled 'Mary Wood the Housemaid'. One story, 'Babay', was reprinted from Mrs Trimmer's *Family Magazine*. Miss More also had reprinted old favourites such as Dr Watt's *Divine Songs for Children*, and Henry Fielding's 'True Example of the Interposition of Providence in the Discovery of Murder'. She was perceptive enough to realize the value of serial stories, always such successful circulation maintainers: 'Next month you may expect a full account of the many tricks and frolics of idle Jack Brown'; and in the next issue, 'Do not forget to inquire for Jack Brown in prison.'

The tracts were distributed through the normal bookselling outlets, and sold at ½d, 1d, and 1½d. Monthly issues were delivered by the publishers to their agents and also to private subscribers—Mrs Montagu, Mrs Boscawen, and other Blue Stockings among them. The Bishop of London allowed his library to be used as a warehouse for the Tracts, some of which 'he gives to every hawker that passes'. Miss More carried the war into the enemy's camp by inducing them to sell her wares. As part of this campaign, local hawkers and pedlars were invited to the opening ceremony of the Tract Repository at Hazard's library in Bath, and 'arrived decently dressed with characteristic ribands in their hats. An assortment of the instructive and entertaining works in poetry and prose were presented to each man by means of a subscription raised by the ladies and gentlemen present.' Originally the publication of the Tracts was subsidized by private subscription in order to allow the promoters to sell them at less than cost price. But the public demand for the Tracts exceeded everybody's wildest hopes. Three thousand were sold in six weeks, and a year later the sales had passed two million. The bound volumes produced for the better-off classes also sold well, and in 1797 Miss More reported that the Tracts were paying for themselves and further subscriptions were unnecessary.

It was after these fatigues and successes that she retired to her country house, Barley Wood near Wrington in the Mendip Hills, where she was joined by her four sisters who had profitably sold their young ladies' seminary in Bristol. Here they started a village Sunday school and also an industrial school to teach girls spinning. Then gradually they established other Sunday and industrial schools in ten surrounding villages, with a total of eight hundred pupils. Many of the farmers, although quite wealthy, were so hard, brutal, and ignorant that they refused to send their children to the schools unless they were paid to do so.

There was disapproval, also, from some members of the upper classes who objected to the very idea of educating 'the poor'. It might divert them from devoting their lives to their appointed tasks, and put notions into their heads beyond the station in life to which they belonged by lowliness of birth. All through the eighteenth century it had been widely accepted that only the leisured classes had leisure pursuits; anything which distracted the labouring classes from their labours was dangerous, likely to upset the economic laws of the country and the class distinctions upon which the social order was based. In his *Essays on the Employment of Time* (1750), Robert Bolton, Dean of Carlisle, mentions the possibility of reading as a pastime for the peasant and the mechanic, and then immediately rejects it: 'No, the advice to him is, *Observe what passes*'.

THE LADY'S DREAM.

THE ENCHANTED STREAM.

XIII. Two plates from *The Keepsake*, 1828, engraved by Charles Heath from paintings by Thomas Stothard, R.A.

XIV. Two engravings from *The Lady's Cabinet*, 1838, illustrating a story and a poem.

THE GOVERNESS.

"JOHN, let the Governess have a glass of wine," said Lady Burnet one day at the dinner-table; "you will find some gooseberry on the side-board." Miss Calder, the person who was thus to be distinguished, by the command of a vulgar-born woman, and now imperious mistress of a weak minded baronet's establishment, from a parcel of spoiled daughters who preferred to taste some exquisite French *liqueur*, had at this time been for several months a member in the capacity named, of the Burnet family; but she had never before met with such a marked and seemingly premeditated insult.

THE VILLAGE SCHOOLMISTRESS.

How doth this picture's art rehme
Of childhood's scenes the buried bloom !
How from oblivion's sweeping stream
Each floating flower and leaf redeem !
From neighbouring tower the iron chime
That told the school's allotted time,
The lowly dome where woodbine crept,
The sanded floor, with neatness swept,
The hour-glass in its gnarled nook,

Hannah More's own ideas about instructing the poor were by no means liberal. She herself described the curriculum she set as 'limited and strict . . . They learn of week-days such coarse works as may fit them for servants. I allow of no writing. My object has not been to teach dogmas and opinions, but to form the lower class to habits of industry and virtue. Principles, not opinions, are what I labour to give them.' Like most of the would-be reformers throughout the century, she believed the prevailing poverty, ignorance, and vice to be a religious problem, not an economic one. It was the spiritual and moral state of the poor that she set about putting to rights. But to do her justice, she was also roused now and again to speak out concerning the spiritual and moral state of the rich.

It must be taken into account that this was a period when the Clergy had virtually abdicated from their responsibilities to their parishioners. They were negligent of their duties, and often worse than negligent in their personal example. Absenteeism from their parishes was a constant cause of scandal. Wilberforce, for whom Hannah More had a great admiration and friendship, campaigned with other reformers against clerical absenteeism. It was very common for one man to hold several livings and perhaps rarely visit any one of them. Younger sons of the aristocracy who had to be provided for somehow, but had no real 'call' to the Church, did not like having to bury themselves in the country away from the delightful distractions of the Town. They would try to wangle dispensations for non-residence on the grounds that it was necessary they should not lose touch with the intellectual intercourse of London literary circles, the advantages of access to learned libraries, and so on. Then there were the 'buck parsons' who contrived to be given livings in convivial sporting neighbourhoods where they could get the kind of rollicking companionship they enjoyed. In *Northanger Abbey* which Jane Austen wrote in 1798, there is no censure of the fact that the hero, John Tilney, only visits his parish at week-ends and other occasional days, although it is understood that he will live at his rectory all the time when he is married. But in *Mansfield Park*, published in 1814 after the Clergy Residence Act of 1810, the plot hinges on the non-residence question. Looking back to this time when Hannah More and her friends and fellow reformers were working on spiritually barren soil, S. C. Hall wrote in his *Book of Memories*:

'Hannah More flourished at a period when religion was little more than a sound in England; when the clergy of the English Church were virtuous only in exceptional cases, and the flocks committed by the State to their charge were left in as utter ignorance of social and religious duties as if they had been really but sheep gone astray; when France was rendering impiety sacred, and raising altars to the worship of Reason; and when in England there were vile copyists—professional propagators of sedition and blasphemy under the names of Liberty and Fraternity.'

Although generally speaking parents were glad to send their children to Sunday school, there were those who needed extra persuasion as is shown by a book, published in 1789, called *Instructions for Cutting Out Apparel for the Poor*. This is a cloth-bound book with thirteen fold-in patterns on a tissue sheet of approximately 15 ins. by 11 ins. when opened. The title-page reads:

'Principally intended for the Assistance of the Patronesses of Sunday Schools and other Charitable Institutions, but U S E F U L in all F A M I L I E S. Containing Patterns, Directions, and Calculations whereby the most Inexperienced may readily buy the Materials, cut out and value each Article of Cloathing of every Size, without the least Difficulty and with the greatest exactness:

'With a P R E F A C E, containing a Plan for assisting the Parents of poor Children belonging to Sunday Schools, to Cloathe them, and other useful observations.

'Published for the Benefit of the S U N D A Y S C H O O L C H I L D R E N at Hertingfordbury in the County of Hertford, where the above Plan has been found to be the best encouragement to the Parents to send their Children to the Sunday School.

'Sold by J. Walter, Charing Cross, London.'

The Preface to the book explains how it came to be published:

'The following little tract has been hastily compiled from a collection of memorandums made for private convenience to save the trouble of repeated calculation and contrivance every time there was occasion to furnish any of the articles hereafter specified. Being much sought after by friends and others concerned in Charitable Institutions, the idea presented itself of committing a few copies to the press, principally for the accommodation of friends . . . it afterwards occured that a profit might ensue from the sale of the remainder, which would increase the fund of the little establishments that first gave rise to the plan itself. The establishments above mentioned are two Sunday Schools, and two Day Schools, or what are generally termed Schools of Industry. So much has been ably written in recommendation of these Institutions, that inferior attempts would be useless. But the difficulty has been to devise a permanent inducement to Parents to send their Children to the former of those useful Seminaries without breaking in too much upon the funds subscribed for their establishment, by donations of money or cloathing, which in the end have been found too often to defeat the Salutary purpose for which they were intended.

'At the Hertingfordbury School of Industry the work materials are all found by the Sunday School Fund. The parents are at the sole expense of teaching the children; viz. 3d a week for each scholar. The parents of the child working each garment have the preference of buying it, at a saving of at least 50% of its normal cost. This provides an Inducement to send Children to the Sunday School and to have them well cloathed.

'As the great object with respect to the poorer sort of girls is to bring them up with the ability to make good servants, and useful mothers to families of their own, the regulation is not only to teach them knitting and plain-work, but to instruct them in the necessary article of *mending* their own things; therefore the parents are directed to send the linen belonging to their families to be repaired.'

There follows an account of a plan for 'Providing for the necessities of poor Lying-in Women'. Lying-in necessities and infants' first clothes were lent for one month, with a week more allowed to return the set clean and in order, as it was received. The most deserving parents were given 'a few things slightly put together of any old materials, if only a few caps and shirts, to give to such parents as are most deserving, when they return the set that has been lent them'. A plan for assistance with the price of bread in severe weather was also in this preface: weekly tickets made out for each family giving the number of quartern loaves or quarters of flour each family consumed—a deduction to 2d a quartern being allowed. They were allowed to choose their own baker (there were no fewer than fourteen bakers in the parish of Hertingfordbury) so that 'By indulging each family in the liberty to purchase of their own tradesmen, all was harmony, gratitude and content. The great secret of success in these respects, seems to be a little attention to the particularities of the lower rank of people, and

NOSEGAY *for the Month of* JUNE

1 *White Lily*   3 *Ranunculus*

2. *Moss Provine Rose*   4 *Honey Juckle*

31. Engraving from the *New Lady's Magazine*, June 1789

to make them feel, as little as possible, their own dependance in the obligation you confer upon them.'

It may seem out of place to have quoted so much from a book that was in no sense a periodical publication. But this Preface so clearly shows contemporary attitudes to 'the poor', and has the same flavour as the many moralizing magazines which were to follow in the wake of Mrs Trimmer's pioneering *Family Magazine*. At the turn of the century such magazines were beginning to come thick and fast. The *Monthly Visitor and Entertaining Pocket Companion and New Family Magazine* ran from 1797 until 1804; the *Female Instructor* came out in 1811 and again each year until 1830; the *Female Preceptor* appeared in 1813, 1814, and 1815. The *Cottager's Monthly Visitor* ran from 1821 until 1856; the *Family Oracle of Health, Economy, Medicine, and Good Living* by A. F. Crell and W. M. Wallace from 1824 until 1828. There was the *Family Magazine* of 1825, and another *Family Magazine* ran from 1834 to 1837, when it was incorporated in *Ward's Miscellany*. The *Christian Lady's Magazine* (1834–49) was edited by Charlotte E. Phelan, who later became Mrs Tonna; and the *Magazine of Domestic Economy and Family Review* ran from 1836 until 1844. The *Library of Fiction, or Family Story Teller* (1836–7) was edited by Charles Dickens and provided lighter fare.

Also in 1836 came *Blackwood's Lady's Magazine or Gazette of the Fashionable World*, which ran until 1860. Presumably the publishers felt that *Blackwood's Magazine* itself was too highbrow for the fair sex, although its editor did in fact condescend to accept contributions from literary ladies. Mrs Hemans and Caroline Bowles (Mrs Southey) were both writing for *Blackwood's* at this time. Even the *Athenaeum*, during 1832, included Mrs Fletcher and Mary Howitt among its contributors. Later it accepted verse from that assiduous lady poet Mary-Jane Jewsbury, contributor to such annuals as the *Literary Magnet*, the *Literary Souvenir*, the *Amulet*, and the *Poetical Album*. Jane Williams wrote in her *Literary Women of England* (1861) that 'Many of the best pieces Mary-Jane Jewsbury ever composed still remain entombed, though embalmed, in the thick quartos of the *Athenaeum*'.

The anonymous editor of the *Female Preceptor*, however, had no advanced notions about women's intellectual interests. This was a periodical that Mrs Trimmer, had she been still alive, would have approved with all her heart, so full was it of pious sentiments. Let us hope that, from her safe seat not far from God's right hand, she was aware of being posthu-

mously honoured by so worthy a publication . . . the January 1814 issue
of the *Female Preceptor* contained this *Memoir of Mrs Trimmer*:

> 'We might, in vain, search the records of ancient and modern history,
> to find a female endowed with more benevolence and worth. In the
> writings of this lady, religion and morality are so happily blended, that
> it seems impossible to practise the one without finding the other ani-
> mate the heart. Her labours have been particularly directed towards the
> lower classes of society who possess not the advantage of cultivated
> minds. With ardency of zeal and strength of persuasion, she has en-
> deavoured to convince them that virtue alone constitutes happiness in
> this life, and that poverty can only be considered as an evil when it is
> united with depravity of mind.'

The *Female Preceptor* was published on the first day of each month and
contained 'Essays, chiefly on The Duties of the Female Sex: with a variety
of Useful and Polite Literature, Poems, etc., embellished with several
beautiful engravings.' It was conducted by A Lady, printed and published
by B. R. Goakman of 9 Church Street, Spitalfields, and sold by a dozen
London booksellers, including Hatchards of Piccadilly, also Ogle of
Glasgow and J. Jones of Dublin. The first bound volume contained a list
of 340 London subscribers, headed by Her Royal Highness the Princess
Charlotte of Wales. It included about thirty men, several of them Rever-
ends. Titled subscribers were placed at the head of each alphabetical section—the *Female Preceptor* was unashamedly snobbish. Country subscribers
were informed that they could have their names inserted in the list by
sending their address (post paid) to the Publisher. The frontispiece to the
first bound volume is of Miss Hannah More, Female Preceptor, to whom all
the volumes are dedicated in admiring phrases: 'To the Literary and accomplished Hannah More, this Work, consisting of Essays, Elegant Moral
Tales, and Poetry, Immediately directed to the Improvement and rational
Entertainment of Females, is respectfully inscribed, by her humble servant,
the Editor.' Further to all that, Hannah More gets a long quotation on the
title page:

> 'A woman should pursue every kind of study which will lead her to be
> intent upon realities—will give precision to her ideas—will make an
> exact mind. She should cultivate every kind of study, which, instead of
> stimulating her sensibility, will chastise it—which will neither create an
> excessive or a false refinement; which will give her definite notions—

will bring the imagination under dominion—will lead her to think, to compare, to combine, to methodize—which will confer such a power of discrimination, that her judgment shall learn to reject what is dazzling, if it be not solid—and prefer not what is striking, or bright, or new, but what is just.'

There is a list of contributors which includes Walter Scott, Lord Byron, Mr Creighton, Miss Edgeworth, Miss Hannah More, Miss Mitford. And the Preface says that 'it shall be the object of the Editor to enhance the value of this work by incorporating as many *original* articles as possible, the production of the brightest ornaments that add to the lustre of British excellence'. But goes on quite shamelessly to say, 'No apology, it is presumed, need be made to those Ladies from whose works several valuable Articles have been drawn. The goodness of their intention in the promulgation of sentiments worthy of countenance, will thus obtain further circulation, and consequently will be very gratifying to the amiable and intelligent authors.' Well, that was one way of keeping the costs down. She would certainly have had to pay—and pay a lot—for Walter Scott's contribution. The Preface concludes:

'Whatever is calculated to extend the view and regulate the fancy, shall receive admission. Of course everything of an immoral or a trifling tendency, will be discarded. The *rationally devout* are here invited to a repast suitable to their taste.'

The rationally devout, cynics may observe, were credited with an insatiable appetite for the subject of seduction. The issue for January 1814 has as its main article: 'Seduction: With an explanation of the causes which give rise to it. Founded upon Facts'. It also has a Poetic Tale composed especially for the *Female Preceptor*, the title of which is 'Seduction'. This is a long poem, ending with the death of the baby and mother in a snowstorm, under the seducer's distracted but dissolute eyes. There is an article called 'Dissipation—or the Pernicious Effects of bad Example. A narrative founded upon Fact'. There is a poem by Oliver Goldsmith:

THE DESERTED FEMALE
She once, perhaps, in village plenty blest,
Has wept at tales of innocence distress'd;
Had modest looks the cottage might adorn,
Sweet as the primrose peeps beneath the thorne;

Now lost to all her friends, her virtue fled,
Near her betrayer's door she lays her head;
And, pinch'd with cold, and shrinking from the show'r,
With heavy heart deplores that luckless hour;
When, idly first, ambitious of the town,
She left her wheel and robes of country brown.

Yet another rending poem was entitled 'The Prostitute,' a long narrative of innocence seduced. But for anguished tearing of the heart strings, the tale ('founded upon facts') of Eliza Dawson can rarely have been surpassed in the history of magazine publishing. It ends: 'As the scene which followed was of a nature too exquisite for description, it must be left for the reader's imagination; the body of the ill-fated victim of lawless passions was, at an early hour the next morning, conveyed to her disconsolate parents' abode; a wet nurse was engaged for the little Edward.' There is an accompanying engraving of the death-bed scene in the garret where she was discovered, too late, after the birth of the baby. The moral of this tale, in addition to the obvious one, was the danger of

'the evils which arise from the present system of education amongst the lower order of the middling class; a boarding school not only unfits them for the performance of their domestic duties, but inspires sentiments of contempt towards their unenlightened parents. The humblest mechanic now considers it necessary to give his daughters a boarding-school education, though he may suffer the greatest inconveniences to defray the expense of it; and a day school where they might not only acquire a knowledge of useful needle-work, but writing, is actually held in sovereign contempt amongst them.'

Too much time was spent in the boarding-schools upon Music, Dancing, and French, and the consequence to the daughters of humble tradesmen and mechanics was

'not to make them capable of earning their own livelihood, for their acquirements are too superficial to enable them to instruct others; . . . but to make them vain of their own superiority, despising admonition by their parents, the home becoming a scene of domestic broils or insipidity, and the circulating library affording the only gratification for the child of imaginary infelicity. School, moreover, that hot-bed where female friendships blossom, and soon ripen into maturity, is frequently the means of introducing a brother, or a cousin, to the acquaintance of the young lady, who, pitying the misery of her situation, from being compelled to associate with unenlightened parents, removes her from such degrading companions and plunges her into misery.'

The heroine, or victim, of the tale which then followed was the daughter of 'an industrious green-grocer' and was seduced by the brother of a rich school-friend in a different station of life. This theme—the dangers of girls making boarding-school friends above their station in life—constantly occurs in eighteenth-century magazine fiction. It was the subject of a letter to the *Sentimental Magazine* in 1773, in which the correspondent complains that although the schools might differ in the fees charged, they one and all provided identical curricula in accomplishments: 'The plan is the same, and the daughter of one of the lowest shopkeepers at one of these schools, is as much miss and young lady as the daughter of the first Viscount at the other.'

There was, however, a growing grumble from articulate women who deplored the general attitude to women's education. In 1777, Mrs Cartwright in her *Letters on Female Education, addressed to a Married Lady*, and Mrs Hester Chapone in *Letters on the Improvement of the Mind*, had demonstrated by their own writings that women *had* minds to improve. Mary Wollstonecraft published her *Vindication of the Rights of Women* in 1792, following on Mrs Catherine Macaulay whose *Letters of Education* (1790) in which she denounced the 'absurd notion of a sexual excellence', had been given a very back-handed compliment by the *Gentleman's Magazine* —'Mrs Macaulay's work is really wonderful considering her sex.' Maria Edgeworth's *Letters for Literary Ladies*, 1795, was followed the next year by her *Parents' Assistant* and in 1798 by *Practical Education,* in which she collaborated with her father. Her novels, meantime, were setting a new standard for women writers, high above that of the main run of fiction in the circulating libraries from which women borrowed most of their reading matter. The critic Jeffrey wrote—'A greater mass of trash and rubbish never disgraced the press of any country than the ordinary novels that filled and supported our circulating libraries down nearly to the time of Miss Edgeworth's first appearance . . . the staple of the novel market was, beyond imagination, despicable, and had consequently sunk and degraded the whole department of literature of which it has usurped the name'. But the 'rabble rout' of the Minerva Press was scattered when Maria Edgeworth's books began to appear.

32. Maria Edgeworth at the desk her father made for her in the library of their Irish country house, Edgeworthstown, near Longford. She always worked here, with a pen given to her by Sir Walter Scott when he visited Edgeworthstown.

Walter Scott visited the Edgeworth family home in Ireland, and became a close friend of Maria. The suggestion has even been put forward by S. C. Hall in his *Book of Memories* that 'to her we are perhaps indebted for the Waverley novels, for it is avowed by Scott that he was prompted by the example of Miss Edgeworth to a desire to do for Scotland what she had done for Ireland'. Certainly by the end of the eighteenth century there was beginning to be expressed a fresh assessment of women's literary capabilities. But as far as the education of girls was concerned, there can hardly be said to have been a break through in spite of all the *Letters* and *Vindications*. For the young, Miss Richmal Mangall's famous *The Questions*, first published in 1798, was original in that it encouraged intellectual curiosity. This little book was the governess's best friend for many years to come. Altogether there were over a hundred London editions, and Longman's last reprint was as late as 1900.

In the general attitude towards women's education, it must be agreed that women were their own worst advocates. They were too humble, accepting and concurring in the traditional belief that they were the inferiors of men. Even Laetitia Barbauld, poetess and authority of some repute upon education, wrote: 'The best way for women to acquire knowledge is by conversation with a father or brother or friend in the way of family intercourse and easy conversation, and by such a course of reading as they may recommend.' She also advised 'visits to genteel families'. Hannah More, in *Strictures* (1799), while warning women to avoid such trash as novels of which the authors 'by the perusal of any three are able to produce a fourth', writes of educating girls, 'Their knowledge is not often like the learning of men, to be reproduced in some literary composition, nor even in any learned profession; but it is to come out in conduct . . . The truth is, women who are so puffed up with the conceit of talents as to neglect the plain duties of life will not frequently be found to be women of the best abilities'.

Lord Kames in his *Loose Hints upon Education*, 1781, wrote that women 'destined by nature to be obedient, ought to be disciplined early to bear wrongs without murmuring . . . to make a good husband is but one branch of a man's duty; but it is the chief duty of a woman to make a good wife'. And it was towards the high purpose of making good wives out of women that the great majority of magazines devoted the greater part of their space. Indeed for women of the poorer classes, being wives—good, bad, or indifferent—was what occupied the major part of their existence through life. The *Female Preceptor* carried a few information columns, including 'Market Prices for Crops', and usually a number of brief news items. One of these, in the issue of July 1815, told of a woman who had had four children in ten months and three days, describing her as 'the wife of an industrious but very poor man'.

Chapter XIII

FASHION PLATES AND MAGAZINES OF THE 1790s

Nicolaus Heideloff flees from the French Revolution to London. His Gallery of Fashion. *Emigré hand-colourists of fashion plates. Children as hand-colourists. The* Fashions of London and Paris. *Madame Récamier in London. The* Lady's Monthly Museum: *profile of Mrs Inchbald; lonely-heart columns; a visit to Bethlehem Lunatic Asylum; criticisms of Sir Walter Scott; distractions of women novelists; notices to contributors. Sketches from King's Bench prison.*

IN Parson Woodforde's Norfolk rectory on 28 September 1792, his niece Nancy wrote in her diary 'Mr and Mrs Custance sent us a brace of partridges. Dreadful times in France. Many are fled for refuge here'. And one of the refugees was Nicolaus Wilhelm von Heideloff. Heideloff came of a family of German painters and was brought up in Stuttgart to be an engraver. In 1784 he went to Paris in the service of Duke Karl Eugen of Wurtenburg, but was soon supporting himself by painting miniatures. When the Revolution came all his rich clients were dispersed, if not guillotined, and he himself fled to England. At first he found work in the bookselling and fine print business of Rudolf Ackermann in the Strand, Ackermann being also of German origin. Then in April 1794, when he was thirty-three years old, he started his own publishing venture, the *Gallery of Fashion*.

This was the first English publication devoted entirely to fashion. Although women's magazines proliferated in the second half of the century, none featured fashion beyond a very occasional costume engraving. Some of the yearly almanacs, museums, and pocket-books had small costume engravings inserted into them; but the only periodical to include regular embroidery patterns and fashion notes, with occasional costume engravings, was the *Lady's Magazine*. This, however, could not be called a fashion magazine, as dress was only one feature amongst many others, and by no means the principal feature. In its first issue, August 1770, the editor of the *Lady's Magazine* did indeed promise to inform his readers of 'every innovation that is made in the female dress . . . and endeavour to render this branch of information more worthy of female attention, by an assiduity which shall admit of no abatement, and by an earliness of intelligence which shall preclude anticipation'. This must have aroused expectations of more fashion information than in the event appeared; but gradually as the years went by the space allotted to matters of dress and the toilet was increased, and the fashion plates became more frequent. These engravings were not usually coloured. An exception was in the issue of April 1771, described in the text as 'a fine Copper-plate, beautifully coloured. Coloured plates extracted from early issues do crop up, but these have most probably been hand-painted by subscribers to the magazine for their own amusement—practising their skill in the essential feminine accomplishment of water-colouring—or, if the subscriber were a professional dressmaker, she would colour them so as to make the clothes look more attractive to her clients. The first in England to be regularly issued in colour by the publishers were those of Heideloff's *Gallery of Fashion*, the plates of which were all hand-coloured aquatints. And doubtless it was the appearance of this beautiful publication in 1794 that spurred the *Lady's Magazine* into issuing its own monthly coloured fashion plates before the year was out.

The *Gallery of Fashion* appeared in monthly parts, and a year's subscription was three guineas. Each monthly part consisted of two aquatints. They were enriched with gold, silver, and other metallic tints which would have been the work of one person alone who did nothing else. In all, nine yearly volumes were published, totalling 217 plates, and each volume also had a hand-coloured allegorical title-page. The final issue was in March 1803. Sacheveral Sitwell in his *Gallery of Fashion* estimates that Heideloff would have employed not more than three or four artists for the handcolouring at his premises, which by November 1794 were moved from Southampton Street to 90 Wardour Street, and in 1799 to John Street, Oxford Road.

Detailed descriptions of the dresses depicted were given for each plate, which might have one, two, or three figures. René Colas says in his *Bibliographie Generale du Costume et de la Mode* that the descriptions were probably given in English, French, and German for all the volumes, although there is only one volume, the sixth, definitely known to exist now with the descriptions in three languages. The number of copies issued was limited to that of the annual subscribers, although a few separate copies were sold at 7s 6d. Vyvyan Holland in his *Hand Coloured Fashion Plates 1770–1899* estimates that an issue would never have been more than 450. Many of the volumes gave lists of subscribers at the back which included, as well as private persons, the names of booksellers who sometimes subscribed for several copies, one taking as many as thirty-six. Subscribers to the first volume included the Princess Royal, the Princess Augusta, the Princess Elizabeth, the Duke of York, and the Empress of Germany. Quite a large number of subscribers were in other countries than England. By Volume IV Her Majesty Queen Charlotte and Prince Edward were on the list. Rudolf Ackermann, Heideloff's old employer, subscribed for four copies, and Messrs Colnaghi and Company took eleven. A later list included the artist John Zoffany, famous for his enchanting conversation pictures.

The fashion plates in the *Gallery of Fashion* could themselves be called conversation pictures. The figures or groups of figures were always shown in charming, very civilized surroundings . . . sitting on a terrace wall or on a garden seat, or taking tea out of doors. They drive out in *phaetons*, recline on *chaises longues* while reading their *billets doux*; they pen little notes at *boudoir* writing tables, and pluck wistfully at harpsichords. They are very, very French, although one plate has Blenheim Palace with Vanbrugh's bridge in the background. The clothes they wear, the muffs and parasols and reticules they carry, the prodigality of ribbons, and plumes in their luxuriant hats, have that touch of chic absurdity that can only be Parisian. But then the fashions of the day were influenced by the aristocratic emigrés from Paris—with whom Heideloff, also an emigré, would be in touch through his years as a miniaturist in Paris. Besides the aristocratic emigrés, those who fled from Paris included many highly skilled workers in the luxury trades, accustomed to waiting upon high society: dressmakers and milliners, fan makers, glove makers, parasol makers, *plumassiers*, makers of artificial flowers. No names of dressmakers or milliners are given with the plates in the *Gallery of Fashion*, but a court-dress depicted in one of them is attributed by Mrs Doris Langley Moore to Madame Beauvais, Queen Charlotte's dressmaker. In his advertisement, Heideloff emphasizes that the dresses depicted 'are not *imaginary* but really *existing* ones'.

Heideloff is likely to have employed some emigré hand-colourists fleeing from the Terror, for coloured fashion plates had been published in *La Gallerie des Modes* in Paris from 1778 to 1787. His first issue named the colourist as Madame Le Beau, but nothing is known of her. She may never really have existed. Her name does not appear in Volume II, and the colouring skill varies very much from issue to issue. Madame Le Beau or no Madame Le Beau, there were clearly various hand-colourists employed.

And at this period there was plenty of other work for these skilled crafts-men and women besides fashion plates. Indeed there must have been in-numerable hand-colourists employed in London, most of them women and young girls since they would accept the extremely low wages paid. Pictures in children's books were usually coloured by children. They sat round a table, each with a little pan of water-colour, a brush, a partly-coloured copy as a guide, and a pile of printed sheets with impressions from wood blocks or copper-plates. One child painted the red wherever it appeared in the guide. Another followed with, say, yellow; the next blue, and so on round the table. It was a methodical way of getting the work done quickly, but no one child had the satisfaction of painting a whole picture.

More expert labour was employed for the expensive travel books that were produced for gentlemen who had visited, or were about to visit, the countries of Europe on the Grand Tour. There were also illustrated books on historic costume, and there were all Ackermann's exquisite publications carrying an immense amount of illustration. Just one of his books, *The Microcosm of London*, involved the hand-colouring of 104,000 aquatint plates. At this time also there were the hand-coloured prints of Rowland-son and Gillray, and it was the great period for sporting and hunting prints. Lithography, which cut out the whole expensive process of engraving as well as the hand-colouring, began to be popular about 1817; and by about 1840 it had almost completely taken over. The process had been introduced to England by Ackermann, and he translated and gave publicity to Sene-felder's treatise on the subject.

The next English publication entirely devoted to fashion appeared in 1798. It was entitled the *Magazine of Female Fashions of London & Paris*, and continued until 1806, the 110 issues being bound into three volumes: 1798–1800; 1801–3; 1804–6. There is no indication of the identity of the editor or proprietor, only that it was 'printed for R. Phillips, 71 St Paul's Church Yard and sold by all Booksellers'. The title-page of the first issue gives a description of the magazine's contents:

'A cheap, useful, and elegant work (to be continued monthly with the other magazines). The magazine of the actually prevailing female fashions of London and Paris for March 1798, containing several coloured figures, four of Ladies in the most prevailing and favourite

London dresses and three of those in the present dresses of the Ladies of Paris with Descriptions.'

Uniquely, the magazine really did contain what its editor promised in his first Introduction. Each issue included at least three plates, two of English fashions, one Parisian; none are signed, and only a few dated. It is interesting to compare the fashions of the two capitals. A few are portrayed on living people. There is Lady Hamilton, for example, with a cameo of Nelson mounted in her head-dress. Madame Récamier, who visited London in 1802, is depicted after the engraving of her by Cosway. It was on this visit to London that Madame Récamier attracted a fever of shocked excitement among the citizens. She promenaded in Kensington Gardens gowned in clinging white muslin *à l'antique* which, it was said, gave her the aspect of a living statue. From this date, English interest in French fashions became intense. London dressmakers still held the position they had gained by the revolution in France; but even while the two countries were at war, English magazines included whatever news they could gather from whatever source about what was being worn in Paris. And as soon as the wars were over, regular information came pouring in. By 1820, the Paris style was so well established in London that the word Parisian had become synonymous with elegance.

In 1806 the title of the *Fashions of London & Paris* was changed to the *Record of Fashion and Court Elegance* and continued as such until 1809. It was published 'under the direction of Mrs Fiske' by Orme, Harris and Walker from 1807 until 1809, the three volumes for these years containing forty-seven coloured fashion plates and a portrait. A contemporary publication of a similar kind but with a much briefer life was the monthly *Mirroir de la Mode*, printed by C. Whittingham for Madame Lanchester of No. 17 New Bond Street, and sold by Messrs Colnaghi & Co—an entirely English publication which let down its pretension of French elegance by a spelling mistake in the title. It ran from January until December 1803, and was then collected into one volume of twenty-five coloured engravings and one frontispiece. These engravings were of very high quality; the text consisted of little more than descriptions of the fashions illustrated, although each month Madame Lanchester included a letter from a correspondent. It is clear from her introduction to the first monthly issue that the cost of the publication was raised by advance subscription:

'Madame Lanchester cannot close this brief but respectful Address,

a. New fancy pattern for working in Colours.

33. Embroidery pattern in the *Lady's Magazine*, 1792

without embracing the Opportunity it offers, of returning her sincere Acknowledgements to the numerous dignified Characters who have honoured her with their Protection. She will only say their Kindnesses are deeply engraven on a Heart, which must cease to vibrate ere it can prove insensible to such magnificent patronage.'

A third fashion publication at this time was the *Elegancies of Fashion & General Remembrancer of Taste & Manners etc.* by Florio Honeysuckle. This was appearing during 1804, published by W. N. Gardiner, but there only appears to have been one volume of twenty-four engraved and colour plates depicting clothes and coiffures.

These three publications were all devoted exclusively to fashion; but there was another magazine, first published in 1798, that contained not only coloured fashion plates and considerable fashion information, but also other women's interest features. This was the *Lady's Monthly Museum*, which continued (changing title in 1829 to the *Ladies' Museum*) until 1832, and was then incorporated with the *Lady's Magazine* and with *La Belle Assemblée* as the *Lady's Magazine & Museum of Belles Lettres*. It had a much longer life than any of the publications devoted entirely to fashion; and for all it was a mixed bag, it was an elegant little magazine. It came out under the imprint of Vernon & Hood, and its full title was:

THE LADY'S MONTHLY MUSEUM;

or

POLITE REPOSITORY OF AMUSEMENT AND INSTRUCTION
Being an Assemblage of whatever can tend to
please the Fancy, interest the Mind, or exalt
the Character of
THE BRITISH FAIR
By a Society of Ladies

The fashion content of the magazine was in a section called *Mirror of Fashion*, and contained two or more plates, a 'General Monthly Statement of Fashion'—'for the dresses we are, as usual, indebted to the taste of Miss Pierpont, Edward Street, Portman Square; and for the Head-dresses to Mr Colley, 28 Bishopsgate'. There was also a report on 'The Parisian Toilet'.

The *Lady's Monthly Museum* carried other engravings besides fashion plates, usually portraits of notable men or women. For example, in the issue of 1 June 1799, there was an engraving of Mrs Elizabeth Inchbald, accompanied by a text that we should now call a 'profile'. It begins rather patronizingly considering she was a living writer of admired talent: 'Whatever her improprieties have been, Mrs Inchbald has been wise enough to direct them uniformly to the improvement of some virtue, or the acquisition of some excellence.' The writer does not, of course, give any indication of what Mrs Inchbald's improprieties were, but it was probably well enough known that as a young girl she had run away to London to become an actress. Her subsequent success as dramatist, novelist, and dramatic critic could never atone for the equivocal position this adventure had placed her in, even though her 'virtue' was reputed to have been preserved through all her early struggles as an actress. The anonymous author of *Public Characters of 1799–1800*, writing in the same year as the *Lady's Monthly Museum* profile, took such pains to extol her moral character that one feels he protested too much, thereby giving his readers suspicions of scandals concealed:

> 'Mrs Inchbald's moral character constitutes her principal excellence; and though useful talents and personal accomplishments, of themselves, form materials for an agreeable picture; moral qualities give the polish that fascinates the heart.'

Of course, no men at that time ever really approved of a woman earning her own living by her pen, and they could never bring themselves wholeheartedly to praise a woman's talents. The three duties of women were to be virtuous, amiable, and beautiful.

Other features of the *Lady's Monthly Museum* included each month a moral tale. For example, 'The Disregarded Precept of Fatal Obstinacy—A Tale with a Moral', which filled no fewer than nine pages. There was a poetry section each month called 'The Apollonian Wreath', there were essays, tales, novels, romances, and biographical memoirs. The tales tended to be Eastern in flavour: for instance, 'Ali, an oriental Tale', and 'The Turtle Dove, from the Arabic'. In this the editor reveals himself (or herself) to have been a little out of touch with public taste, which by this time had tired of the East and moved to European Gothic country. The Black Forest, the Rhine, anywhere gloomy and guilt-ridden such as the Balkans, anywhere craggy like the fearsome Dolomites, these had become the fashionable scene sets for short stories as well as novels. The East, with its glowing colours and pulsating sunshine was out. Unaware, it seems, of the new literary trend, the *Lady's Monthly Museum* ran travel sketches called 'Scenes from the East' through several issues; and a serial story by 'Constance' called 'The Fortune-Hunter' reflected not one flicker of Gothic influence.

There were essays with titles such as 'The Criterion of Virtue', and on the discontent and disappointment awaiting young girls who mixed in social strata higher than their own—the same old theme we have seen crop up in magazines throughout the eighteenth century. It was one such essay that Mrs Morland referred to when Catherine came home after her visit to the Tilneys at Northanger Abbey:

'I hope, my Catherine, you are not getting out of humour with home because it is not so grand as Northanger; that would be turning your visit into an evil, indeed. I did not quite like, at breakfast, to hear you talk so much about the French bread at Northanger . . . There is a very clever essay in one of the books upstairs upon much such a subject, about young girls that have been spoilt for home by great acquaintance —*The Mirror*, I think. I will look it out for you some day or other, because I am sure it will do you good.'

The *Lady's Monthly Museum* carried the same theme further with a 'Deposition on the Present Stagnation of Matrimony'. It attributed this sad stagnation to the elegant and expensive education given to young women beyond the compass of their parents' fortune and stations in life. This piece does not, as in the *Female Spectator* of half a century earlier, warn of the danger of seduction by the brothers of socially superior school friends; it merely deplores that tradesmen's daughters educated at boarding schools become too hoity-toity to marry within their own station in life, but are neither rich enough, nor well-born enough, to marry out of it. Therefore they are destined to remain spinsters, a fate almost worse than seduction— certainly worse in the eyes of romantic young girls.

The magazine also ran a 'lonely hearts' column, that always popular feature of women's magazines. Young ladies were able to pour out their dread of spinsterhood to an unknown friend and beg advice on all matters of the heart. The mentor who operated this column in the *Lady's Monthly Museum* went by the rather unattractive pseudonym of 'The Old Woman'. One correspondent writes to her:

'My dear, venerable, old Lady,
'Your attention to the request of Biddy Wilding, who addressed her

forlorn case to you, and the judicious observations you made upon it for her duction, embolden me to hope you will be equally indulgent to your present correspondent. I have not, like the unfortunate Biddy, to complain of a want of lovers, but of not being able to disengage myself from the pestering importunities of some, whom I can neither encourage with an honest heart, nor yet absolutely turn adrift with any regard to policy, till I have secured the man who is the object of my fondest affection.'

Advice needed, in fact, on the best tactics for keeping them all dangling until one of them is definitely landed, a universal problem with young ladies. If disappointed of the loved one, there must be a *faut de meux*.

The 'Society of Ladies' editing the *Lady's Monthly Museum* was by no means squeamish. Contributions with a strong horror content were not excluded. There was, for example, in a series of 'Visits in London and its Environs', an account of a visit to Bethlehem, the lunatic asylum in Lambeth. It was an account which might certainly have had the effect of persuading young ladies that the wages of seduction were, after all, worse than the frustrations of spinsterhood. A short extract will suffice:

> 'This female was the victim of seduction. Alas! too many of the patients' maladies have originated in that species of cruel depravity, breaking every law, divine and moral; sacrificing the peace, the reputation, the health of many a lovely young creature; leaving her, in the bloom of youth and beauty, weeping over that lamentable fate . . .

> > 'Where partial reason is restored
> > And they themselves, are by themselves deplored

> 'I was told that more than two-thirds of the present female inhabitants of this hospital have been betrayed and deserted by men high in rank. Not quite depraved in vicious courses, the wretched victims, when meditating on their wretched condition, have been finally deprived of their senses, and here found refuge from miseries to which they are no longer sensible. . . . A third piteous object was too terrible to look on. She had lost all sense of conscious shame or feeling, often tore off her garments with such violence, that they were sewed on her body. At the age of sixteen, she had been carried off by stealth from a chamber-window, by a young man of fashion. Robbed of her virtue, she lived

213

with him until she became a deserted outcast; and finally, was admitted to this asylum a confirmed lunatic.'

Strangely enough, the writer of this sketch, which continued with many more horrors, ended his account:

'With an impression rather agreeable than depressing, I took my leave of this well-appointed asylum for the afflicted in mind.

'E.I.S.'

Subsequent instalments in the 'Visits in London and its Environs' series evidently did not reach the same standard of sensationalism, since in a later issue of the magazine the editor (was it still edited by a Society of Ladies ?) writes in the 'Notes to Correspondents' column: 'The continuation of "London and its Environments" is too uninteresting to offer our Readers'. Evidently E.I.S. pitched his interest too high to start with, and could not keep it up.

The *Lady's Monthly Museum* always had a literary section with notices of new publications. In the issue of 1 June 1799, there is a review of *Woodstock: or the Cavalier*, by the author of *Waverley, etc.* which takes a very poor view of this classic:

'The general character of the composition of the Author of Waverley is too well known, as to render any remarks on it quite unnecessary. We shall, however, venture to assert that the historical novel before us is far from being either the best or the worst of the large family of fiction to which it belongs. Several brilliant passages occur and some of the scenes and characters are well delineated, but the general effect is heavy, and the author seems to have performed his task more for the sake of the advantage to be derived from it than from any peculiar partiality for the occupation.'

It can have been no coincidence that the section headed 'Intelligence relative to Literature and the Arts' (in effect a literary gossip column), in the same issue of the magazine, included this paragraph:

'*Waverley Novels*. When the lady of Sir W.S. wants any new expensive dress, or piece of splendid furniture, if on applying to her husband for the money necessary to purchase it, he makes any demur, she instantly tells him "Ye maun write anither novel, Waltie".'

Clearly the magazine had a hate campaign against Sir Walter. He and his disciples in novel writing were hogging the market. In the same issue again, there is a long feature entitled 'Novel Writers, and their Miseries' which contains this paragraph:

> 'As it is evident that periodical works alone divide the public attention and patronage with the Scottish novels, it surely is justifiable, through this means, to seek consolation in this day of mortification and almost extinction . . . We have been swept away by repeated irruptions from the great Borderer and his followers . . . yet we may insist on a right also to be remembered and esteemed, since our talents, although inferior, cannot be deemed contemptible . . . We have, in great measure, succeeded in cleansing our circulating libraries from the puerile and "perilous stuff" which disgraced the succeeding age.'

The article goes on to point out the distractions of housekeeping and constant social interruptions that prevent a woman novelist from devoting her thoughts to authorship. Apart from the style of writing, this article might have appeared in a magazine today:

> 'However rapid may be her mind, or her movements, her hands will not, at the same moment, correct a proof and mend her stockings. She has all the common cares of life to meet, together with the accumulated load of the sorrow she must invent, must dwell upon, must lament—in order that her readers may feel for an hour, what she has felt for a year. Yet the common cares, evils and occupations of life must be endured by her as by others—losses and taxes, hard times, and abridged means, are visitants of her dwelling, and like the rest of her sex, she finds accounts to inspect, children to guide, servants to govern, invalids to nurse, linen to sew, dinners to provide, letters to write, friends to receive, and strangers to conciliate. With a perpetual hurry on her mind, she must yet ensure hours for calm cogitation, half days of quietness, and nights in which the repose demanded by weary nature must be sacrificed to the necessity of writing or thinking in uninterrupted tranquility.'

As with all magazines of the time, the *Lady's Monthly Museum* communicated with its contributors through its columns; and one can imagine with what anxiety the aspiring writer or poet took up the new month's issue to see whether his or her contribution had been used, or whether there were any message about it from the editor. These messages pulled no punches. Many a budding talent must have been so cruelly, so sarcastically nipped, as to prevent any further attempt:

'To Ophelia's Poetry generally, we have but one objection to offer; it transcends our capacity of comprehension.

'We sincerely commiserate the unhappy situation of G.E. G—y, but as we fear his Sonnet is but ill calculated to excite compunction in "Mary's" breast; and would not elevate him as a poet, in the estimation of our readers, we decline its insertion.

'We recommend to T.W. and some other of our rhyming Correspondents, a careful perusal of the "Art Poetica" of Horace before they next attempt to write poetry.

'We must request our Correspondents will pay some attention in their communications to the art of writing. We have often as much difficulty to decipher their writing as to understand their meaning.

'One of our Correspondents solicits our correction of his Essay; but our so doing has been rendered impractible by the closeness of the lines as well as of the writing itself; indeed the sheets so transmitted are, to us, almost illegible; and would be returned for transcription had we been favoured with the writer's address.'

Occasionally there is praise and encouragement:

'G.H. will perceive that we have received both his parcel and his letter. We accept with pleasure his promise of becoming a frequent correspondent.'

But even regular correspondents have to be reprimanded:

'The poetry of Charles M— is received, and part of it designed for insertion. We, however, most heartily wish he had attended to our lately oft-repeated request, and had sent his communications in a less crowded and confused state; in which case he need not have "feared" what is now really a fact, that "he has written much further than we will", or indeed, can "read".'

Sometimes the message was brief, but baffling:

' "Sonnet to a Nightingale" by H. is inadmissible.'

In the issue of April 1826 there was a letter written from the King's Bench Prison, in which the correspondent says that he and other prisoners having 'formed a Reading-society at Mr Gordon's library, and in the coffee room, we have made some acquaintance of a very agreeable and desirable nature. Mr Gordon has proposed that each member of the Society should commit his history to paper and that, under feigned names, it should be transmitted to the magazine, that thus many might be taught by the experience of the few. May I therefore request you state if we may calculate in your acquiescence, that no time may be lost in the needful correction and punctual transmission of these sketches from Life? I am, Mr Editor, your obedient servant, *Observer*.'

The reply was favourable: 'In answer to *Observer's* letter, the editor has to express his full conviction of the interest and beneficial consequences which the offered communication must combine. If the tale be but faithfully and honestly told, "Scenes from Life" possess an interest beyond romance, and impress a lesson a novelist can never teach. We therefore encourage *Observer* to forward us the promised Sketches at his earliest convenience.' The editor by this time seems to be a man, not a Society of Ladies.

In the issue of 22 May 1826, the first sketch from the King's Bench Prison was inserted. The editor's encouragement had not included any promise of payment, and one wonders whether the debtors would have realized that women's magazines contrived to get most of their contributions for nothing. The fact that no more sketches from prison appeared after this first one seems to suggest that they were disappointed about payment. It is possible, of course, that they did submit further *Sketches from Life* but that the editor decided they were too 'faithful' to be suitable for his polite female readership. On the other hand, ladies who enjoyed that earlier account of a visit to Bethlehem lunatic asylum can scarcely have been very squeamish.

Chapter XIV

PERIODICALS OF THE NEW CENTURY

La Belle Assemblée, *Bright new ideas for magazine make-up*. Le Beau Monde.
Ackermann's Repository of Arts. *Mrs M. A. Bell: her Magazin de Modes;
her connection with* La Belle Assemblée. *The* World of Fashion. *John
Mitford's journalistic activities. The* Lady's Magazine *accepts Miss
Mitford's* Our Village. *Townsend's* Quarterly Selection of Parisian Costumes.
The Lady's Pocket Magazine. *Sales of bound volumes affected by the
'Annuals'.*

ᘉᖙᖙᖙᖙᖙᖙᖙᖙᖙᖙᖙᖙᖙᖙᖙᖙᖙᖙᖙᖙᖙᖙᖙᖙᖙᖙᖙᖙᖙᖙᖙᖙᖙᖙ

JOHN BELL's great talents were employed at their best in raising the
standard of typography, illustration and layout of periodical publishing. This is what made him of such importance in the history of magazines, and what made his beautiful periodical *La Belle Assemblée* such a
landmark. Charles Knight wrote, in *Shadows of the Old Booksellers*, 'Bell's
draughtsmen and engravers were not selected for their cheapness, but for
their excellence. His love of innovation was really awful'. Leigh Hunt
described him as 'a speculator in elegant typography' and wrote of him in
his *Autobiography*:

> 'He possessed no acquirements, perhaps not even grammar; but his
> taste in putting forth a publication and getting the best artists to adorn
> it was new in those times, and may be admired in any. All his original
> training and experience lay in type founding and book publishing, and
> he instinctively felt the importance for a periodical to appeal to the eye
> as well as to the intellect or to the appetite for gossip and scandal, news
> and notions, curious facts and extravagant fancies. And he was a pioneer
> in that kind of publication so much in vogue in later days, by which
> the multitude is introduced to the best literature, and made to feel an
> interest in it by means of illustrations executed by good artists.'

*La Belle Assemblée, or Bell's Court and Fashionable Magazine, Addressed
Particularly to the Ladies* was launched in 1806. It was a lavishly elegant
ancestor of the glossy magazines of today, with an excellently varied

34. Title page of *La Belle Assemblée*, January 1807

content. The price was three shillings, which was a great deal more in terms of real money than the price of present-day fashion magazines. It was a royal octavo, thus considerably larger in page size than the *Lady's Magazine*, and much larger than the pocket-sized *Ladies' Monthly Museum*. It had a whole section devoted to London and Paris fashions, with two engraved plates folded face to face, or one which folded to equal two plates. In the early days of the magazine the fashion plates were attributed. For example, in June 1806 'The Prevailing Spring Fashions' were 'drawn by Devis from the Elegant Designs of Madame Lanchester and engraved by Mitan expressly for *La Belle Assemblée*'. This was the Madame Lanchester who had been responsible for the *Mirroir de la Mode* from January to December 1803.

There was a great deal in the magazine besides fashion. And it was the combination of fashion with literary content that made it so successful. In this John Bell is thought to have been influenced by the success of Le Brun's *Journal de la Mode et du Gout, or Amusements du Salon et de la Toilette*. This popular publication, first issued in Paris on 25 February 1790, contained poetry, a serial romance, an airette, and a coloured fashion plate with descriptions; and it was the first French periodical to combine a literary content with fashion information. John Bell, introducing his first issue of *La Belle Assemblée* to 'The Public, our Readers, and Correspondents' wrote: 'We flatter ourselves that we have introduced a material improvement, so far as method, arrangement, and elegance of display, which may be considered as enticements to writers in periodical publications. Communications, and correspondence, therefore, are ardently invited.'

One of John Bell's bright new ideas in make-up was to provide *La Belle Assemblée* with two separate supplements. The first was a literary supplement containing extracts from recently published works in *belles lettres*, history, poetry, and so on. For this there was a title page at the end of each volume so that when the section of sixty-four pages was completed it could be incorporated with the volume or be bound separately. The second supplement was a monthly compendium of advertisements—'literary, fashionable, and domestic'—'addressed to the elegant, polite, and economical'. Each section was bound, at any rate for the first few numbers, in a brilliant orange wrapper; and a title page for the volume was given free with the completing monthly issue, engraved with a decorative frame. The advertisement section was planned to be such an attractive feature in its

MIDDLETON AND INNES,
HABERDASHERS AND LINEN DRAPERS,
No. 192, Fleet-Street, corner of Chancery-Lane,

SELL WHOLESALE AND RETAIL,

Every kind of Bengal and Madras Muslins; Long Cloths and Calicoes; British and Scotch Muslins, Muslinets, Dimities, Quiltings, and Jeans; Irish Linens and Scotch Hollands; Russia, Scotch, Irish, Lancashire and Yorkshire Sheeting; Scotch, Irish, and Hamburgh Damask and Diaper Table Linen; Hukabaks, Diaper, Russia and Scotch Tweeling; Patterbons, Silesias, Pomeranias, Hessians, and every kind of Household Linen; Flannels, Baizes, and Swanskins; India, Norwich and Muslin Shawls and Handkerchiefs; French, Scotch, and Irish Cambricks and Lawns; Lawn Pullicat and printed Pocket Handkerchiefs; Counterpanes and Quilts; Nankeens and Ginghams; Bombazeens and Black and White Lutestrings; Gauzes, Crapes, and Tiffinys; Alamodes and Sattins for Cloaks; Peleng Sattins, Persians, Sarsnets, Ribbons, and Feathers; Black, Blond, and Thread Laces and Veils; Women and Children's Cotton and Silk Hose; Men's Black and White Silk Hose; Chip, Leghorn, and Straw Hats; Men and Women's Gloves; English Poplins; Muffs, Tippets, and Fur Trimmings.
Millinery, and every article in Haberdashery.

INSURANCE AGAINST FIRE.
PHŒNIX FIRE-OFFICE, LOMBARD-STREET, LONDON.

The firm support which the PHŒNIX OFFICE continues to receive from its numerous Friends demands the thanks of the Directors.

This Office has ever been impressed with an ardent desire to give encouragement to the Agricultural Interests of the Kingdom; and the Directors rely, that the regulations which they from time to time have introduced for that purpose, will be satisfactory to the Public, and secure the continuance of its Favour and Patronage.

N.B Persons insuring for Three Hundred Pounds or upwards, will not be charged for the Policy
By order of the Directors,   H. A HARDY,
Secretary of the Country Department.

ACCOMMODATION COACHES.

Worthing, Brighton, and Horsham, to London, Accommodation Coaches, set out every morning from the Nelson Hotel, and New-Inn, Worthing; and from the Star and Garter, Brighton, at seven o'clock: arrive at the Swan and Crown Inns, Horsham, at ten o'clock; and at the White Bear, Piccadilly, and Bell Savage, Ludgate-Hill, at five o'clock in the afternoon; and return every morning from the above Inns at 7 o'clock.

Cheapest House in London for the best Manufactured

BOOTS AND SHOES,

Equal to any bespoke, No. 60, St. Martin's-le-Grand, three doors from the Castle and Falcon Hotel.

T. BRADSHAW respectfully returns his most sincere thanks to his Friends and the Public, for the very liberal Encouragement he has hitherto met with, and assures them no effort in his power shall be wanting to merit a continuance of the same. At the same time particularly informs them, he has just manufactured a fashionable and prime assortment of the following Articles, calculated for the present and ensuing Season, viz.

	£	s	d
Prime Calf-Leather Jockey Boots	1	16	0
Black-Strap Three quarter Boots ..	1	14	0
Best Calf Hessian Boots	1	15	0
Cordovan Boots	1	5	0
Ditto Jockey Boots	1	10	0
Gentlemen's Strong Shoes	0	9	0
A great variety of neat ditto......	0	7	6

An extensive Assortment of Ladies' Kid, Morocco, Jean, and Velvet Slippers, of every description, from 4s. 6d. per pair, and upwards.

Anxious to give the utmost satisfaction, he is particularly careful in manufacturing every Article under his own Inspection; and as the establishment of this Concern depends upon the quality of the Article, a single trial will convince a discerning Public that his Boots and Shoes are—*Superior to any bespoke.*

N.B. A great Assortment of Boys and Children's Shoes, Shooting-Gaiters, Black Cloth ditto, Japan Blacking, &c.

Merchants, Captains, and others, supplied on the shortest Notice.

London: Printed by and for J. BELL, Southampton-street, Strand. October 1, 1806.

35. First page of the advertisement section of *La Belle Assemblée*, October 1806.

own right that subscribers would value it as a permanent directory 'co-existent with and forming an integral part of the work, to be bound up and preserved with it'. Bell claimed that it possessed a 'prominence and an order, together with a grace and splendour in display never before attempted'. And he was justified in his claim, for there was literary distinction in the publishers' announcements, set out in beautiful typography. Some of the commercial advertisements, such as the finely displayed prospectus of tea companies, were equally elegant. A four-page advertisement for Urling's Lace had a fine steel engraving of the shop at 329 Strand with samples of real lace inserted in place of the detail in the shop window.

La Belle Assemblée also included a song with music, engraved for each number—always a popular publisher's bonus. Another regular feature was intelligence from foreign courts: 'In order to render the work an amusing and instructive emporium of elegant erudition, regular correspondence is established at Paris and at the other polished courts of the Continent.' There was also an engraved portrait of some prominent personage, usually aristocratic, and a 'familiar miscellany' of anecdotes about celebrities—literary, artistic, and military—in fact, a gossip column. The contents usually included contributions called 'Lectures on Useful Sciences': pneumatics, hydrostatics, botany, astronomy, culinary research. There were papers on politics and there was poetry; also accounts of places of interest in London, such as museums. A section at the end contained the fashion plates, embroidery patterns, reports on dress and on the fine arts. Births, marriages, and deaths concluded each issue.

The volumes were completed half-yearly; but before the second volume had come out an important change was forced by competition. John Bell's own son, with whom he had quarrelled, started a rival publication in October 1806. John Browne Bell, as the son was named, produced his magazine with exactly the same format as *La Belle Assemblée*, and gave it a title that was exactly the same as that of one of the sections of his father's magazine: *Le Beau Monde*. These similarities, together with the similarity of the publishers' names, made it easy for newsagents to substitute the new publication for the original; and *Le Beau Monde* had the advantage of offering its readers hand-coloured plates, not only of costumes but also of furniture, carriages, and other gentlemenly possessions. There were other features aimed at attracting male readers: descriptions and reports of new 'sporting attire for gentlemen', details of newly-designed coaches and equipment, accounts of race meetings.

Perhaps this attempt to include the interests of both sexes in one magazine was too ambitious, or perhaps it was a psychological mistake at that moment of time. It is noticeable that quite a number of magazines addressed to gentlemen and ladies were launched towards the close of the eighteenth century and the beginning of the nineteenth, and that all of them were short-lived. On the other hand, the relative failure of John Browne Bell's publication may have been simply because he did not have his father's long experience as a publisher nor his instinctive flair for giving the fashionables what they wanted. At any rate *Le Beau Monde* did not thrive. John Browne Bell started the *National Register* in 1805; and in January 1809 made an attempt to revive his dying fashion magazine by redesigning it entirely and re-issuing it as Vol. I, No. I of *Le Beau Monde and Monthly Register*. But this only lasted for ten numbers.

At his father's death in 1831 and his own final disinheritance, John Browne Bell started a Sunday paper in direct imitation of *Bell's Weekly Messenger*, calling it *Bell's New Weekly Messenger*, and ran it in competition with his late father's original Sunday paper. Later on, in 1843, it became the *News of the World*. Then, as now, this newspaper devoted much space to murders, luscious rapes, and all kinds of lurid crime. It can be seen as yet another unfilial gesture to his father's shade when one remembers John Bell's insistence with his own Sunday newspaper that it should be suitable for the whole family and contain nothing 'to invade female delicacy'.

To return to *La Belle Assemblée*, the rivalry of *Le Beau Monde* had the effect of making John Bell introduce illustrations in colour into his publication. It is surprising that he had not done so before since colour plates were a feature that the public was beginning to expect to find in high-class fashion publications. French and German fashion periodicals had for some time carried colour plates, and Heideloff's *Gallery of Fashion* had forced the *Lady's Magazine* to hand-colour its fashion engravings. The *Lady's Monthly Museum* had carried coloured plates since its first number in 1798. It seems completely out of character that John Bell, with his interest in illustration and the display side of magazine publishing, did not from the beginning have colour fashion plates in *La Belle Assemblée*. As it was, with the impudent rivalry of *Le Beau Monde*, he brought out his issue for December 1806 in two editions: price 2s 6d with plain plates, or 3s 6d coloured. In the next number, January 1807, there were a colour and a plain engraving on each of the two pages of fashions. A further introduction at this time, continued in each subsequent issue, was a pair of engravings in outline 'after such ancient and modern masters as Raphael and Sir Benjamin West'. These seem to have been too highbrow to be popular, and after a few months it was reported that since the plates had failed to interest the feature was being abandoned.

In 1809 another rival to *La Belle Assemblée* came into the field. This was Ackermann's *Repository of Arts, Literature, Commerce, Manufactures, Fashion and Politics*, a beautiful publication that was very much more than a modish magazine. Indeed, it was a prestige periodical, 'humbly dedicated by permission to His Royal Highness the Prince of Wales by his grateful and obedient servant Rudolf Ackermann'. It was almost certainly subscribed to more by men than by women, although it contained some features intended especially to appeal to feminine readers. William Combe contributed a series under the title of 'The Female Tatler'; and his 'Letters between Amelia in London and her Mother in the Country' appeared monthly. They were later issued in book form. Amelia was a young lady of fashion, and the letters were amusing and lively. This was the William Combe who was author of the enormously popular 'Doctor Syntax's Tours', written in 'rhyming, rambling, rickety, ridiculous poetry'. There were three tours: 'In search of the Picturesque'; 'In Search of Consolation'; 'In Search of a Wife'. The illustrations were by Rowlandson. In point of fact, it was the illustrations that gave the ideas for the text. Ackermann bought a series of drawings from Rowlandson depicting Dr Syntax in situations calculated to exemplify his hobby-horsical search for the picturesque, and handed them over to William Combe, who was then in the King's Bench prison. This seems to have been more or less Combe's permanent home after he had swiftly dissipated a large fortune he had inherited shortly after completing a classical education at Eton and Oxford. Rees and Britton say in their *Reminiscences of Literary London* that he edited a newspaper from the prison, with weekly meetings of contributors held after dark. But as we have seen, he was by no means the only editor to have conducted a publication from that address.

Each monthly issue of Ackermann's *Repository of Arts* carried two very good fashion plates, sometimes more, intended to be clear guides to ladies and their dressmakers; and there were numerous other plates of furniture and silverwork, paintings, portraits, and objets d'art. The fashion plates were hand-coloured aquatints and each had its accompanying detailed description in the text. Several of the early numbers invited textile manufacturers to send in patterns of any new dress materials they were making,

36. First page of a ballad in *La Belle Assemblée*, June 1823

saying that 'if the requisites of Novelty, Fashion and Elegance are united, the quantity necessary for this magazine will be ordered.' The quantity would not be great, for the purpose was to paste small fabric patterns on settings described as 'an allegorical woodcut'; but the publicity would be excellent, as descriptions of the fabrics chosen were given on the page facing the woodcut, with names and addresses of their manufacturers. The idea may well have been inspired by Urling's lace advertisements in *La Belle Assemblée*.

Ackermann's *Repository* was certainly a formidable rival to *La Belle Assemblée*, and it maintained its remarkably high standard throughout its twenty-one years of existence. John Bell's magazine also upheld its own high standards, although they were rather less cultural than those of the *Repository*. The decade from 1810 to 1820 is considered to be the greatest period of *La Belle Assemblée* and during these years the fashion department came under the direction of Mrs Mary Ann Bell. It consisted of two illustrated pages in each issue, depicting morning, evening, and town dresses, walking costumes, seaside bathing dresses, headdresses, spencers, pelisses, corsets, all with their detailed descriptions, and all credited as being 'the sole inventions of Mrs M. A. Bell'. For ten years this redoubtable lady dominated the fashion pages, in which readers were invariably directed to her dress-shop, the *Magazin de Modes*, first at 22 Upper King Street, Bloomsbury, then from 1815 at 26 Charlotte Street, Bloomsbury—not the present Charlotte Street but a street north of Bedford Square. Later she moved to the even more fashionable location of 52 St James's, where she was favoured with the patronage of the Duchess of Kent. As a retailer she was undoubtedly assisted in this upward journey in the social scale of shopkeepers by her close connection with *La Belle Assemblée*. Not only were her dress designs featured in the magazine, but the text made it quite clear that all the accessories shown—everything from tippets and muffs to feathers, bonnets, and gloves—were obtainable at her shop.

Corsets were a particular speciality, Mrs Bell being credited as 'sole inventress' of all she sold. Her famous Circassian Corset was named after the Persian Ambassador's 'favourite companion' whom he purchased at Constantinople and who came with him on a visit to London, much to the consternation, curiosity, and amusement of the Court of St James's. Mrs Bell recommended her Circassian Corset as a 'most desirable and healthful stay to those who are inclined to corpulency'. Presumably the Ambassador's favourite companion was plump. The corset was described as:

'giving to the form that ease and gracefulness which supports of steel and whale-bone must inevitably destroy . . . it is the only one which displays, without indelicacy, the shape of the bosom to the greatest possible advantage; giving a width to the chest which is equally conducive to health and elegance of appearance'.

It was also the perfect aid to a good figure when sea-bathing. An aquatint in *La Belle Assemblée* in the issue of August 1814 shows a lady wearing the *Circassian Ladies' Corset and Sea Side Bathing Dress* on the cliffs, below which there are bathing boxes on the beach. Unfortunately these interesting garments are modestly concealed by a wind-blown négligé. The fair bather wears a bonnet whose shape suggests that it would serve better as a buoy than a bathing cap.

The identity of Mrs M. A. Bell was something that John Bell's biographer, Stanley Morison, was unable to trace when he was writing his *John Bell*. He said the initials were for Mary Ann; and while believing she must have been a family connection of the magazine's proprietor since she was so much involved with it, he said, 'There is no indication that John Bell was ever married or had children.' But in his *English Newspapers*, published two years later in 1932, the late Mr Morison definitely states that John Browne Bell was John Bell's son, born in 1779. He must have come by some more information, and it seems reasonable in the light of this to suppose that Mrs M. A. Bell was either John Bell's wife or his daughter-in-law, although she is not mentioned in this second book. The marriage might have been concealed from readers of John Bell's publications so that there would be no suspicion of nepotism in using them as vehicles for advertising her Magazin de Modes. Her name first appeared in John Bell's Sunday newspaper, the *Weekly Messenger*, in announcements of her millinery shop in Bloomsbury. And her name disappeared from *La Belle Assemblée* in 1821 when John Bell was seventy-six years old. It was then that he sold the magazine and it began appearing as a 'New Series' under the imprint of J. P. and C. Whitaker of Paternoster Row. In 1832 the title became the *Court Magazine & Belle Assemblée* and the Hon. Mrs Norton was appointed editor. In 1837 it was absorbed by the *Lady's Magazine & Museum of Belles Lettres,* which became from 1838 to 1847 the *Court Magazine & Monthly Critic & Lady's Magazine & Museum of Belles Lettres*—one of the longest titles in the history of magazines.

Meanwhile Mrs Bell, having lost her valuable connection with *La Belle*

37. Embroidery pattern for collars from the supplement to the *Lady's Magazine*, 1816

Assemblée when John Bell sold it, bobbed up again in close association with an entirely new publication. This was the *World of Fashion and Continental Feuilletons—Dedicated Expressly to High Life, Fashionables, and Fashions, Polite Literature, Fine Arts, the Opera, Theatre, etc*. A monthly, it clearly owed a great deal to the pioneering of *La Belle Assemblée* and Ackermann's *Repository*. But it was more exclusively a woman's magazine than they were. Its contents were virtually all concerned with fashion or fashionable life. Regular features included 'High Life and Fashionable Chit Chat, Etc.'; 'On Dits of Fashion'; 'Continental Notes and On-Dits'; 'Newest London and Parisian Fashions.' It had a large page size, and the costume plates contained up to six figures. The best of these appeared early in the magazine's life, and were engraved by W. Alais; but the majority of them were inferior copies of French plates.

When Mrs Bell joined the *World of Fashion* at its outset in 1824, its publishers were given as Mr Anderson and Mr Bell. Stanley Morison says in his *John Bell* that the identity of this Mr Bell is 'a mystery'; but it seems very likely that this was once more John Browne Bell. By 1830, when the *World of Fashion* was being 'edited by several Literary and Fashionable

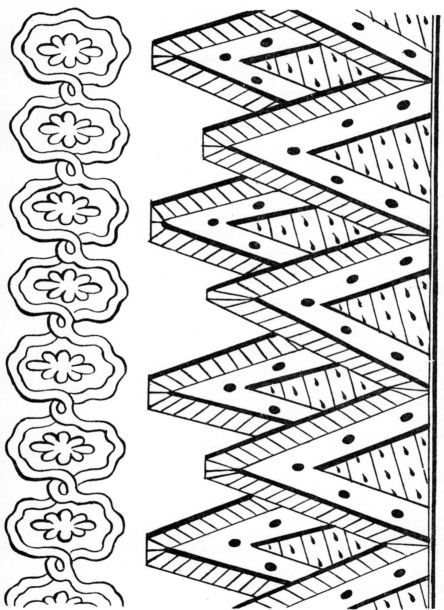

38. Embroidery pattern for 'an Entire new Frill for the Throat, or Border for the Bottom of a Dress', *La Belle Assemblée*, February 1807

Characters', it was announced as being published by Mr Bell, 3 Cleveland Row, St James's; and it was to this address that Mrs Bell had moved her shop from Bloomsbury:

> 'This publication is indebted to Mrs Bell, removed to No. 3 Cleveland Row, opposite St James's Palace, for the designs and the selection of Fashions, and the Costumes of all Nations which regularly embellish it. Mrs Bell's Magazin de Modes is replete with every fashionable article; and there is a daily and constant succession of novelties in Millinery, Dresses, etc., and at most moderate prices. Mrs Bell's patent corsets are unrivalled, and very superior to all others; they impart an indescribable grace to the figure.'

By the 1840s the magazine was 'embellished' with as many as six plates, 'comprehending all the London and Paris fashions' for the month. But Mrs Bell had retired by then, or been dropped, or died, for there is no advertising for her shop, which was such a considerable feature of the earlier volumes. In April 1846 the magazine began appearing under new direction: 'The Editorship of this Magazine is now entrusted by the Proprietors to a Lady of great Acquirements.' The sub-title became a *Monthly Magazine of the Courts of London and Paris, Fashions and Literature, Music, Fine Arts, the Opera, and Theatres; Embellished with the latest London and Parisian Fashions and costumes of all Nations, etc.* It was printed and published by J. B. Bell, at No. 299 Strand.

The *World of Fashion* attracted a very satisfactory amount of advertising, particularly advertising of shops, dressmakers, and trades connected with fashion, beauty, the toilet, and health. The advertisements were confined to a special section, and fashion plates were kept separate from the literary matter. It is reasonable to assume it had a wide circulation—it was sold by all the leading booksellers in England (Gray and Fell of Piccadilly is especially mentioned) and also in Dublin, Edinburgh, Paris, New York—'and by booksellers in any part of the world'. The public was also advised that it could be forwarded on the first of each month to the East and West Indies on application to the publisher. The magazine continued until 1851, and then from 1852–79 was renamed the *Ladies' Monthly Magazine and World of Fashion*. Finally, from 1880 to 1891 it became *La Mode Elegant or the World of Fashion.*

There were a number of other new publications launched in the period

THE
LADY'S MAGAZINE,
OR
Entertaining COMPANION for the FAIR SEX.

Vol. 47, N°. 2, for FEBRUARY, 1816.

EMBELLISHMENTS.
1. The LADY of the ROCK.
2. Fashionable COSTUME.
3. PATTERN for the FRONT of a DRESS.

CONTENTS.

The Lady of the Rock, (*With a Plate*) page 51
Caroline, or the Blessings of Adversity, 51
Timur, 56
Linnæus, 59
English Courage and Loyalty, 60
Such Things Are, or Mrs. Clairville, 62
Whimsical Letter, 66
The Lady's Answer, 67
Courage and Rashness, 67
The Author's Portfolio, 69
Professional Character of Sir Joshua Reynolds, 74
Hogs in Boots, 76
French Infidel reclaimed, 76
Cardinal Ximenes, 77
Northern Fisheries, 77
Pun, 78
The Propensity to magnify the idea of Self, 78
Soldiers, 78
Epitaph, 78
American Advertisement, 78
German Women, 78
Clerical Residence, 79
The Harmattan, 79
Hung for leaving his Liquor, 80
Honey Moon, 80
God Save the King, 80
Large Emerald, 80
Poetical Prescription, 80
Gambler's Wit, 80
Catherine II. and her Consort, 81
Swedish Travelling, 82
Bamborough Castle, 83

EMINENT PERSONS LATELY DECEASED.
The Earl of Buckinghamshire, 83

General Sir G. Prevost, Bart. 83
Sir Edward Crofton, 83
Caleb Hartland, 83
Dr. Vincent, 84
Phineas Bond, Esq. 84
Dr. Zouch, 84

POETRY.
Glory gain'd and Peace restor'd, 85
Temper, 85
Sonnet, 85
Imitation of a Hebrew Melody, 86
Translation from Griselda, 86
Stanzas from the Persian, 86
The Exile's Balm, 87
On the Death of the Hottentot Venus, 87
Mary Lee, 87
The Inmost Recess of Heaven, 87
Young Greyhounds playing in the Snow, 88
On entering a Lady's Room, 88
Epigram, 88
To ———, 88
Dispar et Idem, 89
Solution to a Charade, 89
Rebus, 89
On a recent Affair at Drury Lane Theatre, 89
Beauty compared with Flowers, 89
FASHIONS for March, 89

DRAMATIC INTELLIGENCE.
King's Theatre, 90
Theatre Royal Drury Lane, 91
Theatre Royal Covent Garden, 92
Books recently published, 92
Literary Intelligence, 92
CHRONICLE, 93
Births, 96
Marriages, 96
Deaths, 96

LONDON:

Printed for G. and S. ROBINSON, No. 25, Paternoster Row,
where Favors from Correspondents continue to be received.

39. Contents page from the *Lady's Magazine*, February 1816

between the end of the Regency and the accession of Queen Victoria. Some were short-lived, including an English version of the *Petit Courrier des Dames* called *Fashion as it Flies or The Ladies' Little Messenger of Parisian Fashions*, which appeared in 1823 and carried many engravings. There was the *New British Ladies' Magazine* of 1819; also the *New Bon Ton Magazine or Telescope of the Times*, 1818–21, which was edited by John Mitford, a cousin of Mary Russell Mitford who wrote *Our Village* and near relative of Lord Redesdale. The *New Bon Ton Magazine* was more of a gossip sheet than a fashion magazine, and John Mitford also edited a short-lived *Scourge* (there had been three previous attempts at a paper of this title in 1719, 1752 and 1780) and the *Quizzical Gazette, Extraordinary and Wonderful Advertiser*, which ran for eight numbers only in 1825. It was revived in 1831 as the *Quizzical Gazette and Merry Companion*. John Mitford drank himself to death in 1831—with gin, not a fashionable drink at that time.

Miss Mitford's father gambled away several small fortunes, one of which was a £20,000 prize that she herself had won in a lottery when she was ten years old. She had reason to be thankful to the *Lady's Magazine* because it was in its pages that *Our Village* first appeared. It had been rejected by Campbell who was then editor of the *New Monthly Magazine*, and by the editors of several other periodicals. After it appeared as a series of sketches in the *Lady's Magazine*, these were collected into one volume and published in 1823. From that time on, as S. C. Hall wrote in his memoirs, 'Miss Mitford never after had occasion to beg acceptances from her pen.' She came to spend quite a lot of time in London, and was regarded as an amusing curiosity in sophisticated literary circles—a dumpy little figure with a very round face and very short skirts. The poetess L.E.L. (Laetitia E. Landon) called her 'Sancho Panza in petticoats'; but S. C. Hall says that when she spoke 'her pleasant voice, her beaming eyes and smiles, made you forget the wide expanse of face; and the roly-poly figure, when seated, did not appear really short'. After the success of her tragedy *Rienzi* she became 'a little grand and stilted . . . receiving those who wished to be introduced to her seated *en reine*'. Macready called *Rienzi* an extraordinary tragedy 'for a woman to have written'—*for a woman*, the usual reservation. In 1837 Lord Melbourne granted her a literary pension of £100, that is, £200 less than he awarded that same year to Lady Morgan, who is generally credited as having been the first woman to be granted a literary pension.

Townsend's *Quarterly Selection of Parisian Costumes* began in 1823 and

40. First page of a ballad in *La Belle Assemblée*, 1823

continued from 1825 to 1888 as a monthly selection. This was a publication devoted entirely to fashion. There was no reading matter apart from descriptions of the plates, so it was probably subscribed to mainly by dressmakers and other professionals in the fashion trade. It consisted of six plates delicately coloured, selected from the most recent Parisian publications, the descriptions of the costumes being given in English. It was held in high esteem, for Townsend chose his plates with great discrimination. Most of the earlier ones originally appeared in *Le Journal des Dames et des Modes* and in *Le Petit Courrier des Dames*. There was a brief period during which he saved money by using inferior plates executed in London, but this policy evidently did not pay off for he soon reverted to the superior imported plates. The *London and Paris Ladies' Magazine of Fashion* ran from 1828 to 1891, and there was also the *Ladies' Pocket Magazine*, an annual appearing for the years 1825 to 1839.

This was one of Joseph Robin's publications, issued from Bride Court, Bridge Street. Its fashion plates, although hand-coloured, were very poor; they were supported by brief jottings called 'Cursory Remarks' on English and French fashions, and a section called 'The Ladies' Toilet'. The literary content of the magazine was of a higher standard than its fashion content. For example, the volume for 1828 (which is dedicated to the poetess Miss L. E. Landon as 'a tribute to Female British Genius') had a story by Leigh Hunt, 'The Venetian Girl', and one of Charles Lamb's Elia essays: 'A Bachelor's Complaint about the Behaviour of Married People'. It also had the first instalment of a series by Coelebs the Younger named 'The Bachelor's Budget'. Presumably the pseudonym was chosen in satirical vein after Hannah More's novel *Coelebs Search of a Wife*, published in 1808.

The Introduction to the volume of the *World of Fashion* for 1828 revealed that the sales of yearly bound volumes of magazines were beginning to be adversely affected by the new fashion for 'annuals'. These lavish productions for the Christmas trade began to make their appearance from the beginning of the 1820s. The editors of the *World of Fashion* ('several Literary and Fashionable Characters') announced:

'We feel convinced the specimen we now present to you, liberal patrons, will be in your eyes superior to the prettiest "Annual" and the neatest "Pocket-book" (and they are all very daintily devised this year); never did the Roman, in his most "palmy state", offer the *strenae*, or little presents, (auguring happiness to his friends from month to month) with more unalloyed joy, than we should our *Forget-us-nots,* our *Pledges of Friend-ship,* our *Friendship's Offerings* to you; nor would gallant Frenchmen fly with greater alacrity to deposit his *étrennes* at your feet than we to lay upon your tables the *Cupid's Album, Jewels, Remembrances, Amulets, Souvenirs,* pledges of our esteem.'

They then gave some extracts from *Cupid's Album,* published by Sherwood & Co.; and later in their 'High Life and Fashionable Chit Chat' column came back to the annuals again, saying:

'Lady Charlotte B . . . . has quite put some of her high-life acquaintance into a flutter by writing on 'Flirtation', so uneasy has the cap fitted some she has placed it on. We suppose you little care as long as you have such pretty verses as these transmitted you by L. . . . . from that pleasing little volume *Cupid's Album*:

TO AN AUTHORESS WRITING
When stained with ink that lip I view,
  Where joys their fragrant sentry keep;
Much I lament their alter'd hue,
  And curse the quill that soil'd thy lip.'

Many pretty lips, most of them well-known in Society, were soiled in the task of editing and contributing to the annuals over the next two decades. Lady Blessington came virtually to depend upon her earnings from them to ward off the creditors from the magnificent portals of Gore House. She toiled on, scribbling literally for her life, until everything crashed about her in 1849, by which time the era of the annuals was virtually over.

The annuals, although they do not come under the category of periodicals, have a place in this narrative since many of them were edited by women. Moreover, they provided a new outlet for women writers, an elegant prestige outlet in which their work appeared in company with that of many well-known authors, men as well as women. Intellectuals might scorn the annuals, but there were very few writers of the day who did not, sooner or later, contribute to these decorative drawing-room volumes.

Chapter XV

THE ANNUALS, THEIR EDITORS
AND CONTRIBUTORS

A publishing phenomenon. Harrison Ainsworth's introduction to the first
Keepsake. *Frederic Schoberl's editorship of Ackermann's* Forget-Me-Not
and Friendship's Offering. *Writing to pictures. S. C. Hall and the* Amulet.
Famous contributors to the annuals. Sir Walter Scott's payments. The Hon. Mrs
Norton, novelist, journalist, and editor. The Book of Beauty *edited by L.E.L.*
Her poetry and other writings. Gossip breaks her engagement. Marriage on the
rebound and tragic death.

ﻌﻌﻌﻌﻌﻌﻌﻌﻌﻌﻌﻌﻌﻌﻌﻌﻌﻌﻌﻌﻌﻌﻌﻌﻌﻌﻌﻌﻌﻌﻌﻌﻌﻌﻌﻌ

T HE annuals were a publishing phenomenon. Elegant volumes bound
in watered silk, in velvet, or tooled morocco leather, they began
appearing in the early 1820s, and each year from then on until the
end of the 1830s produced several new titles. Wordsworth referred to them
as 'The ornamental annuals, those greedy receptacles of trash, those
bladders upon which the boys of poetry try to swim'. Yet he was a contributor to some of the annuals himself, when he was offered what he considered a sufficiently handsome payment for thus demeaning his muse.

It was social snobbery that secured the success of the annuals. They
owed their peculiar prestige to the social position of their editors, to the
status of the literary lions and lionesses who contributed to them, and to
the engraved portraits of Society beauties which appeared in them. 'If
publications of this nature proceed as they have begun,' wrote Harrison
Ainsworth in an introduction to the first number of the *Keepsake*, published
towards the end of 1827 for 1828, 'we shall soon arrive at the millennium
of souvenirs. Instead of engravings, we shall have paintings by the first
masters; our paper must be vellum; our bindings in opal and amethyst;
and nobody must read us except in a room full of luxury, or a bower of
roses.' George Eliot makes a reference to the *Keepsake* in *Middlemarch*
which, although written in 1871 is set in the early part of the century:
' "I wonder which would turn out to be the silliest—the engravings or the
writing here", said Lydgate, turning over the pages of the *Keepsake*
quickly. "Do look at that bridegroom coming out of church: did you ever

see such a 'sugared invention'—as the Elizabethans used to say? Did any haberdasher ever look so smirking? Yet I will answer for it the story makes him one of the first gentlemen of the land." '

Highbrows liked to contend that to people of taste the annuals were an offence, yet they cannot all be dismissed as meretricious trivia. Their production was for the most part excellent; and many of the innovations in book-making and binding during this period were first tried out in the annuals. They were illustrated with steel engravings of unquestionable quality, sometimes of exquisite delicacy. Some of the vignettes which decorated their pages are considered the equal of any in book production, and it has been said that steel engraving reached its zenith in the annuals, declining with them at the mid-century. Woodcuts then became fashionable again and were used to illustrate the 'Books of the Sixties' which followed the annuals as drawing-room delights.

The literary content of the annuals takes rather more defending. There can be no denying that they tended to publish 'the worst poems by the best authors'; and it cannot be disputed that some famous writers saw the annuals as a profitable wastepaper-basket for 'the sweepings of their desks'. Generally speaking, the prose was of a higher standard than the verse, which was described with some justice by a contemporary critic as resembling the poet's corner of a country newspaper. It is not impossible to find worthwhile prose pieces; more difficult to find good verse. There were occasional exceptions. Thomas Hood, who edited the *Gem*, published in it his weirdly powerful poem 'The Dream of Eugene Aram'. But much of his verse in the annuals was simply written to go with engravings already chosen, and his most quoted one, 'I remember, I remember', which first appeared in *Friendship's Offering*, would qualify admirably for the provincial poet's corner:

> I remember, I remember,
> The house where I was born,
> The little window where the sun
> Came peeping in at morn;
> He never came a wink too soon,
> Nor brought too long a day,
> But now, I often wish the night
> Had borne my breath away!

Thomas Hood's 'Ruth' was first published in the *Forget-Me-Not* annual, in which Hogg's 'Skylark' also made its debut. The poet with the greatest number of contributions to the annuals was Barry Cornwall (Bryan Waller Proctor), friend and biographer of Charles Lamb. His total was no fewer than ninety-four poems in twelve different annuals. The best known of the prose contributions were the 'Imaginary Conversations' of Walter Savage Landor, which made their first appearance in the *Keepsake*.

The idea of the annuals germinated from the ladies' pocket-books and almanacs which had been published spasmodically for over a hundred years. One of the earliest of the annuals was called the *Graces* after a ladies' pocket-book of that name. It will be remembered that pocket books were a successful part of William Lane's publishing activities at the Minerva Press. His *Ladies' Museum* appeared ten times between 1773 and 1819, his *Ladies' Mirror* intermittently from 1785 to 1818, and his *Ladies' New and Elegant Pocket Book* came out three times between 1811 and 1818. There were many more produced by other publishers. Harrison Ainsworth, referring back to the pocket books in his introduction to the first *Keepsake* wrote:

'One aspect of the pocket-books it must be owned, it would be difficult to improve. Those delicate little engravings of landscapes and country seats, at the heads of the pages in the *Regent's Pocket Book* were in particular a happy thought. The graces of vignettes, however, are endless. Mr Stothard could turn any pocket book into a nest of Cupids. Every subject might have its allegory, and every allegory be crammed full of beauties. Flowers, outlines, portraits, antiques, miniature copies of Claude and Poussin, such as have been lately poured forth at Paris, all these, and fifty other things, might be put in greater requisition.'

Then he comes to the annuals:

'It struck somebody, who was acquainted with the literary annuals of Germany, and who reflected upon this winter flower-bed of the booksellers—these pocket books, souvenirs and Christmas presents—that he would combine the spirit of all of them, and omitting the barren or blank part, produce such a pocket book as had not been yet seen. Hence arose the *Forget-Me-Nots*, the *Literary Souvenirs,* the *Amulets*, and the *Keepsakes*, which combine the original contribution of the German annual with the splendid binding of the English Christmas present.'

The first English annual to be planned, although not the first to be published, was called the *Literary Souvenir*, and it may well have been inspired by Robert Southey's *Annual Anthology*, a collection of literary pieces without illustrations, which appeared in 1799 and 1800. Southey himself admitted that he got the idea from similar collections that had been published in France and Germany. But these French and German anthologies included steel engravings illustrating some well-known book. The *Almanack de Gotha*, for example, had a series in the 1820s illustrating Walter Scott's novels, then so fashionable all over Europe. And when Rudolph Ackermann, himself of German origin, published the *Forget-Me-Not* at the end of 1822 for 1823, he openly declared his purpose was to rival 'the elegant and tasteful productions of the continent'. As the already famous publisher of finely illustrated books and of the superb *Repository of Arts*, he was well equipped to surpass them.

Ackermann's first number of the *Forget-Me-Not* contained a diary section which accounted for the great part of its pages. In the following year his *Friendship's Offering or Annual Remembrancer* was actually made in the form of a diary. Both these annuals were edited by Frederic Schoberl. J. Fitzgerald Molloy says in his biography of Lady Blessington, published in 1897:

> 'These two publications which contained poems and sketches whose worthlessness would now prevent their admission into the poorest of our magazines, were fairly well illustrated, interleaved with sheets of blank paper, bound in tinted wrappers of the same material, and sold for 12s. (These paper-bound annuals were enclosed in a cardboard case). Their success begot competition, and with rivalry they improved. The bindings kept pace with the contents; tinted paper was no longer used being discarded for silk-covered bindings of gorgeous colour; silk in time gave place to velvet and morocco leather. Prices, which began at 12s bounded to a guinea with the first issue of the *Keepsake*, whose second number cost its proprietors £1,600.'

This £1,600 was for the literary contributions alone.

In their second year of publication, both the *Forget-Me-Not* and *Friendship's Offering* were brought out without any diary section at all, their whole contents devoted to literature and art. It was the same with the *Literary Souvenir*, edited by Alarcic Watts, first issued in 1824 for 1825. The *Amulet* of the following year was edited by that prolific writer and journalist S. C. Hall, who was responsible in 1832 for commissioning Lady Blessington's 'Conversations with Byron' for the *New Monthly Magazine*.

The *Anniversary* was a guinea annual started in 1828 as a rival to the *Keepsake* which had been the first at that price. Its editor was the Scots writer Allan Cunningham, who was able to get many eminent authors to contribute, in particular Scottish writers such as Lockhart and Hogg. Robert Southey wrote a poem on his own portrait in the *Anniversary*, and Theodore Hook, editor of *John Bull* published his sketch entitled 'The Splendid Annual'—the splendid annual being the Lord Mayor of London.

Early in the era of the annuals large sales were achieved. Frederic Schoberl, editor of the *Forget-Me-Not*, announced in 1827 that 10,000 of the previous issue had been sold. It was then a small gilt-edged volume in green-glazed figured boards, in a slip-in case of the same design. In 1833 the green boards and slip cover were abandoned in favour of a red silk binding such as had been introduced by Charles Heath in the *Keepsake*. Schoberl did not go for famous names. He asserted that as a rule the merit of a contribution was in inverse ratio to the fame of the author. His policy was to have plenty of keen young contributors all interested in extending the sale. The general practice at first was for the editor of an annual to commission literary contributions and select pictures to be engraved more or less at random, the pictures and text having no relationship to each other. But it soon became more usual to buy the engravings first and then ask someone to write a poem or a story to fit the picture. This may seem now a strange way of going about things, but at that time steel engravings were the new and fashionable thing. A popular picture by a modish painter would be eagerly run after by editors who would pay the artist from £20 to £120 for permission to reproduce his painting. Then the engraver was paid anything up to 200 gns. for his work. S. C. Hall, who edited the *Amulet, a Christian and Literary Remembrancer*, recorded: 'For *The Crucifixion* after Martin, engraved by Le Keux, that gentleman received from me 180 guineas (size 7 in by 4 in) making the cost of the print, including the sum paid for the drawing, 210 guineas. For the embellishments alone in that number the publishers had to pay nearly 1,200 guineas. And yet, strange to say, that was the only volume of the whole series of the *Amulet* that yielded a profitable return upon the capital expended and the labour bestowed.' S. C. Hall's editorship of the *Amulet* was, in point of fact, a disastrous episode in his life, since he was a partner as well as editor. The first volume was published in the autumn of 1826 and ten more volumes followed; but as he recalled in his *Retrospect of a Long Life*, 'By 1837 the "fashion" for annuals had ceased, and the *Amulet* was discontinued. The publishers became bankrupt, and I was made responsible for the accumulated debts of the publication. This terrible event utterly ruined me, and I had to begin life again.'

Charles Heath, the famous engraver who was proprietor of the *Keepsake* and later of *Heath's Book of Beauty*, toured the country in the early days to coax literary contributions from celebrated authors. Most of them at first felt themselves to be too celebrated to contribute; but usually their dignity was undermined by the temptation of seductively large fees. Wordsworth, who has said amongst other withering comments that 'It would disgrace any name to appear in an annual', could not resist haggling for a big price for the few lines of his that appeared in *Winter's Wreath*. He had the reputation of being 'a great haggler'. Thomas Moore boasted that he had rejected a fee of 600 guineas for 120 lines of prose or verse for the *Keepsake*—which led Lockhart to remark that it was doubtful which was the greater fool, Heath who made the offer or Moore who refused it. Lockhart also wrote in his life of Sir Walter Scott that Heath gave him £500 for the hundred pages of *The House of Aspen* and *My Aunt Margaret's Mirror* and added, 'But Sir Walter regretted having meddled in any way with this toy shop of literature, and would never do it again, though repeatedly offered very large sums.' Mrs Newton Crosland said it was reported that Sir Walter 'received four hundred guineas for the short story he contributed to the first *Keepsake*; and allowing for perhaps a little exaggeration, there is no doubt he obtained a large sum for the few pages from his pen that appeared'. If this were really correct, it would seem to have been madness on the part of Heath, since in the first issue of the *Keepsake* all the contributions were anonymous, by the policy of the editor, Harrison Ainsworth. Ainsworth said that his idea in keeping his contributors anonymous was so that their work would be judged on its own merits, unaided by the previous reputation of the writers, 'though literary idlers will probably find amusement in tracing the hand of particular authors in their respective contributions'. It is possible that through the promise of anonymity he was able to persuade contributions from haughty authors who would not have written for an annual under their own names. More likely the anonymity was a way of implying that his authors were famous but in fact paying only small sums to younger unknown writers who would, unlike the scornful famous ones, give of their best. What is very evident when one reads his first *Keepsake* is that the standard of contribution is noticeably superior to later ones and to most of the other annuals. Of course it is quite probable that Ainsworth wrote most of the pieces himself. There is a brilliant satirical sketch on the Blue Stockings called 'The Conversazione'. And there is this description of a bust of Bacchus:

'Gigantic, earnest, luxuriant, his head a very bower of hair ivy; his look a mixture of threat, and reassurance, and the giving of pleasure; the roughness of wine is in his eyes, and the sweetness of it on his lips. Annibal Caracci would have painted such a face, and grown jealous when his mistress looked at it. Such did Bacchus appear when Ariadne turned pale with loving him; and he said, with divine insolence in his eyes, "Am I not then better than a mortal?"'

The illustrations in this first number of the *Keepsake* were engraved by Heath from paintings by Thomas Stothard and F. P. Stephanoff; and it is made clear that the stories and poems which accompany them were commissioned to be written especially for them. This may seem like prostitution to modern writers, but there is a great deal of sensitive imagination in, for example, the story which accompanies Stephanoff's picture 'The Inconstant' as this short extract will show:

'Isadora's eye dwelt lightly and carelessly on the garish scene around her. Her heart was formed to echo to love, not to splendour; and the gay society offered her no charm, for it wanted him whose presence could alone make it acceptable. Everyone, who has loved, knows with what a fond and almost proud consciousness the heart will seclude itself from the community of crowds and assemblies and withdrawing, as it were within itself, enjoy with pensive satisfaction its internal world of recollections.'

F. Mansel Reynolds took over the editorship of the *Keepsake* from 1829 to 1835, and at first continued Ainsworth's policy of anonymous contributions. But Charles Heath, as proprietor, soon introduced a new policy in seeking fashionable names as distinct from celebrated ones, believing social glamour to have more sales appeal than literary fame for the kind of readers who bought annuals. He also conjectured, rightly as it turned out, that given an editor with the right circle of acquaintance, he or she would be able to cajole titled people to contribute gratis. A fashionable hostess was the obvious answer. And so he appointed the Honourable Mrs Norton to edit the volume for 1836, and then Lady Emmeline Stuart Wortley the four volumes from 1837 to 1840. Finally, and most fruitfully, the Countess of Blessington, who proved to be an irresistible cajoler of fashionable contributors—and even of celebrated literary men.

Mrs Norton had already had experience of editing. She had edited *La Belle Assemblée* for John Bell from 1832, and the *English Annual* from 1834. She was also a contributor to many other periodicals, including *Fraser's Magazine*, which had an extremely high reputation in literary circles. Grand-daughter of Richard Brinsley Sheridan the playwright, she inherited his Irish charm and wit, although her wit sparkled more brightly in conversation than on paper. Certainly she had her literary detractors. But from the point of view of publicity for his annual, Heath could not have chosen a more vivid personality. The name of Caroline Norton was on everyone's lips—a society beauty, harried by gossip and scandal, rumours and counter-rumours. She was always hot news, even before the blazing sensation of the divorce action brought in 1837 by her husband, in which Lord Melbourne was cited as her lover. Although Mrs Norton's innocence was proved in court, her name had been bandied about in every scurrilous news sheet and by every society wit and common or garden gossip-monger. The divorce case was followed by a final separation from her husband.

Women rarely had a good word to say for Caroline Norton. Lady Eastlake, a regular contributor to the *Quarterly Review* who mixed a great deal in literary circles, said she used her eyes 'ably and wickedly'. But later on, when the scandals had dwindled and the dust of the divorce case was long settled, Caroline had earned sufficient reputation as a poet for a *Quarterly Review* critic in 1840 to call her the Byron of Modern Poetesses— a romanticism that was subsequently employed by many other critics. The reviewer placed her first in a list of ten British women poets, Elizabeth Barrett coming second. She was never rated highly as an editor. The *New Monthly Magazine* commented on the first issue of the *Keepsake* published under Mrs Norton's editorship: 'However much we may desire to say of a lady only that which is pleasant, we are compelled to state that the change (from the editorship of F. M. Reynolds) has not been advantageous to the work . . . the volume is made up of mere nothings.' The *New Monthly Magazine* allowed her only one triumph—that of persuading Thomas Moore to contribute. But since they were both Irish this is unlikely to have been at all difficult. For the rest, the critic's opinion was that she had not succeeded in improving the *Keepsake* in any particular, nor in 'giving dignity to the class of works to which it belongs'.

" I sit upon the green grass and
Beneath the willow tree
My haunt it is the lonely grave
And let that be my answer be ..

L.E.L

41. Laetitia Elizabeth Landon, the poetess L.E.L.

Other critics were equally damning, and the *Keepsake* under Caroline Norton's editorship was compared unfavourably with the *Book of Beauty*, which was launched by Charles Heath in 1833 under the editorship of L.E.L. (Miss Laetitia E. Landon) and continued from 1834 under Lady Blessington. L.E.L. in fact wrote the entire letterpress in the first issue, for which Heath paid her £300. She was already a popular poetess of the bittersweet strain, writing long, highly coloured dramatic verse. Her 'Impovatrice', published in 1824, reached six editions in its first year. She also successfully edited Fisher's *Drawing-room Scrap-Book* and was its sole contributor of text from the first number in 1832 until her marriage in

1839. Fisher collected the illustrations, which had mostly appeared in other works so that there was no great outlay on artists' fees, and L.E.L. wrote suitable verses or stories to go with them. There were upwards of thirty pictures in each volume: 'It is not an easy thing', wrote L.E.L. in the introduction to the first, 'to write to prints selected rather for their pictorial excellence than their poetic capabilities, and mere description is certainly not the most popular species of composition.' But she was a facile versifier, and soon became accustomed to writing to any picture set before her. Perhaps the reason she was so successful at it was because, as it was said, 'she hit no higher than the public taste'. She did complain, however, in a letter to Mrs S. C. Hall, that so many of the engravings were views of eastern scenery and antiquities and that 'mellifluously to mention the bare names of the places required something like an effort of genius . . . How my ingenuity has been taxed to introduce the different places! and, pray, forgive this little tender effusion of vanity, I do pique myself on contriving to get from Dowlutabad to Shusher, and Penawa, and the Triad Figure in the Caves of Elephants, and from thence to Ibrahim Padshah's tomb, etc.'

Laman Blanchard wrote in his biography of L.E.L., published only two years after her death,

'From the commencement of the annuals, there was scarcely one (although each season produced its new ones) that did not secure the attraction of her initials. From several of these, such as the *Literary Souvenir* and the *Forget-Me-Not*, etc. she derived sums considerable enough to show that it was no immutable decree of fate by which poetry and poverty had been made inseparable companions, and that in the judgement of experienced publishers, her writings retained their charm over the gentle purchaser, in spite of their profusion. She also wrote uninterruptedly in verse and prose for the *Court Journal* over a period of about three years. It was the *New Monthly Magazine*, however, that obtained by far the most finished of her poetical efforts—the subjects being her own and not her publisher's. From 1836 she annually added to the beauty of Mr Schloss's *Fairy Almanac*; and princesses have rarely been hailed in such hearty and passionate strains as in L.E.L.'s *Birthday Tribute to the Princess Victoria*, which appeared in May 1837.'

L.E.L. did not have the romantic background nor the position in Society that Caroline Norton had, nor her beauty. Her father had died in financially embarrassing circumstances, and she lived at 22 Hans Place as a lodger in the house of the Misses Lance, who kept a boarding-school for girls which Laetitia herself had attended as a child. She had earned her living by her pen for a long time, also providing for her mother; and at the time she started writing for the annuals she was already well known in literary circles. As early as 1821 she was a regular contributor of verse to William Jerdan's *Literary Gazette*—indeed, she was only fifteen when that highbrow journal first published a poem signed L.E.L. She published her first novel *Romance and Reality* in 1831, and in 1835 another novel, *Ethel Churchill*, was extremely popular. Her prose output for the annuals was considerable, but it was as a poet that she was most widely known.

The vein of her poetry was that of the prevalent romanticism of the period. Jane Williams in her *Literary Women of England* (1861) describes it as having been 'extraordinarily popular with young and old . . . full of melancholy forebodings, the weariness and despondency of baffled hopes and blighted affections—but its picturesque, chivalrous, and beautiful imagery touched the poetic nerve in every heart, and touching thrilled it. Although she was neither a plagiarist nor an imitator, her inspiration is obviously Byronic. The want of consistent truthfulness, and the indulgence of reverie spoilt her fine mind, as dodder spoils the rose.' As time went on L.E.L. explored some less melancholy veins; and of one 'fine and lofty' poem in the *Drawing-room Scrap-Book* another critic wrote:

'Miss Landon seems to have discovered, at last, that genius can have some nobler aims than to plant along the road of life an avenue of yews and cypresses. It may be that she has exhausted her varieties of melancholy phrase and, in sheer necessity, begun to think that there are other things to be adorned besides the sepulchre.'

Disraeli, who may or may not have known that her family home had been in Old Brompton, described L.E.L. as 'the personification of Brompton—pink satin dress and white satin shoes, red cheeks, snub nose, and hair *à la Sappho*'. He met her at a soirée at Bulwer Lytton's house, when there was 'a large sprinkling of Blues', amongst them Lady Morgan (author of *The Wild Irish Girl*), the Hon. Mrs Norton, and Mrs Gore, the writer of fashionable 'silver-fork novels', whom he described as 'a very sumptuous personage looking like a full-blown rose'. A month later he again met L.E.L. at Bulwer Lytton's, looking quite different: 'She had thrown off Greco-Bromptonian costume, and was perfectly *à la Française*, and really looked quite pretty.' Brompton evidently had a reputation for intellectual

42. The house in Hans Place where L.E.L. lodged

exhibitionism long before the aesthetic movement of the 1870s when
Punch christened it 'Passionate Brompton'.

It was most unusual for a young gentlewoman at that time not to have
a family background and home, and the equivocal position of L.E.L.
inevitably led to rumours. One of these was that she spent a remarkable
amount of time at the house of William Jerdan during the period that she
was contributing to his *Literary Gazette*. Later her name was connected
with that of another married man, the writer and editor Dr Maginn, who
helped her with the editorship of the *Drawing-room Scrap-Book*. It was the
gossip about Maginn which led to her breaking off her engagement to
marry John Forster (later the biographer of Oliver Goldsmith and Charles
Dickens), with whom she was deeply in love. Her life ended tragically in
June 1839, at the age of thirty-six. She died of prussic acid poisoning four
months after her marriage to Mr George McLean, Governor of the Gold
Coast. He was a man with totally different interests and sympathies from
her own, whom she had met in London shortly after the breaking of her

engagement to Forster. It was never proved whether her death in Cape Coast Castle was suicide, an accident, or an act of revenge by her husband's discarded native mistress.

Poor L.E.L. was really the victim of the social hypocrisy of her time. Although the morals of society were permissive for all who were able to maintain an impeccable social façade, there was no mercy for women whose position was precarious. They were considered fair game for the wits and the gossips. Michael Sadleir describes the vulnerability of L.E.L.'s position in his *Bulwer and his Wife*: 'It is essential to remember that her appearance in literary London as a very young woman with no protective background to speak of and a living to earn was, in 1820, a most unusual appearance. In consequence, comments on her behaviour and gossip as to her indiscretions must be very considerably discounted in advance. She was in herself a phenomenon so startling as almost by her very existence to be a scandal.'

L.E.L. herself was acutely sensitive and resentful of the jealousy that literary success by a woman aroused in the other sex. In a letter to Mrs S. C. Hall she wrote: 'Envy, malice, and all uncharitableness—these are the fruits of a successful literary career for a woman'.

Chapter XVI
WRITING WOMEN OF THE 1830s

Lady Blessington edits the Book of Beauty. *Her equivocal ménage
at Gore House; her unceasing literary toil; her earnings. Mrs Gore's 'silver fork'
novels. Sydney Owensons'* Wild Irish Girl *and other writing; her social success
and marriage to Sir Charles Morgan. First literary pension awarded to a woman.
Lady Blessington's tact with contributors. Camilla Toulmin's visit to
Gore House. Collapse of the Gore House establishment; Lady Blessington's
death in Paris. Her niece continues the* Book of Beauty. *Mrs Newton Crosland
edits* Friendship's Offering. *Women's magazines of the 1830s; Victorian
domesticity sets in.*

HEATH's appointment in 1834 of Marguerite, Countess of Blessington, to the editorship of his *Book of Beauty* in place of L.E.L. proved to be rewarding in every way. She had already won literary praise through publication in the *New Monthly Magazine* of her *Journals of Conversations with Lord Byron*, the first instalment of which appeared in July 1832. Of these Leigh Hunt later wrote in his autobiography, 'Her Ladyship's account of Lord Byron is by far the best and most sensible I am acquainted with. Her writings, indeed, throughout, though not of a nature qualified to endure, were remarkable for a judgement as well as benevolence for which many would not give credit to an envied beauty.'

Lady Blessington had recently, on the death of her husband, returned from the Continent and set up house with Count d'Orsay, who had married her stepdaughter. This ménage à trois was naturally the subject of unceasing gossip and surmise, which was by no means lessened when Harriet d'Orsay left her husband and sought the protection of her father's relatives. Lady Blessington's place in Society was in any case equivocal owing to the mysteries veiling her early life. She had not been free to marry Lord Blessington until the death of the husband whom she had been forced by her father to marry at the age of fifteen and from whose brutalities she had fled soon after.

There had, of course, been gossip about the previous editor of the *Book of Beauty*. But L.E.L. was not such a conspicuous figure, and if you are going to have a gossiped-about person as an editor you may as well have gossip on a gorgeous scale, with a glamorous Countess as the magnet for rumours. Moreover, Lady Blessington applied herself to her editorship in a thoroughly efficient and industrious manner. She wrote to authors, artists, and engravers. She selected pictures and portraits for engraving, and then forwarded the engraved copies to writers asking them to supply stories or verses to go with them. She herself wrote innumerable verses and sketches for this purpose. The *Book of Beauty* also contained articles and essays independent of the plates, and she coaxed or flattered some of the greatest writers of the time to contribute—Thackeray, Wordsworth, Bulwer Lytton, Walter Savage Landor, Disraeli, Sir Walter Scott—as well as fashionable novel writers like Mrs Gore and Lady Morgan. Gradually her drawing-room at Gore House, Kensington, became a meeting place for authors, poets, essayists, artists, engravers, publishers, editors and critics. High rank mingled with young talent, painters were introduced to patrons, authors met editors and publishers, and critics met the writers and actors they critized. Among regular visitors were Bulwer Lytton, Macready the actor and manager, the elder Disraeli and his son, Barry Cornwall, Captain Marryat, Thomas Campbell, Harrison Ainsworth, and Albany Fonblanque, the eminent political writer who was editor and proprietor of the *Examiner*.

While continuing to edit the *Book of Beauty*, Lady Blessington undertook in 1836 to write the entire letterpress for another annual, *Gems of Beauty*; and in 1840 she took over the editorship of the *Keepsake*. In that same year she brought out the second part of her *Idler in Italy* and published a novel, *The Belle of the Season*. Writing in 1804 to a friend she said,

> 'When I tell you I have no less than three works passing through the press, and have to furnish the manuscript to keep the printers at work for one of them, you may judge of my unceasing and overwhelming occupation, which leaves me time neither for pleasure, nor for taking air or exercise enough for health. I am literally worn out, and look for release from my literary toils more than ever slave did from bondage.'

William Jerdan, who as an old friend and literary adviser was likely to know, says that she made between £2,000 and £3,000 per annum for some years—a very large earned income indeed for those days. She must certainly have been the most highly paid woman in the country, apart from eminent courtesans. When Charles Dickens invited her to contribute to the *Daily News*, launched in 1846, she asked £800 a year to supply 'any sort of intelligence she might like to communicate of the sayings, doings, memoirs, or movements of the fashionable world'. This was considered extravagant by the managers of the paper, and she was offered £400 a year certain, or £250 for six months, when the arrangement would be renewed if satisfactory. This she accepted, but at the end of the six months John Forster, who had taken over from Dickens as editor, terminated her appointment.

At the time of her first involvement with the annuals, she was at the height of her literary demand. Her biographer J. Fitzgerald Molloy wrote in *The Most Gorgeous Lady Blessington* that in 1836 Lady Blessington expected, and got, £800 from a publisher for a novel, whereas Caroline Norton only got £250. Mrs Gore was assessed lower still: only £120, in spite of her being unquestionably the most talented novelist of the three. Women writers, it is palpably evident, were paid according to social status rather than literary ability. Mrs Catherine Grace Gore's witty and satirical novels of fashionable life gave an acutely observed picture of Regency society. She pin-pointed for especial dissection those people who, in her own words, 'exulted in the consciousness of superior self-possession and knowledge of the world; and of that nameless something or nothing, which constitutes the airy elegance of *bon ton*'. Quite apart from their period interest, her novels can be read with great enjoyment today.

This genre of fiction, sometimes called 'fashionable novels', sometimes 'silver-fork novels', provided aspirants to Society with the rules of the game, the language, the manners and modes—and the pitfalls. The new aristocracy of money, bred by the prolonged wars with France, anxious above all things to emulate the old aristocracy, made great parade of culture and *comme il faut*. Some of them were already in the second generation, since even before the *nouveaux riches* who emerged during the wars there were the cash barons created by a lavish distribution of titles which began in the 1760s. By the beginning of the new century London society was already infiltrated with socially ambitious families who, having made their fortunes and been ennobled during the preceding fifty years, were acquiring the necessary social polish to give them the confidence they needed to mix with the *bon ton*. It was this infiltration that fascinated Mrs Gore, and that she was so skilful at satirising in drawing-room conversations—as, for example, in *Mothers and Daughters*:

'A Sir Westland Somebody—or Sir Somebody Westland;—one of our commercial upstarts—as rich as the Bank, and as vulgar as Oxford Street.'

'My dear Tichborne!—prithee present me. I adore a brute who is both vulgar and opulent; any qualification which enables one to despise a rich man ensures one such a delicious personal triumph! Pray present me!'

Theodore Hook's *John Bull* and Charles Molloy Westmacott's *Age* prospered through their near-libellous comments on social climbers. These merciless scandal sheets were largely fed by blackmailers and by fake fashionables who were the paid spies of Society, feeding back all the innuendo and gossip they could gather. It was a series of malicious paragraphs in the *Age* that began the pressure on Lady Blessington which caused the first cracks in the magnificent façade of her Gore House establishment.

The female side of this upsurging society was just as anxious as the male to scale the social heights, but wives and daughters had to employ different methods. If they failed to get invited to the right 'evenings' to meet the right people, one method they could attempt was to attract fashionable notice by contributing to one of the annuals. For the most part, it is true, editors of annuals required their contributors to have either literary fame or social position; but they usually had to pay high fees to fame, and sometimes to position also. In contrast, the climbers were able to pay (if not directly in money, in some other kind of accommodation) for the privilege of having their poems or stories seen by the aristocratic readers. They could be asked to pay even more to have their portraits included.

The height of ambition for female literary climbers was to be included among the Blue Stockings. The Regency Blues were neither so well read in the classics nor so well versed in mythology as the original Blue Stockings of the eighteenth century, and most of them had taken up literature for the sake of the money they might be able to earn. Lady Dacre held gatherings of fashionable Blues, and so also did the Countess of Morley. These two literary *grandes dames* were not writers themselves, but it amused them to patronize literary aspirants who were also aspirants to Society. To acquire a *reputation du salon* was an intoxicating experience, although very often an ephemeral one. A more humble aspiration was to contrive to have a foreword to your book written by a titled lady. This, in those Society-ruled days, was sufficient to get it published. Whereas in the previous century novel writing was not done by the best people, it had now become a fashionable hobby. In 1818 Lady Charlotte Bury noted in her diary: 'People of *ton* have taken to writing novels; it is an excellent amusement for them, and also for the public.'

The most notable of the genuine writers among these latter-day Blues were Caroline Norton, L.E.L., Mrs Gore, Lady Blessington, and Lady Morgan. Lady Morgan was known everywhere as 'The Wild Irish Girl', after her novel of that name published in 1806. Born in 1777 she was the daughter of Robert Owenson, an actor and theatre manager in Dublin. She used to say that her father was frequently 'torn to prison', and her mother on the point of beggary, and that she, Sydney Owenson, had provided for herself from the time she was fourteen. She became a governess in two families before her writing became remunerative. The first book she published, in 1801, was a novel called *St Clair* and for remuneration she received four copies of the book. *The Novice of St Dominic* published by Sir Richard Phillips was a success, which led him to offer £200 for the first edition of *The Wild Irish Girl* and £50 more for the second and third editions. Then, hearing that Miss Edgeworth's publisher was going to make a rival bid, he raised his offer by another £50. Although rhapsodical and sentimental, it contained descriptions of considerable imaginative power, and there was something about it that caught the popular fancy. In less than two years it ran into seven editions. In 1809 Sydney Owenson had another success with a four-volume novel called *Woman, or Ida of Athens*, whose appreciative readers included Jane Austen. She went to France in 1815 and afterwards produced a book dealing with travel, politics, and society called *France* which went through four editions in one year. On the strength of this success, Colburn offered her £2,000 for a similar book on Italy, which was published in 1821.

Sydney Owenson was not a beautiful Irish girl. A contemporary described her as 'hardly more than four feet high, with a slightly curved spine, uneven shoulders and eyes, she glided about in a close-cropped wig, bound by a fillet or solid band of gold, her face all animation, and with a witty word for everybody'. Another writer alluding to the 'unevenness' of her eyes said, 'they were, however, large, lustrous and electrical'. When Sydney Owenson was thirty-five she married Charles Morgan, an obstetrician who was a friend of Jenner. He was some five or six years younger than his bride, reasonably prosperous, and was knighted on the day they married—to her great satisfaction. In 1837 Lord Melbourne, on Lord

43. Lady Morgan's residence, Kildare Street, Dublin

Morpeth's solicitation, granted Lady Morgan the first literary pension ever conferred on a woman writer. This was a generous £300 a year 'in acknowledgement of the services rendered by her to the world of letters'.

In most people's opinion the award was both unmerited and unnecessary. Her husband was well off, and her writing was fluent and facile rather than distinguished; sometimes it was positively slipshod. Her countryman, John Wilson Croker, accused her in the *Quarterly Review*, either directly or indirectly, of 'licentiousness, profligacy, irreverence, blasphemy, libertinism, disloyalty and atheism'. That seems a bit steep, even from the pen of an Irishman; but the *Quarterly* seems to have been particularly malicious about Lady Morgan. Of her book on Italy another *Quarterly* critic wrote: 'Notwithstanding the obstetric skill of Sir Charles Morgan (who we believe is a male midwife), this book dropt all but stillborn from the press.' In contrast, Lord Byron praised it as 'fearless and excellent'.

In 1839 Sir Charles and Lady Morgan deserted Dublin society and went to live in London, where they launched into an intoxicating whirl of social engagments. Sydney adored the flattery she received, and in this new life found no time to write. Her last novel *Woman and her Master*, although published in 1840, was written before she left Ireland. It was described as 'rather poor vapouring'—Lady Morgan's triumph was one of personality, not of literary talent. In old age she was described as 'a little humpbacked old woman, absurdly attired, rouged and wigged; vivacious and somewhat silly; vain, gossipy, and ostentatious; larding her talk with scraps of French, often questionable in their idiom, always dreadful in their accent, exhibiting her acquaintance with titled people so prodigally as to raise a smile'. The journalist S. C. Hall, who knew her well, wrote:

'She was created for society, enjoyed and lived in society to the last. Nothing annoyed her so much as being invited to a *small party*. She liked the crowded room, the loud announcement, and the celebrity she had earned. Her vanity was charming; it was different from every other vanity. It was so naïve, so original, and she admitted it with the frankness of a child. "I know I am vain, but I have a right to be so. It is not put off and on, like my rouge." And again: "Look at the number of books I have written! Did ever woman move in a brighter sphere than I do? My dear I have three invitations to dinner today; one from a duchess, another from a countess, and a third from a diplomatist—I will not tell you who—a very naughty man, who, of course, keeps the best society in London. Now what right have I, my father's daughter to this? What am I? A pensioned scribbler! Yet I have gifts that Queens might covet . . . Princes and Princesses, celebrities of all kinds, have presented me with the *souvenirs* you see around me, and *they* would make a wiser woman vain." '

This was a very different experience of the woman writer's lot than that of poor L.E.L. If Sydney Owenson had come to London unprotected by a husband and dependent upon her own earnings for board and lodging, it might have been a different story; she might then have experienced the

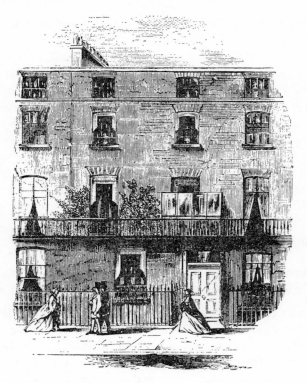

44. Lady Morgan's residence, William Street, London

'envy, malice, and all uncharitableness' that L.E.L. maintained were 'the fruits of a successful literary career for a woman'. With no one to pull strings for her, she would almost certainly not have been granted that £300 literary pension, although her need of it would have been very much greater.

Lady Morgan for all her wild success was not as a writer in the same class as Mrs Gore. Mrs Gore published *Women As They Are or The Manners of the Day* in three volumes anonymously in 1830, and this is generally considered to have been the first of what were called 'fashionable novels' or 'silver-fork novels'—although claims are sometimes made for Theodore Hook's *Sayings and Doings*, 1824. Hook, in his position as editor of *John Bull*, was at the receiving end of a bountiful flow of information about the dissipations and decadences of Society—all the material he needed for a fashionable novel. He pioneered the method of presenting in fictional form a blend of realism, epigram, and unlikely plot that became a popular form of 'silver-fork' fiction for two decades. Mrs Gore's novels, on the other hand, were of a higher standard altogether. Bulwer Lytton, himself born into the Society she depicted, wrote of her: 'She was a remarkably clever woman, and her novels have a merit that has never been sufficiently appreciated. She preceded Thackeray, and as she knew good society infinitely better than he did, her satire makes his like caricature.' Mrs Gore does not seem to have been deflected from her novel writing to contribute to the journals or magazines, but she edited Heath's *Picturesque Annual* for the year 1840, and again in 1843.

When Lady Blessington took over the editorship of the *Book of Beauty* from Caroline Norton, she set about enrolling well-known women writers. Unlike her predecessor, she was able to establish warm relationships with women as well as with men. One of the women writers she gathered into her glamorous fold was Mrs S. C. Hall, whose husband was editor of the *Amulet* amongst his other literary activities, and who herself later edited the *Juvenile Forget-Me-Not*, for which she gathered contributions from many distinguished writers, including Mrs Hemans, Mrs Opie, Miss Mitford, and Mrs Hofland. Mrs S. C. Hall became a constant contributor to Lady Blessington's annuals and a frequent afternoon caller at Gore House. She was completely captivated by the charm of her editor and fell under the spell that never failed to work upon intelligent people of both sexes. She wrote of Lady Blessington:

'I had no means of knowing whether what the world said of this beautiful woman was true or false, but I am sure *God* intended her to be good, and there was a deep-seated good intent in whatever she did that came under my observation. She never lost an opportunity of doing a gracious act or saying a gracious word. There was great satisfaction in writing for her whatever she required, labours became pleasures from the importance she attached to every little attention paid to requests, which as an editor she had a right to command.'

Mrs Newton Crosland was another professional journalist who wrote for the annuals during most of the time they were in fashion—that is, for about twenty years. Born Camilla Dufour Toulmin, her father had died when she was eight years old leaving his widow and daughter unprovided.

Before she was twenty years old, William Chambers accepted a contribution from her for *Chambers' Journal*, and helped her find her feet in journalism. She was a contributor to *Chambers' Journal* for more than fifty years, and contributed poems, essays, historical notes, biographical sketches, and other miscellanea to periodicals such as *Bentley's Miscellany*, the *People's Journal*, the *London Journal*, the *Old Monthly Magazine*, *Ainsworth's Magazine*—and later to Douglas Jerrold's *Magazine*, and the *Illustrated London News*. She also published a number of novels. In her book of reminiscences, *Landmarks of a Literary Life*, she wrote, 'From the year 1838 Lady Blessington had accepted little poems of mine for her *Book of Beauty*, always with gracious notes of acknowledgement.' Gracious notes of acknowledgment had, in very truth, to satisfy many young writers in the later days of the annuals, even if in the hey-day of their prosperity there was more material payment. 'When Christmas came round I received, as I had done for many years, a present from Lady Blessington, usually of jewellery. It was in this way she requited many of her contributors, for the evil days had set in when the publishers were more parsimonious than of old.'

Charm was undoubtedly Lady Blessington's chief asset as an editor, and many examples have been recorded of her tact in dealing with rejections, her long courteous letters of explanation. For example, young Charles Mathews who submitted a long poem:

> 'A thousand thanks my dear Charles for the verses which are beautiful but, alas, a *leetle* too warm for the false prudency of the public taste. Were I to insert them I should have a host of hypercritical hypocrites attacking the warmth of the sentiments of the lines, and the lady-editor: and therefore I must ask you to give me a tale, or verses more prudish— prettier ones you can hardly give me. I have been so long a mark for the arrows of slander and attack, that I must be more particular than anyone else: and your pretty verses, which in any of the annuals could not fail to be admired, would in a book edited *by me* draw down attacks. I keep the verses for they are too beautiful not to find a place in my album. What a misery it is, my dear Charles, to live in an age when one must make such sacrifices to cant and false delicacy, and against one's own judgement and taste.'

It is sad that we shall never be able to read those verses that were a '*leetle* too warm', nor know from them exactly what the 'cant and false delicacy' of the day considered unacceptable.

'Tis thine, to mould us to thy will.
Bid the heart tremble, or be still
As Ocean, when the Storm is o'er
And waves come dying to the Shore,
Feb 3rd 1836 — Marguerite Blessington

45. The lady editor's handwriting, in which she dashed off her effusive little notes to contributors

Lady Blessington's charm in dealing with her contributors may be a leetle too sugary for our taste, but it must have been a pleasing contrast to the cavalier attitude of most editors of that day. One of the women who edited a rival annual used to boast that when an author, despairing of getting a reply to his letters, at length called in person to demand his manuscript she 'sent down a drawer full of detached manuscripts to him in her hall, desiring he would take what he pleased'. At the beginning of the *Keepsake* for 1834, that is during F. M. Reynold's editorship, there is this notice to contributors: '*It is particularly* requested that copies will be retained of all MSS. addressed to the Publishers for insertion in the *Keepsake*, as the editor begs leave to state, most explicitly, that *he cannot undertake to return rejected articles.*' This attitude would be bad enough today; but in those days everything had to be handwritten, and there were no carbon copies.

Mrs Newton Crosland described in her memoirs her first experience of 'writing to a plate'. Lady Blessington had sent her the merest outline of a portrait with the request that she would write a few verses to it:

'I knew not what to do. The engraver's work was not sufficiently advanced for me to divine whether the face was full of dignity and intelligence, or only revealed the beauty of youth; of course one of these attributes it must have been expected to possess. I took counsel with one or two intimates as to the propriety or prudence of my calling on Lady Blessington instead of writing to her about the plate, and the offer of a friend to drive me in her carriage to Gore House decided the matter.

259

Many subsequent visits I paid, but always there was the same formality. The great carriage gates were always shut, and it was someone from the stable who answered the loud bell from a small side door. He never knew if his mistress was at home, but took the card that was presented, and in a few minutes the visitor was admitted into the courtyard. The hall door was flung wide open by a powdered footman in a gorgeous livery of green and gold, and the name passed on to another servitor—both were upwards of six feet in height. This second footman ushered me, on my first visit, into the library, where the hostess advanced to meet me in the most cordial manner possible. Explaining the object of my visit I gained all the information necessary and, I believe, had a more advanced sketch sent me; at all events, some lines of mine on a lady's portrait appeared in the *Book of Beauty* for 1843. When I left, Lady Blessington pressed my hand in both of hers, saying, "Look on me as an old friend" and invited me to come and see her again. I own I was gratified and charmed by my reception, and, prudent or imprudent, I for some years made an afternoon call at Gore House every few months.'

Prudent or imprudent—this, of course, refers to Lady Blessington's doubtful position in Society and the unconventional ménage at Gore House, which made it an undesirable place for a young girl to frequent. On one afternoon visit Camilla Toulmin (as she then was) stayed to dinner as a thunderstorm made it difficult for her to leave; and on another day she was invited again, when Lady Blessington said they were expecting Prince Louis Napoleon, Lord Brougham, Mr Disraeli, and 'some other friends, whom perhaps I should like to meet. Under ordinary circumstances I am not quite sure what I should have done; but it so happened that I considered myself pledged to be at home that evening as Mr and Mrs William Chambers, who were in town, had promised to drop in at teatime if they could one evening that week.' It seems incredible that this young journalist should have foregone the opportunity of meeting such a dazzling selection of guests for the mere *possibility* of old Mr and Mrs Chambers calling, even though William Chambers had helped her to start her journalistic career. But she makes it clear that she would have hesitated about the propriety of accepting the invitation to dine at Gore House in any case. Looking back as an old lady writing her memoirs she says, 'I have often thought that it was all for the best that I could not stay to dinner on that occasion. I might have been drawn into the vortex of the Gore House set a great deal more than was good for me; but it pained me to fancy that I might have been suspected of only fabricating an excuse.' Whether or not this was suspected, she was never invited to dine again.

Charles Heath, the proprietor of the *Book of Beauty* and the *Keepsake*, died insolvent in 1847, owing Lady Blessington £700. And in the spring of 1849 the Blessington–d'Orsay household was finally wrecked in a sea of debts. A sheriff's officer entered Gore House with an execution put in by Howell & James, a shop which supplied much of the furnishings of the house, and it was hourly expected that a whole army of other creditors would foreclose. Count d'Orsay, who had his own list of creditors, fled with his valet to Paris. Lady Blessington effected a life insurance for a large amount which she handed to the most importunate of her creditors, and the contents of Gore House, furniture, pictures, objets d'art and all her jewels were auctioned to settle the rest of her debts. Lady Blessington died only a few months later in Paris of 'an enlarged heart'. Sentimentalists interpreted this diagnosis as a broken heart.

Her niece, Marguerite Power, carried on the editorship of the *Keepsake* with the help of Mrs Newton Crosland. It was the latter who did most of the proof-correcting and corresponding with authors, since Miss Power lived chiefly in Paris after her aunt's death. Most of the well-known contributors continued to write for the *Keepsake*, knowing that Miss Power needed the money; and the seven volumes under her editorship were, Mrs Crosland contended, of a good standard—contributors including Thackeray, Elizabeth Barrett Browning, Robert Browning, H. F. Chorley, Tennyson, Mrs S. C. Hall, Eugene Sue, Madame Emile de Giradin and de Lamartine—'the little French articles being a pleasant innovation'. Mrs Newton Crosland also became assistant editor of *Friendship's Offering* when Leitch Ritchie was the ostensible editor but was more occupied with politics and other writing. She received a share of the editorial salary, corresponded with authors, corrected proofs, read manuscripts, and commissioned poems, stories, or sketches to go with plates already chosen. Sometimes she wrote these herself, if a writer failed to get his work in on time.

The last issue of the *Keepsake*, that of 1857, ended the era of the annuals. It was not only that they had gone out of fashion, but they had been killed by cheaper productions that were by then flooding the market. The annuals were essentially for the Christmas trade, and because they had large sales in Britain's Indian empire, as well as in America and the Colonies, they were produced by the end of July to be shipped for the long voyage round the Cape. With the opening up of the quicker 'overland' route to India, as it was called, Anglo-Indians were able to participate in the influx of cheap literature, and orders for expensive books fell off. Mrs Newton Crosland contrasts these new cheap publications with the higher standards of the annuals: 'Articles for the best annuals, whether paid for by a publisher's cheque or not, were always written for educated and cultivated readers. If a classical or mythological allusion or reference to world-famous *belles lettres* was made, there was reliance it would be understood; whereas when the flood of literature for the masses set in, a different order of things began to prevail. I remember the editor of a highly successful cheap publication saying to me, in reference to what I was doing for him, "Do not appear to teach, but at the same time do not give your readers credit for knowing anything".' And looking back in *Landmarks of a Literary Life* Mrs Newton Crosland wrote an affectionate defence of the annuals:

'It is now the fashion to sneer at and scorn these publications; but they fell out of favour, I am persuaded, not from deterioration of quality, but because the era of cheap literature was slowly advancing, and publishers could not pay distinguished authors liberally, and engravers such as the Findens and Heath the high prices they demanded, and still compete with five-shilling Christmas books, which were in a very few years to be superseded by shilling holiday numbers of magazines. It is within my own knowledge that for many years authors were exceedingly well paid when writing for or editing the Annuals. It is easy to talk of such and such an author giving but the "sweepings of his study" to these richly illustrated gift-books, but why should he have done so when the guerdon was so satisfactory? Brief the articles often were, but where goldsmiths work the dust is of value. Publications with contributions by Bulwer Lytton, Walter Savage Landor, Mrs S. C. Hall, William and Mary Howitt, Disraeli, Lord John Manners, the present Duke of Rutland, Mrs Hemans, L.E.L., Barry Cornwall, Mr Ruskin—who did not disdain *Friendship's Offering* for some of his very early but really beautiful poems—and a host of other writers of sterling merit could not be worthless.'

She could have added Charles Dickens, Captain Marryat, Mrs Maberly and Lord William Lennox. Lord Melbourne contributed a translation from the Greek of *The Power of Bacchus* to the *Drawing-Room Scrapbook*, and Elizabeth Barrett Browning contributed to *Finden's Tableaux*, a folio

46. 'Walking Dress—a pelisse robe of lavender peau de soie; rice straw bonnet with green peau de soie crown.' From the *Ladies' Cabinet of Fashion, Music, and Romance,* May 1838. Hand-coloured in the original.

annual edited first by Mrs S. C. Hall and then by Mary Russell Mitford. Indeed everybody who was anybody in the close, introspective circle of early Victorian literary society was at some time or other seduced into contributing to the annuals—either by money, or by snobbery, or by ambition for notice, or by feelings of friendship, or simply because they feared that if they did not contribute people would think that they had not been invited to do so.

Although the annuals were serious competitors to the yearly bound volumes of magazines, they did not, of course, in any way conflict with the weekly or monthly issues as they appeared. There were many periodicals for women during the twenty years when the annuals flourished. The ones which had been established for longest were the *Lady's Magazine*, the *Lady's Museum*, and *La Belle Assemblée*; then came the *World of Fashion* and the *Court Magazine*. There were the specialist fashion publications: the *Ladies' Fashionable Repository*, Townsend's *Quarterly*, and the *London & Paris Ladies' Magazine of Fashion*. Newcomers during the 1830s in their order of appearance were the *Lady's Pocket Magazine*, the *Magazine of the Beau Monde*, the *Royal Ladies' Magazine*, the *Ladies' Cabinet of Fashion*, the *New Monthly Belle Assemblée*, the *Christian Lady's Magazine*, the *Lady's Gazette of Fashion*, the *Magazine of Domestic Economy and Family Review*, and *Blackwood's Lady's Magazine*.

Most of the longer-lived publications kept their own characteristics through their whole life-span. In 1815 the *Lady's Magazine* was still scolding its contributors and would-be contributors—'The Orphan's Prayer' is not sufficiently correct for publication—and was still having cuts at Sir Walter Scott:

ON SCOTT'S POEM ENTITLED WATERLOO
How prostrate lie the heaps of slain
On Waterloo's immortal plain!
But none, by sabre or by shot,
Fell half so flat as Walter Scott—
Though none with magic spear or shield
E'er fought like him on Flodden Field.

The fiction is still on the same themes: 'Unfounded Jealousy'; 'Caroline, or the Blessings of Adversity'. There were improving essays—'On the Reward which Seldom Fails Attending the Performance of Maternal Duties, and the Happiness which Arises from Filial Obedience'; and there

47. 'Bridal Dress in India muslin over white peau de soie; veil of India muslin bordered with lace and embroidery.' From the *Ladies' Cabinet of Fashion, Music, and Romance,* May 1838. Hand-coloured in the original.

were beginning to be articles on quite daring controversial topics, such as: 'The Moral Expediency of Prohibiting the Intermarriage of the Offending Parties in Adultery considered'.

The *Ladies' Cabinet of Fashion, Music, and Romance* was very much on the same lines as the *Lady's Magazine*, although only pocket-sized. It was edited by Margaret and Beatrice de Courcy, published by G. Henderson, Old Bailey, and carried four coloured plates each month. These were crudely executed and not in the same class as those in the *Lady's Magazine*, although they improved in later years. It also carried steel engravings, and these were of excellent quality. Their subjects were the romantically picturesque scenes so fashionable at the time—ruins, castles, 'awful' mountains and 'dreadful' ravines. Occasionally the engravings illustrated stories in the magazine. Some numbers carried pages of music. These may have been a more regular feature than they seem, since they were frequently taken out of the issues before binding. The volume for 1833 has *The Last Words of Byron* set to music:

> The splendour of the poet's lyre,
> The eloquence of fame,
> The spirit's intellectual fire—
> The glory and the name—the name—
> The glory and the name.

One can well imagine this being extracted from the magazine and kept in the music album, ready for an evening when some handsome baritone was of the party.

Other features of the *Ladies' Cabinet* included a serial story, short stories, instructive articles, poetry. The poetry was in the sad, sentimental bitter-sweet vein, with melancholy titles such as 'The Wreck of Beauty', 'A Woman's Truth', 'The Child's Funeral', 'The Dying Girl'. All these are titles taken from one year's volume, so the cumulative effect over the years must have been very lowering to the spirits. 'The Dying Girl' tells the old, old story of innocence betrayed, the story that was repeated again and again in one form and another, in verse or in fiction, or in moralizing tale, throughout the magazines of the eighteenth century and after:

> THE DYING GIRL
> I weep—but 'tis not that I grieve
> This sweet and sunny world to leave;
> I mourn the barter of my youth
> For treason in the form of truth.

I deem'd not that this weary breast
So soon should wander to its rest;
But quick life's vital chain decays
When falsehood's mildew on it preys.
I felt the rust within my soul
Gnaw link from link—so snaps the whole!

Thou wilt be near when I am laid
In the dark churchyard's darkest shade;
But place no stone to tell the spot,
For was I not in life forgot?
And this proud spirit would disdain
The sighs that come, when sighs are vain;
The tears—his tears—which would not flow,
Till she for whom they fall was low!

And let no summer blossoms wave
To mock my lone and lowly grave;
Roses torn rudely from their bed,
Crush'd, broken, scentless, wither'd, dead,
Fling on my grave, and they shall be
In their bruis'd beauty, types of me!
Enough—but oh! if near this way
His steps—they will—should ever stray,
Tell him,—and chide not—that in death
The tremblings of my latest breath
Falter'd—to curse him? No—oh no—
The words would choke me in their flow!

Deep in my soul I love him still,
Through slight and suffering, wrong and ill.
Tell him the prayer, breath'd long and last,
Was peace and pardon for the past;
That pausing on the verge of time—
May Heav'n forgive me if 'tis crime—
My last, my fondest thoughts were his—
My dying pray'r—his future bliss!

A sketch at the end of the 1838 volume of the *Ladies' Cabinet* shows that
the Beatrice and Margaret de Courcy who edited it were mother and
daughter. It is called *At Home*:

48. 'Dinner Dress of straw-coloured velours épinglé, over an under dress of white satin. Scarlet toque of an antique form, profusely ornamented with ostrich feathers.' From the *Ladies' Cabinet of Fashion, Music, and Romance,* March 1838. Hand-coloured in the original.

Madam: Well, my dear Margaret, have you examined that packet of books your Papa was so kind to send us.

Margaret: Oh yes, Ma, they are all new works, and all written by ladies; delightful isn't it.

de Courcy: Good morning, ladies, I see you are already busy with the books.

Margaret: Oh, yes, and we are quite delighted at the idea of their appertaining to our own hitherto much despised sex. If you gentlemen or 'Lords of the Creation', as you are modestly pleased to call yourselves, don't look very sharp we shall soon carry everything our own way in literature and politics as well as millinery and pie-making.

de Courcy: That you surely will Margaret. I verily believe the great millennium of the reign of women upon earth is fast becoming about, what with female sovereigns and female writers.

Madam: There's Mrs Trollope literally devouring the globe, anatomizing in a six weeks' tour the social, moral and political condition of a country, and bringing home a panoramic view of each city in Europe, for the enlightenment of her friends and the replenishing of her coffers.

de Courcy: Did you remark the fillip she gets from Miss Martineau, who has succeeded her in *Americanizing*? A Yankee Bookseller encouraging the diffident political economist to write the domestic manners of friend Jonathan, said, 'Oh you must have seen a good deal, and then you can *Trollopize* a little, and so make a very readable book'.

Margaret: By the by, Mrs T. seems to have stepped into the shoes of Lady Morgan. Has she given up touring and book-making?

de Courcy: Can you ask such a question? the ruling passion is strong in death; you know Lady Morgan is almost blind, but she still twaddles on, as witness a farrago of absurdities called *The Princess* published last year.

Madam: But she was clever, and I hear she has, what with the profits of her writings and £300 a year pension, a clear income of £1,000 per annum.

de Courcy: An additional proof of the gullibility of the public.

Margaret: Fie you naughty man. You are too severe upon us ladies—jealousy of course. But you know Miss Pardoe has been to Constantinople—have you read her *City of the Sultan*?—How did you like it?

49. 'Dinner Dress in green velvet lined with white satin, worn over a white satin petticoat. Chapeau a l'Agnes Sorel of black velvet, adorned with a bird of Paradise.' From the *Ladies' Cabinet of Fashion, Music, and Romance,* April 1838. Hand-coloured in the original.

de Courcy: As a fly does treacle. I was smothered by its turgid sentimentality, its rose hues and rose odours, and all that sort of thing. I
believe we have now enumerated the whole constellation of female
book-makers.

Margaret: No! No! there's Miss Landon, a poetess, novelist, *New
Monthliest*, Annualist, in short a very miracle of versatility.

de Courcy: True, true, I had forgotten. But what I mean is we have had
enough of them for the present.

Enough of them then for the present, literary women. We have followed
them into the first year of the Victorian age, and from then on they became
more and more Victorian, less and less individual. De Courcy might be
predicting the great millennium of the reign of women to be at hand, but
as things turned out the progress women had made in the eighteenth
century was halted, even reversed. Women were to remain subject to men
for a very long time to come; and for the most part they accepted their
subjugation dutifully, as became intellectually inferior creatures.

By the same token, as the century progressed, women's magazines
became ever more obsessively domestic. Even before Victoria came to the
throne, the social climate had changed, the atmosphere for women had
begun to get claustrophobic. There had been a reaction to the permissive-
ness of the Regency period; and the influence of the narrow-minded,
newly-rich industrialists and their families from the North, many of whom
belonged to evangelical sects, was beginning to permeate through middle-
class society. All this was reflected in the publications of the 1830s. Consider the annuals, how much they embodied of what we now think of as
Victorian. Take only their editors' practice of choosing the illustrations
first and then commissioning stories or verses to go with them, how essentially this seems to belong to the period when every picture had to tell a
story. The de Courcy's *Ladies' Cabinet* was a prudish publication, and
many of the magazine titles of the 1830s are indicative of the way things
were going. In 1832, for example, there was the *Maids, Wives, and Widow's
Penny Magazine* edited by Mrs C. Baron-Wilson, whose very name suggests a middle-class lady with ideas about what would be good for the
'deserving poor'. Six years later there was a magazine simply called the
Young Widow—short-lived, as one might expect. After all, even in those
days of high death rates, such a restricted class of reader cannot have
offered at all a promising circulation potential, nor an attractive proposi-

tion to advertisers. From 1834 to 1839 there was the *Christian Lady's Magazine* edited by Miss Charlotte E. Phelan. In 1836 the *Magazine of Domestic Economy* was launched and ran economically for eight years; and in 1838 there appeared the *Servant's Magazine, or Female Domestic's Instructor*. This publication flourished for thirty-one years. It must surely have been the mistresses who bought it for their servants. The servants themselves would have appreciated a more escapist magazine for their few off-duty hours, something a little less on the job.

As the magazines narrowed their horizons, the journalists became more parochial. There were, of course, women writers in other fields—writers of novels, *belles lettres*, poetry, travel books—many of them held in high regard. But those who worked for newspapers and periodicals were spoken of scornfully as 'penny-a-liners'. Somehow this term seems to have an even more contemptuous ring to it than the 'scribbling females' of a century earlier. And indeed the scribbling females were of another breed. They at least wrote with fire and venom, not mincing their words nor their matter. Most of the penny-a-liners wrote so puerilely, about such trivialities, and were so unprofessional, as to deserve to be held in contempt. When Arnold Bennett was editor of *Woman* he wrote a little book called *Journalism for Women* (1898) in which he said:

'In Fleet Street there are not two sexes, but two species—journalists and women journalists, and we treat the species differently. Women are not expected to suffer the same discipline, nor are they judged by the same standards. In Fleet Street femininity is an absolution, not an accident.'

Before Victoria, as we have seen, women writers depending upon their pens for a living had to be both tough and talented to survive at all. They were literally writing for their lives, and they neither expected nor received absolution.

Chronological List of Periodicals Mentioned in the Text

In the various sources consulted, minor differences occasionally occur, and in such cases the date given here is that which has the most supporting evidence. Differences in cataloguing can come about through eighteenth-century monthly magazines being normally issued on the first day of the month following the month which is printed on them: thus the number designated December of one year would usually be issued on 1 January of the next. Annual publications—such as almanacks, miscellanies, ladies' pocket books, and the 'Annuals' of the early nineteenth century—tended to be issued in December of the previous year: thus the issue designated, say, 1820 would in fact be published in December 1819, or some time earlier in order to catch Christmas mails to countries overseas.

Editors' names are given here only when they constitute part of the title (in such cases they were usually pseudonyms), or in order to distinguish between two periodicals of the same or very similar title. Otherwise, editors' names, if known, will be found in the text.

1690–6	*The Athenian Gazette, or Casuistical Mercury* (after No. 1, entitled *Athenian Mercury*)
1691–2	*The London Mercury* (after No. 8, *Lacedemonian Mercury*)
1692–4	*The Gentleman's Journal, or the Monthly Miscellany*
1693	*The Ladies' Mercury*
1694	*The Ladies' Dictionary, by John Dunton*
1696–7	*The Night-Walker, or Evening Rambles in Search after Lewd Women*
1696	*Pegasus*

1704–1840	*The Ladies' Diary, or The Women's Almanack* (then 1840–71 united with the *Gentleman's Diary* as *The Lady's and Gentleman's Diary*)
1705	*The Wandering Spy*
1707–10	*The Monthly Miscellany, or Memoirs for the Curious*
1708–11	*The British Apollo, or Curious Amusements for the Ingenious*
1709–11	*The Tatler*

| 1709–10 | *The Female Tatler*, by Mrs Crackenthorpe |
| 1709 | *The Whisperer*, by Mrs Jenny Distaff |

1710–14	*The Examiner*
1710	*Records of Love, or Weekly Amusements for the Fair Sex*
1711	*The Freethinker*, printed by J. Baker
1711–12	*The Spectator*
1711	*Delights for the Ingenious, or A Monthly Entertainment for the Curious of Both Sexes*
1711–12	*The Protestant Post Boy*
1713	*The Guardian*, by Richard Steele
1714–18	*The Lover*, by Marmaduke Myrtle, Gent
1714	*The Spinster*, by Rachel Woolpack
1714	*The Reader*
1715	*The Lover*, to which is added *The Reader*
1715–16	*Town Talk, In a Letter to a Lady in the Country*
1715	*The Englishman*
1716	*Tea-Table*
1716	*The Orphan*
1716	*Chit Chat*, by Humphrey Philroye
1716	*The Charitable Mercury*
1717	*The Scourge*
1718–19	*The Freethinker, or Essays on Ignorance*, by Ambrose Phillips
1718	*The Lover and Reader*, by the Author of the *Tatler* and *Spectator*
1719–20	*The Orphan Reviv'd, or Powell's Weekly Journal*
1719	*The Weekly Medley, or Gentlemen's Recreation*
1719	*The Plebian*

1720	*The Theatre*, by Sir J. Edgar (Richard Steele)
1720–1	*The Free Thinker*
1722–4	*Bibliotheca Literaria*, ed. S. Webb
1723–4	*The Visiter*
1723	*The Young Ladies' Miscellany, or Youth's Innocent and Rational Amusement*
1724	*The Tea Table*, by Mrs Eliza Haywood
1727	*The Ladies' Journal* (Dublin)
1728	*The Parrot*, by Mrs Penelope Prattle

| 1731–1907 | *The Gentleman's Magazine, or Monthly Intelligence* |

274

1732–85	*The London Magazine, or Gentleman's Monthly Intelligencer*; then *The New London Magazine*, 1785–97
1732–3	*The Friendly Writer and Register of Truth*, by Ruth Collins (pseud.)
1733	*The Bee, or Universal Weekly Pamphlet*
1733	*The Lady's Magazine, or Monthly Intelligencer*
1736–7	*The Country Magazine, or The Gentleman's & Lady's Pocket Companion*
1737–8	*The Nonsense of Commonsense*
1737–9	*Commonsense*
1738–9	*The Lady's Magazine, or the Compleat Library*
1741–52	*The Family Almanack*, by Nicholas Culpepper
1741–1840	*The Gentleman's Diary, or the Mathematical Repository* (then united with the *Ladies' Diary* 1840–71)
1744–6	*The Female Spectator*
1746	*The Parrot, with a Compendium of the Times*
1747	*The Lady's Weekly Magazine*, by Mrs Penelope Pry
1749–50	*The Traveller's Magazine, or Gentleman's & Lady's Agreeable Companion*
1749	*The Palladian*
1749–53	*The Ladies' Magazine, or the Universal Entertainer*, by Jasper Goodwill of Oxford, Esq.
1749–1844	*The Monthly Review*

1750–2	*The Rambler* by Samuel Johnson
1750–3	*The Midwife, or Old Woman's Magazine*
1752	*The Lady's Curiosity, or Weekly Apollo*, by Nestor Druid
1752–65	*The Gentleman's & Lady's Palladian*, by J. Tipper
1755–6	*The Old Maid* by Mary Singleton, Spinster
1756	*The Young Lady* by Euphrosine
1756–79	*The Critical Review, or Annals of Literature* (intermittently)
1757–79	*The Gentleman & Ladies' Diary & Palladian*
1758–60	*The Grand Magazine of Magazines, or Universal Register*
1758–60	*The Universal Chronicle* (containing the *Idler*)
1759–63	*The Lady's Magazine, or Polite Companion for the Fair Sex* (Goldsmith)
1759	*The Bee*
1759	*The Busy Body*

1759–60   *The Weekly Magazine, or Gentleman's & Lady's Polite Companion*
1759–71   *The New Royal Magazine, or Gentleman's & Lady's Companion*

1760   *The British Magazine*, edited by Smollett
1760   *The Monthly Melody, or Polite Amusement for Gentlemen & Ladies*
1760–1   *The Imperial, or Complete Monthly Intelligencer*
1760   *The Royal Female Magazine* (containing the *Meddler*)
1760–1836 *The Public Ledger*
1760–1   *The Lady's Museum* (Charlotte Lennox and Hugh Kelly)
1760–7   *The British Magazine, or Monthly Repository for Gentlemen & Ladies*
1761–5   *The Court Magazine, or Royal Chronicle* (then the *Court & City*; then *The Court, City, & Country*)
1761–1866 *Saint James' Chronicle*
1762–70   *The Universal Museum, or Gentleman's & Lady's Polite Magazine of History, Politicks, and Literature*
1763   *The Country Magazine, Calculated for the Gentleman, the Farmer, & his Wife*
1764   *The Court, City & Country Magazine*
1765–9   *The Court Miscellany, or Ladies' New Magazine,* by Matilda Wentworth & others (then to 1771 *The Gentleman & Lady's New Magazine*)
1769   *The Ladies' Complete Pocket-Book*

1770–1832 *The Lady's Magazine, or Entertaining Companion for the Fair Sex*
1771–9   *The Ladies' Own Memorandum Book, or Daily Pocket Journal*
1772   *The Gentleman's & Lady's Magazine,* by James Tytler (monthly)
1772   *The Gentleman & Lady's Weekly Magazine*
1772–1937 *The Morning Post, or Cheap Daily Advertiser*
1773–5   *The Sentimental Magazine, or General Assemblage of Science, Taste, etc.*
1774–5   *The Monthly Miscellany, or Gentleman & Lady's Compleat Magazine*
1774–1820 *The Ladies' Museum, or Complete Pocket Memorandum Book* (William Lane, intermittent annual).
1775–86   *The Lady's & Gentleman's Diary* (Carnan)
1775   *The Matrimonial Magazine, or Monthly Anecdotes of Love & Marriage*

1776   *The Gentleman & Lady's Magazine in French & English*

1776–86   *The Lady's & Gentleman's Diary, or Royal Almanack*, by Reuben Burrow

1776–9   *The British Gazette & Public Advertiser*

1777   *The Magazine à la Mode, or Fashionable Miscellany*

1777–8   *The Gentleman's & Lady's Museum*

1779–80   *The Mirror*, by Henry Mackenzie (Edinburgh; other editions up to 1827)

1779–1805 *Johnson's British Gazette & Sunday Monitor* (1805–14 *Johnson's Sunday Monitor & British Gazette* (& *London Recorder*); 1814–29 *The Sunday Monitor & London Recorder*)

1780–8   *The Novelists' Magazine*, by James Harrison

1780   *The Weekly Mirror*, by James Tytler

1781–2   *The Lady's Poetical Magazine* (annual, also in 1791)

1785–1818 *The Ladies' Mirror, or Mental Companions* (intermittent annual)

1786–95   *The New Lady's Magazine, or Polite & Entertaining Companion for the Fair Sex*

1786–7   *The New Novelists' Magazine*

1786   *The Fashionable Magazine, or Lady's & Gentleman's Recorder of New Fashions*

1787   *The Female Guardian*

1787–94   *The World, or Fashionable Gazette*

1788   *The Court, City, & Country Magazine, or Gentleman & Lady's Universal and Polite Instructor*

1788–9   *The Family Magazine*, ed. Mrs Sarah Trimmer

1788–1800 *The Lady's Daily Companion* (annual)

1789   *Lady's Gazette & Evening Advertiser*

1789–90   *The Oracle, or Bell's New World*

1791   *The Novelist* (then from second monthly issue renamed *The Polite Repository, or Amusing Companion*)

1791–6   *The Bon Ton Magazine, or Microscope of Fashion & Folly*

1792–6   *The Carlton House Magazine, or Annals of Taste, Fashion & Politeness*

1792–1925 *Boyle's Fashionable Court Guide* (with changes of title until merged with *Webster's Royal Red Book*, 1925)

1793   *The Female Mentor*

1794–1803 *The Gallery of Fashion*
1794   *The Pocket Magazine, or Elegant Repository of Useful & Polite Literature*
1795–6   *The Bouquet, or Blossoms of Fancy*
1795–1810 *The Monthly Mirror, Reflecting Men & Manners*
1795   *The Lady's New & Elegant Pocket Magazine, or Elegant & Entertaining Companion for the Fair Sex*
1796   *The Lady's Pocket Magazine, or Elegant & Entertaining Companion for the Fair Sex*
1796–1896 *Bell's Weekly Messenger*, continued as *Country Sport*
1797–1804 *The Monthly Visitor & Entertaining Pocket Companion & New Family Magazine*
1798–1806 *The Magazine of Female Fashions of London & Paris*
1798–1828 *The Lady's Monthly Museum* (then 1929–32 *The Ladies Museum*; then united with *The Lady's Magazine*)
1799–1800 *The Young Gentleman's & Lady's Magazine, or Universal Repository of Knowledge*

1803   *Mirroir de la Mode* by Madame Lanchester
1804   *The Elegancies of Fashion & General Remembrancer of Taste & Manners*, by Florio Honeysuckle
1806–32   *La Belle Assemblée, or Bell's Court & Fashionable Magazine* (continued as the *Court Magazine & Belle Assemblée* to 1837, then incorporated with the *Ladies' Magazine & Museum*, etc.)
1806–10   *Le Beau Monde, or Literary & Fashionable Magazine* (then *Le Beau Monde & Monthly Register to 1810*)
1806–9   *The Record of Fashion & Court Elegance*
1809–95   *Ladies' Fashionable Repository*
1809–29   *Ackermann's Repository of Arts, Literature, Commerce, Manufactures, Fashion, and Politics*
1809–1967 *The Quarterly Review*

1811–30   *The Female Instructor* (annual)
1811–18   *Ladies' New & Elegant Pocket Book, or Young Women's Companion* (intermittent annual)
1811–15   *The Scourge, or Monthly Expositor of Imposture & Folly*
1813–15   *The Female Preceptor*
1814   *The Domestic Magazine*

1814   *Female* (annual, also 1815 and 1816)
1814–81   *The New Monthly Magazine*
1815–18   *The British Lady's Magazine & Monthly Miscellany*
1817–   *Blackwood's Magazine*
1817–62   *The Literary Gazette*
1818–21   *The New Bon Ton Magazine, or Telescope of the Times*
1819–21   *The Ladies' Literary Cabinet*
1819   *The New British Lady's Magazine*

1820–31   *The London Journal*
1820–84   *The New Monthly Magazine*
1820–92   *John Bull*
1821–56   *The Cottager's Monthly Visitor*
1821–3   *The Mirror*
1822–5   *The Album* (quarterly)
1822   *The Gazette of Fashion & Magazine of the Fine Arts*
1823–88   *Townsend's Quarterly Selection of Parisian Costumes* (from 1825 monthly)
1823–47   *The Forget-Me-Not*
1823–47   *The Mirror of Literature, Amusement and Instruction*
1823   *Fashion as it Flies, or The Ladies' Little Messenger of Parisian Fashions* (English version of the *Petit Courrier des Dames*)
1824   *The New Female Instructor*
1824   *The Graces*
1824–44   *Friendship's Offering, or Annual Remembrancer*
1824–51   *The World of Fashion* (cont. as the *Ladies' Monthly Magazine and World of Fashion* 1852–79, then as *Le monde Elegant, or the World of Fashion,* 1880–91)
1825–39   *The Ladies' Pocket Magazine* (annual)
1824   *Miroir des Modes Parisiennes*
1824–8   *The Family Oracle of Health, Economy, and Good Living*
1825–43   *The Age*
1825   *The Quizzical Gazette, Extraordinary & Wonderful Advertiser*
1825–35   *The Literary Souvenir, or Cabinet of Poetry & Romance*
1825–37   *The Family Magazine*
1826–37   *The Amulet, or Christian & Literary Remembrances*
1826–8   *Graham's Casket, Ladies' & Gentleman's Magazine*
1827–42   *The Court Magazine & Monthly Critic*

1828–91   *The London & Paris Ladies' Magazine of Fashion*
1828–32   *Winter's Wreath* (then absorbed in *Friendship's Offering*)
1828–57   *The Keepsake*
1828–1921 *The Anniversary*
1828–30   *The Bijou*
1828   *The Athenaeum*
1829–37   *The Juvenile Forget-Me-Not*
1829–32   *Affection's Offering*
1829–32   *The Ladies' Museum* (formerly *Lady's Monthly Museum*; from
           1832–7 united with the *Lady's Magazine* as *The Lady's
           Magazine & Museum of Belles Lettres*; then 1838–47 united
           with the *Court Magazine* as *The Court Magazine & Monthly
           Critic and Lady's Magazine & Museum of Belles Lettres*)

1830   *The Female Instructor, or Young Woman's Friend & Companion*
1830   *The Iris—A Religious & Literary Offering*
1830   *The Family Magazine*
1830–5   *The Lady's Pocket Magazine*
1830–82   *Fraser's Magazine for Town & Country*
1830–3   *Affection's Gift*
1831–5   *The Comic Offering, or Ladies' Melange of Literary Mirth*, ed. by
           Louisa H. Sheridan
1831   *The Quizzical Gazette & Merry Companion*
1831   *The Remembrancer*, ed. by T. Roscoe
1831–43   *The Magazine of the Beau Monde, a Monthly Journal of Fashion*
           (then *Le Nouveau Beau Monde* 1844–61; then merged in *Lon-
           don & Paris Ladies' Magazine of Fashion & Polite Literature*)
1831–5   *The Royal Ladies' Magazine and Archives of the Court of St
           James's*
1832–7   *The Christian's Penny Magazine*
1832–46   *Knight's Penny Magazine*
1832–7   *The Lady's Magazine & Museum of Belles Lettres*
1832–45   *Heath's Picturesque Annual*
1832   *The Isis, A London Weekly Publication edited by a Lady of the
           Rotunda* (E. S. Carlile)
1832–54   *The Drawing Room Scrapbook*
1832–3   *The Ladies' Penny Gazette*

1832–70   *The Ladies' Cabinet of Fashion, Music & Romance* (from July 1852 vols. of this identical with those of the *New Monthly Belle Assemblée and The Ladies' Companion*, except title pages)

1832   *The Boudoir, or British Magazine*

1832–3   *The Maids, Wives & Widows* (*penny*) *Magazine*; continued as *The Weekly Belle Assemblée, etc.* 1833–4 (running title *The Penny Belle Assemblée*); from 1834–70 *The New Monthly Belle Assemblée*, etc., also including from July 1852 *The Ladies' Cabinet & the Ladies' Companion at Home & Abroad.*

1832–54   *Chamber's Edinburgh Journal* (then cont. as *Chamber's Journal*)

1833–49   *Heath's Book of Beauty*

1833   *Le Beau Monde Reviv'd*, ed. J. Belcher

1834–7   *The Family Magazine* (incorp. in *Ward's Miscellany*, 1837)

1834–70   *The New Monthly Belle Assemblée* (from July 1852 identical with *The Ladies' Cabinet & the Ladies' Companion at Home & Abroad*)

1834–8   *The English Annual*

1834–94   *The Ladies' Gazette of Fashion*

1834–49   *The Christian Lady's Magazine*

1836–60   *Blackwood's Lady's Magazine & Gazette of the Fashionable World*

1836–44   *The Magazine of Domestic Economy* (from 1843–4 *and Family Review*)

1836–7   *The Library of Fiction, or Family Story Teller*, ed. Charles Dickens

1836–40   *Gems of Beauty*

1837–68   *Bentley's Miscellany*

1837–41   *Finden's Tableaux of the Affections*, ed. Mrs S. C. Hall and Miss Mitford

1837   *Le Miroir de Paris et Londres*

1837–8   *Ward's Miscellany*

1838–69   *The Servant's Magazine, or Female Domestic's Instructor*

1838–47   *The Court Magazine & Monthly Critic, & Ladies' Magazine & Museum of Belles Lettres*

1838   *The Young Widow*

1839–70   *The Ladies' Cabinet of Fashion, Music, & Romance* (from 1852 identical to *New Monthly Belle Assemblée* except title pages)

Bibliography

When a book is edited with considerable introduction and notes, it is listed here under the name of the editor as well as that of the author.

ALICE ACLAND. *Caroline Norton*. Constable, 1948.

ALEXANDER ANDREWS. *The History of British Journalism*. Richard Bentley, 1859.

ANON. *Fables for the Female Sex*. R. Francklin, 1744.

ANON. *Public Characters*: Vol. I, 1798–9; Vol. II, 1799–1800; Vol. III, 1800–1; Vol. IV, 1801–2; Vol. VII, 1805. R. Philips.

JOHN ASHTON. *Social Life in the Reign of Queen Anne*. Chatto & Windus, 1883.

MARY ASTELL. *A Serious Proposal to the Ladies for the Advancement of their True and Greatest Interest* (1694). Richard Wilkin, 1697.

JANE AUSTEN. *Northanger Abbey*. First published 1818.

ROBERT BAGE. *Hermstrong* (1796). The Folio Society, 1960.

GEORGE BALLARD. *Memoirs of Several Ladies of Great Britain, Who Have Been Celebrated for Their Writings or Skill in the Learned Languages, Arts and Sciences*. W. Jackson, 1752.

IRIS BARRY (ed.). *Memoirs of Mrs Laetitia Pilkington, 1712–50, Written by Herself*. 1st ed., 1748–54. Reprinted by George Routledge, 1928.

APHRA BEHN. *All the Histories and Novels written by the late Ingenious Mrs Behn, Intire in One Volume*. 6th Edition. J. D. & M. Wellington, 1718.

APHRA BEHN. *The Rover*. Edited by Frederick M. Link. Edward Arnold, 1967. (First published, 1677).

APHRA BEHN. *Poems Upon Several Occasions, with a Voyage to the Island Of Love*. R. Tonson & J. Tonson, 1684.

ARNOLD BENNETT. *Journalism for Women*. John Lane, the Bodley Head, 1898.

DOROTHY BLAKEY. *The Minerva Press, 1790–1820*. The Bibliographical Society at the University Press, Oxford, 1939.

LAMAN BLANCHARD. *Life and Literary Remains of L.E.L.* Henry Colburn, 1841.

JAMES BOSWELL. *The Life of Samuel Johnson, LL.D., with His Correspondence and Conversations*. Edited by Edward Malone. James Blackwood, 1807.

Boswell's London Journal, 1762–3. Prepared for the press by Frederick A. Pottle, Heinemann, 1950.

ANDREW BOYLE. *An Index to the Annuals,* Vol. I, *The Authors, 1720–1750.* Privately printed by Andrew Boyle (Booksellers) Ltd, 1967.

JOHN BRITTON and THOMAS REES. *Reminiscences of Literary London from 1779–1853.* Suckling & Gallaway, 1896.

FRANCES BURNEY. *Evelina, or The History of a Young Lady's Entrance into the World.* Introd. and notes by Annie Raine Ellis .Bohn's Novelist's Library, 1881.

THE REV. THOMAS CAMPBELL. *Diary of a Visit to England,* Feb.–May 1775. Edited by James Clifford. Cambridge University Press, 1947.

GEORGE E. G. CATLIN. *Introduction to The Rights of Women,* by Mary Wollstonecraft. Everyman Edition, 1929.

DAVID CECIL. *Two Quiet Lives* (Part 1, 'Dorothy Osborne'). Constable, 1948.

COLIN CLAIR (ed.). *Literary Anecdotes of the Eighteenth Century,* by John Nichols F.S.A., Centaur Press, Fontwell, Sussex, 1967.

A. S. COLLINS. *Authorship in the Days of Johnson, 1726–80.* Robert Holden, 1927.

A. S. COLLINS. *The Profession of Letters, 1780–1832.* Routledge, 1928.

MRS NEWTON CROSLAND. *Landmarks of a Literary Life, 1820–92.* Sampson Low, Marston & Co., 1893.

HENRY CURWEN. *A History of Booksellers—The Old and the New.* Chatto & Windus, 1873.

MARGARET DALZIEL. *Popular Fiction One Hundred Years Ago.* Cohen & West, 1957.

MARY DAVYS. *Familiar Letters Betwixt a Gentleman and a Lady* (1725). Augustan Reprint Society, No. 54, 1955.

ISAAC DISRAELI. *The Curiosities of Literature.* Frederick Warne, 1839.

W. HEPWORTH DIXON (ed.). *Lady Morgan's Memoirs.* Wm H. Allen & Co., 1863.

JUDITH DRAKE. An Essay in Defence of the Female Sex. Third edition. A. Roper and R. Chavel, 1697.

JOHN DUNTON. *The Life and Errors of John Dunton, Citizen of London.* J. Nichols, Son & Bentley, 1818.

JOHN DUNTON. The Ladies Dictionary; being a General Entertainment for the Fair Sex. Printed at the Raven in the Poultry, 1694.

ANNIE RAINE ELLIS. Introduction to *Evelina,* by Frances Burney. Bohn's Novelists' Library, 1881.

JOHN FORSTER. *The Life & Times of Oliver Goldsmith* (1848). 7th edition. Bickers & Son, 1878.

H. R. FOX-BOURNE. *English Newspapers, Chapters in the History of Journalism.* Chatto & Windus, 1887.

DOROTHY GARDINER. *English Girlhood at School.* Oxford University Press, 1929.

M. D. GEORGE. *London Life in the Eighteenth Century.* Kegan Paul, French, Trubner, 1925.

WILLIAM GODWIN. *Memoirs of Mary Wollstonecraft.* Constable's Miscellany, 1928.

OLIVER GOLDSMITH. *Collected Works.* Edited by Friedmann. Vol. III, *Specimens of a Magazine in Miniature.*

MRS C. G. F. GORE. *Mothers and Daughters.* Richard Bentley, 1834.

S. C. HALL. *Retrospect of a Long Life, from 1815 to 1883.* Richard Bentley, 1883.

S. C. HALL. *A Book of Memories of Great Men & Women of the Age, From Personal Acquaintance.* Virtue & Co., 1876 (new edition).

ROBERT HALSBAND. *The Life of Lady Mary Wortley Montagu.* Clarendon Press, 1956.

ROBERT HALSBAND (ed.). *The Nonsense of Commonsense,* 1737–8, by Lady Mary Wortley Montagu. Northwestern University, Evanston, 1947.

ELIZA HAYWOOD. *History of Miss Betsy Thoughtless.* Harrison & Co., 1783 (first published 1751).

GEORGINA HILL. *Women in English Life from Mediaeval to Modern Times.* Richard Bentley, 1896.

VYVYAN HOLLAND. *Hand Coloured Fashion Plates, 1770 to 1899.* Batsford, 1955.

JOHN CAMDEN HOTTEN. *The Life and Adventure of the Author of 'Doctor Syntax'* (Introduction to *Doctor Syntax's Three Tours,* by William Combe). John Camden Hotten, Piccadilly, Undated.

DEREK HUDSON. *British Journalists and Newspapers*. Collins, 1945.

F. KNIGHT HUNT. *The Fourth Estate: Contributions towards a History of Newspapers, and of the Liberty of the Press*. David Bogue, 1850.

LEIGH HUNT. *Autobiography*. Edited by J. E. Morpurgo, Cresset Press, 1949 (first published 1860).

ELIZABETH INCHBALD. *A Simple Story*. G. G. J. & J. Robinson, 1791.

MASON JACKSON. *The Pictorial Press: Its Origins & Progress*. Hurst & Blackett, 1855.

MURIEL JAEGER. *Before Victoria: Changing Standards & Behaviour, 1787–1837*. Chatto & Windus, 1956; Penguin, 1967.

R. BRIMLEY JOHNSON. *Blue Stocking Letters*. John Lane, 1926.

M. G. JONES. *Hannah More*. Cambridge University Press, 1952.

JULIA KAVANAGH. *English Women of Letters: Biographical Sketches*. Hurst & Blackett, 1863.

CHARLES KNIGHT. *Shadows of the Old Booksellers*. Peter Davies, 1927 (first published 1865).

CHARLES LAMB. *Essays of Elia*; and *Last Essays of Elia*. Methuen, 1935.

CHARLES LAMB. *Letters*. Edited by E. V. Lucas. Methuen, 1935.

JAMES LAVER. *Fashion & Fashion Plates, 1800–1900*. King Penguin Books, 1943.

JAMES LAVER. Preface to *Harriette Wilson's Memoirs of Herself & Others*. Peter Davis, 1929.

Q. D. LEAVIS. *Fiction & the Reading Public*. Chatto & Windus, 1965 (first published 1932).

W. S. LEWIS. Introduction to *The Castle of Otranto*, by Horace Walpole (1764). Oxford University Press, 1964.

S. R. LITTLEWOOD. *Elizabeth Inchbald & Her Circle (1753–1821)*. David O'Connor, 1921.

E. V. LUCAS (ed.). *Letters of Charles Lamb*. Methuen, 1935.

JAMES PELLER MALCOLM. *Anecdotes of the Manners and Customs of London During the 18th Century*. Longman, Hurst, Rees, and Orme, 1810.

DOROTHY MARSHALL. *Eighteenth Century England*. Longmans, 1962.

DOROTHY MARSHALL. *English People in the 18th Century*. Longmans, 1956.

GERTRUDE TOUNSHEND MAYER. *Women of Letters*. Richard Bentley, 1894.

J. FITZGERALD MOLLOY. *The Most Gorgeous Lady Blessington*. 4th ed., Downey & Co., Covent Garden, 1897.

DORIS LANGLEY MOORE. *Fashion through Fashion Plates, 1771–1970*. Ward Lock, 1971.

LADY MARY WORTLEY MONTAGU. *The Nonsense of Commonsense, 1737–38*. Northwestern University, Evanston, 1947.

SYDNEY, LADY MORGAN. *Memoirs, Autobiography, Diaries, & Correspondence*. Edited by W. Hepworth Dixon. William H. Allen, 1863.

SYDNEY, LADY MORGAN. *Passages from my Autobiography*. Richard-Bentley, 1859.

STANLEY MORISON. *The English Newspaper, 1632–1932*. Cambridge University Press, 1932.

STANLEY MORISON. *John Bell, 1745–1831*. Cambridge University Press, 1930.

J. E. MORPURGO (ed.). *The Autobiography of Leigh Hunt*. Cresset Press, 1949.

JOHN NICHOLS F.S.A. *Literary Anecdotes of the Eighteenth Century*. Edited by Colin Clair. Centaur Press. Fontwell, 1967.

KATE O'BRIEN. *English Diaries and Journals*. Collins, 1947.

DOROTHY OSBORNE. *Letters to Sir William Temple (1652–4)*. Edited by Edward Abbott Parry. J. M. Dent, Wayfarer's Library, undated.

CHARLES PEBODY. *English Journalism and the Men Who Have Made It*. Cassel, Petter, Galpin & Co. 1882.

LAETITIA PILKINGTON. *Memoirs of Mrs Laetitia Pilkington, 1712–50, Written by Herself*. 1st edn 1748–54 Reprinted 1928 with introd. by Iris Barry. George Routledge & Sons, 1928.

MARJORIE PLANT. *The English Book Trade*. George Allen & Unwin, 1965.

FREDERICK A. POTTLE (ed.). *Boswell's London Journal, 1762–3*. Heinemann, 1950.

JAMES PRIOR. *Life of Oliver Goldsmith M.B.* John Murray, 1837.

PETER QUENNELL. Introduction to John Cleland's *Memoirs of a Woman of Pleasure (Fanny Hill)*, first published 1749. G. P. Putnam's Sons, New York, 1963.

ANN RADCLIFFE. *The Mysteries of Udolpho; A Romance Interspersed with some Pieces of Poetry.* 6th edn. in 4 vols, Longman, Hurst, Rees and Orme, 1806 (first published 1794).

WALTER RALEIGH (ed.). *The Complete Works of George Savile, 1st Marquess of Halifax.* Oxford University Press, 1912.

THOMAS REES and JOHN BRITTON. *Reminiscences of Literary London from 1779–1853.* Suckling & Gallaway, 1896.

CLARA REEVE. *The Old English Baron.* (1778), first published as *Champion of Virtue,* 1777. Edition printed by C. & W. Thompson, Sheffield; sold by Longman, Hurst & Co., London.

SAMUEL RICHARDSON. *Pamela,* or *Virtue Rewarded,* First published 1740.

MICHAEL SADLEIR. *Blessington d'Orsay—a Masquerade.* Constable, 1933.

MICHAEL SADLEIR. *Bulwer and His Wife. A Panorama, 1803–36.* Constable, 1931.

MICHAEL SADLEIR. *Things Past.* (Essay entitled *All Horrid—Jane Austen and the Gothic Romance*). Constable, 1944.

GEORGE SAVILE, 1st MARQUESS OF HALIFAX. *The Lady's New-Year's Gift or Advice to a Daughter,* 1700. (Included in the 'Complete Works' in *Miscellanies.* Edited by Walter Raleigh, Oxford University Press, 1912).

SACHEVERELL SITWELL. *Gallery of Fashion, 1790–1822.* B. T. Batsford, 1949.

RICHARD STEELE (ed.). *The Ladies' Library, Written by a Lady,* 3 vols. 1714.

JONATHAN SWIFT. *Journal to Stella.* Edited by Harold Williams. Oxford University Press, 1963.

JAMES D. SYMON. *The Press and Its Story.* Seeley, Service & Co., 2 vols. 1914.

MRS THOMSON. *Recollections of Literary Characters & Celebrated Places,* 2 vols. Richard Bentley, 1854.

J. M. S. TOMPKINS. *The Popular Novel in England, 1770–1800.* Constable, 1932; Methuen, 1969.

MRS SARAH TRIMMER. *Life and Writings of Mrs Trimmer,* 2 vols. F. C. & J. Rivington, & J. Johnson & Co., 1816.

C. E. VULLIAMY. *English Letter Writers.* Collins, 1945.

ADA WALLAS. *Before the Blue Stockings.* George Allen & Unwin, 1929,

HORACE WALPOLE. *The Castle of Otranto.* Oxford University Press. 1964 (first published 1764).

IAN WATT. *The Rise of the Novel: Studies in Defoe, Richardson, and Fielding.* Chatto & Windus, 1957; Peregrine Books, 1963.

CHARLES WELSH. *A Bookseller of the Last Century, Being Some Account of the Life of John Newbury.* Griffith, Farren, Okeden & Welsh, 1885.

CYNTHIA L. WHITE. *Women's Magazines, 1639–1968.* Michael Joseph, 1969.

FRANCIS WILLIAMS. *Dangerous Estate—The Anatomy of Newspapers.* Longmans, Green, 1957.

HAROLD WILLIAMS. (ed.) *Swift's Journal to Stella,* 2 vols. Oxford, 1963.

JANE WILLIAMS. *The Literary Women of England.* Saunders, Ottley, & Co., 1861.

HARRIETTE WILSON. *Memoirs of Herself and Others.* Peter Davis, 1929 (first published Stockdale 1825).

MARY WOLLSTONECRAFT. *A Vindication of the Rights of Women.* Everyman, 1929. (First published 1792.)

VIRGINIA WOOLF. *The Common Reader.* 1st Series, Hogarth Press, 1968; 2nd Series, Hogarth Press, 1965.

REFERENCE BOOKS and PERIODICAL PUBLICATIONS

Bibliographie Générale du Costume et de la Mode, by René Colas. Libraire René Colas, 8 rue de l'Odéon, Paris 8.

British Union Catalogue of Periodical Publications.

An Index to the Annuals, 1820–1850, Vol. I, *The Authors.* By Andrew Boyle. Privately printed by Andrew Boyle (Booksellers) Ltd., Worcester, 1967.

The Cambridge Bibliography of English Literature, Vols. I, II, III.

The Cambridge History of English Literature.

The Diarian Miscellany. Extracts from the *Ladies' Diary* from 1704–73, in 5 vols by Charles Hutton F.R.S., Professor of Mathematics in the Royal Military Academy, G. Robinson & R. Baldwin, 1775.

A Dictionary of Printers and Printing, with the *Progress of Literature,* by C. H. Timperley, H. Johnson, 1839.

Lowndes Bibliographer's Manual of English Literature. Revised by Henry H. Bohn, 1858.

Dictionary of National Biography.

The London Mercury, Oct. 1931, Vol. XXIV, No. 144. 'The New Lady's Magazine of 1786' by Geoffrey Tillotson.

Publication of the Modern Languages Association of America, Vol. XLVIII (1933): 'Early English Periodicals for Ladies', 1700–60, by Bertha Monica Stearns.

Tercentenary Handlist of English and Welsh Newspapers, Magazine, and Reviews, Section I, *The Times*, 1920.

British Museum Periodical Publications Catalogues.

Bound volumes of weekly, monthly, and annual publications, chiefly in the British Museum Library and the Fawcett Library, but some belonging to private owners. Unbound issues of eighteenth-century periodicals are extremely rare, and I am therefore particularly grateful to Miss L. V. Paulin, F.L.A., County Librarian of Hertfordshire, for lending me unbound monthly issues of *The Lady's Magazine*, July to December 1781, in her personal possession.

I must also record my gratitude to Miss Mildred Surry, A.L.A., Librarian of the Fawcett Library, for permitting me to reproduce many illustrations in this book from original volumes in the library.

INDEX

Abedelazar, 19
Ackermann, Rudolf, 204, 206, 224, 239
Addison, Joseph, 55–7, 62, 67, 170
Adventures of Roderick Random, 111, 126
Adventures of Sir Launcelot Greaves, 126
Advertisements, 150, 186; section in *La Belle Assemblé*, 220; in *Repository of Arts*, 224–6; in World of Fashikn, 230
Advice to a Daughter, 33–5
Age of Reason, 191
Age, The, 252
Agnes de Castro, 24
Ainsworth, Harrison, 159–61, 236, 238, 241, 250
Ainsworth's Magazine, 258
Albert, van der, 20
Albina, 173
Almanacks, 156–7; 238
Almanack de Gotha, 239
Almyna, 58
Almira, 27
Amelia, 106
Amulet, The, 197, 239, 240–1
Andrews, Alexander, *quoted*, 144, 180, 184, 185
Anecdotes of the Manners & Customs of London during the 18c., *quoted*, 38
Annesley, Elizabeth, 25
Anniversary, The, 240
Annual Anthology, The, 239
Annual Register, The, 113, 123
Annuals, The, 234–5; 236–63; 271
Apology for the Life of George Anne Bellamy, 177
Artist, The, 172
Astell, Mary, 27, 40–5; 89
Athenaeum, The, 197
Athenian Gazette, The, 26
Athenian Mercury, The, 26–31
Athenian Oracle, The, 30
Athenian Spy, The, 28

Austen, Jane, 57, 162–3; on fashion, 163; Gothic vogue, 170; *Lover's Vows*, 173; *Northanger Abbey*, 170, 193, 212; 253
Authorship in the Days of Dr Johnson, *quoted*, 80

Bage, Robert, 169
Baker, Thomas, 60–1
Ball, Hannah, 188
Bath Herald & Register, *quoted*, 173
Bath Intrigues, 73
Bathoe, William, 110
Baldwin, A., 60, 61
Baldwin, Mrs, 27
Ballard, George, *quoted*, 45
Barber, John, 62–3; 93, 94
Barbauld, Mrs, 174, 188, 203
Barnes, Mrs, 27
Baron-Wilson, Mrs C., 271
Le Beau, Madame, 206
Le Beau Monde, 222–4
Beauvais, Madame, 206
Bee, The, 119–21
Behn, Aphra, 19–20; 74, 78, 87; novel potted for *Ladies' Magazine*, 107; *Oroonoko* dramatized, 123
Beighton, Henry, 27
Bell, John, 177–82; 185–6; 218–27
Bell, John Browne, 222–3; 227, 228–30
Bell, Mrs M. A., 226–30
Bellamy, George Anne, 177
Bellamy, Daniel the Elder, 75
Bellamy, Thomas, 165
Bell's British Theatre, 174
Belle's Strategem, The, 137
Bell's New Weekly Messenger, 223
Bell's Weekly Messenger, 185–6; 223, 227
Belle of the Season, The, 250
Belle Assemblée, La, 134, 186, 218–27; advertisements, 220–2, 226; fashion dept., 226; Mrs Norton editor, 243; 264

Bellpine, Mrs, 38
Bennett, Arnold, 272
Bentley's Miscellany, 115, 258
Betsy Thoughtless, The History of Miss, 104
Bibliographie Generale du Costume et de la Mode, 205
Bibliotheca Literaria, 79
Birthday Day, The, 173
Blagdon, Barbara, 40
Blanchard, Laman, *quoted*, 245
Blackwood's Lady's Magazine, 197, 264
Blackwood's Magazine, 197
Blessington, Countess of, 235, 239, edits *Keepsake*, 243; edits *Book of Beauty*, 249–51; literary earnings, 250–1; *Book of Beauty*, 257–61
Blue Stockings, 35, 86, 134, 135–8; satyrized in the *Keepsake*, 242; Regency, 252–3
Boldini, 185–6
Bolton, Mrs, 27
Bolton, Robert, Dean of Carlisle, 192
Book of Beauty, The, 244, 249–50
Book of Memories, *quoted*, 193, 202
Books of the Sixties, 237
Boscawen, Mrs, 136
Boswell, James, 109, 111, 117; on Blue Stockings, 136
Bowles, Caroline (Mrs Southey), 197
Brereton, Thomas, 80
Brewman, Draper, 185
Bridges, Elizabeth, 162
British Classics, Harrison's, 156
British Gazette & Sunday Monitor, 184–5
British Magazine, The, 124–6; 132, 144
British Recluse The, 73
British Theatre, The, (Elizabeth Inchbald), 172
Broadsheets, 190–1
Brooke, Frances Moore, 115–16
Browning, Elizabeth Barrett, 243, 261, 262
Browning, Robert, 261
Le Brun, 220
Budgell, Eustace, 119
Bulwer and His Wife, 35, 248

Burnet, Bishop, 42
Burney, Dr, 136, 180
Burney, Frances, 117, 135–6; 136, 167, 174, 180
Burrow, Reuben, 156–7
Bury, Lady Charlotte, 253
Busybody, The, 119–20
Bute, Henry, 178–9
Bute, Lady, 86–7
Byron, Lord, 199, 249, on Lady Morgan, 256; 266

Calprenède, Sieur de, 74
Campbell, Dr Thomas, 113
Campbell, Thomas, 250
Cappe, Mrs Catherine, 188
Carey, Mrs, 38
Carnan, Thomas, 108, 156–7
Carter, Elizabeth, 81, 117, 134–5; 136
Cartwright, Mrs, 201
Castle of Otranto, The, 132, 169
Cave, Edward, 79–81, 135
Cecil, Lord David, *quoted*, 88
Cecilia, 136
Centlivre, Susannah, 25, 87
Chamber's Journal, 258
Chambers, William, 258, 260
Chap Books, 190
Chapone, Mrs Hester, 137, 191, 201
Charitable Mercury, The, 64
Charlotte, Prince of Wales, 198
Charlotte, Queen, 136, 206
Cheap Repository Tracts, 190–2
Cheek, Mrs Grace, 27
Chesterfield, 3rd Earl of, 34
Chesterfield, 4th Earl of, 27, 33, 34
Chit Chat, 56
Christian Lady's Magazine, The, 197, 263, 272
Chorley, H. F., 261
Cibber, Colley, 93
Cibber, Mrs, 123
City of the Sultan, 269
Clarissa, 89, 134
Cleland, John, 90, 111

Clergy Residence Act, 193
Coelebs in Search of a Wife, 137, 234
Cockburn, Catherine (née Trotter), 24, 81
Coffee houses, 30, 72, 86, 113
Colas, René, *quoted*, 205
Collins, A. S., *quoted*, 80
Colnaghi & Co., 206, 208
Combe, William, 224
Commonsense, 88, 91
Conscious Lovers, 76
Connoisseur, The, 116, 156
Congreve, William, 24
Coote, Mr, 128
Corbauld, R., 155
Cornwall, Barry (Bryan Walter Proctor), 238, 250, 262
Correspondent, The, 167
Cottager's Monthly Visitor, The, 197
Court and City Magazine, The, 118
Court, City, and Country Magazine, The, 118
Court Journal, The, 245
Country Magazine, The (1736), 83-6
Country Magazine, The (1763), 127
Court Magazine, The, 118, 264
Court Miscellany, The, 118, 128
Court Magazine and Belle Assemblée, The, 227
Court Magazine and Monthly Critic, The, 227
de Courcy, Beatrice and Margaret, 267-71
Cowley, Mrs Hannah, 173-4; 181
Crabbe, George, 148
Critical Review, The, 111, 113-14
Criminal trial reports, 106, 151
Croker, John Wilson, 254
Croom, Mrs, 27
Crosland, Mrs Newton, 241, 257-8, writing for Annuals, 259-60; assist. editor of *Keepsake*, 261-2
Cudworth, Damaris (Lady Masham), 27, 40
Cunningham, Allan, 240
Cupid's Annual, 235
Curiosities of Literature, 20, 87

Curtis, Mrs, 27
Curwen, Henry, 110

Dacier, Madame, 134
Dacre, Lady, 252
Daily Gazetteer, 88
Daily News, The, 251
Davenport, R. A., 156
Davis, Mrs, 27
Davys, Mary, 71-2
Defoe, Daniel, 42, 74
Delaney, Mrs, 135
Delights for the Ingenious, 49-50
Deserted Daughter, The, 172
Diary of a Visit to England, 113
Dickens, Charles, on Minerva Library, 167; 197; 251; 262
Dictionary of Printers & Printing, 186
Disraeli, Benjamin, 250, 260, 262
Disraeli, Isaac, 20, 25, on Lady Mary Wortley Montagu, 87, 250
Divorce, Mrs Haywood's advice, 101
Doctor Syntax's Tours, 224
Dodsley, publisher, 93, 119
Drake, Judith, 42
Drawingroom Scrapbook, The, 244, 246, 247, 262
Druid, Nestor, 107
Duncombe, John, *quoted*, 115
Dunton, John, 25-32, *Pegasus*, 55; and Mrs Malthus, 63; on Mrs Sowle and Mrs Harris, 64

Eastlake, Lady, 243
Easy Lessons for Children, 188
Edgeworth, Maria, 199, educational writings, 201; novels, 201-2; Sir Walter Scott, 202; 253
Edinburgh Review, The, 154
Education of Women, The (Defoe), 42
Education, of women and girls, 37-52; 75-6; 117-18; 134; 198-203
Education of the poor, 188-98
Elegancies of Fashion & General Rembrancer of Taste & Manners, 210

Eliot, George, 236
Elopements, 32, 35, 98, 133
Elstob, Elizabeth, 45
Emmeline, 178
English Annual, The, 243
English Chronicle, The, 169
English Newspapers, quoted, 227
Englishman, The, 56
Englishwomen of Letters, quoted, 169
Essay in Defence of the Female Sex, 42
Essay on Man, 81, 134
Essay papers, 55–7; *The Parrot*, 77–8; *Female Spectator*, 95–103; *Lady's Curiosity*, 107; *Old Maid*, 116
Essays on the Employment of Time, 192
Este, Rev. Charles, 181
Ethel Churchill, 246
Ethelinde, 178
Evelina, 135, 138
Examiner, The, 62–3; 250

Fairy Almanac, The, 245
False Delicacy, 118
Familiar Letters, 71–2; 138
Familiar Letters Betwixt a Gentleman & Lady, 71–2
Family Magazine, The (of 1825, 1830, and 1834–7) 197
Family Magazine, The (Mrs Trimmer's), 189–90; 197
Family Oracle of Health, Economy, Medicine & Good Living, 197
Fancourt, Rev. Samuel, 110
Fanny Hill, 90, 111
Fatal Falsehood, The, 173
Fatal Friendship, The, 24
Father's Legacy to his Daughter, A., 35
Fashion as it Flies, 232
Fashion plates, 121, 129, 132; in *Ladies' Museum*, 161; in *Lady's Daily Companion*, 163; in *Lady's Magazine*, 204–5; *Gallery of Fashion*, 204–6; 207, 208, 210; in *Lady's Monthly Museum*, 210; in *Belle Assemblée*, 220; 226; in *Le Beau Monde*, 223; *Ackermann's Repository*,
224; in *World of Fashion*, 230; 232, 234, 265
Fashion reports, 121, 129, 163; in *Lady's Magazine*, 204–5; in *Belle Assemblée*, 220, 226; in *World of Fashion*, 230
Fell, Margaret, 40
Female Dunciad, The, 73
Female Preceptor, The, 197–201; 203
Female Quixote, The, 117
Female Spectator, The, 95–103; 108
Female Tatler, The (Thomas Baker), 60–1
Female Tatler, The (Mrs Manley), 57, 59–62
Female Tatler (in *Ackermann's Repository*), 224
Feminead, The, or *Female Genius*, 115
Fielding, Henry, 89, 103, 110, 191
Fielding, Sarah, 86
Finden's Tableaux, 262
Fiske, Mrs, 208
Fitzherbert, Mrs, 179
Fisher's Drawingroom Scrapbook, 244–5
Fletcher, Mrs, 197
Fonblanque, Albany, 250
Forster, John, *quoted*, 113, 114, 124, engagement to L.E.L., 247, 251
Forget-Me-Not, The, 237, 240, 245
Fraser's Magazine, 115, 243
Frederick & Caroline, 167
Freeman, Jean, *quoted*, 173
Free Thinker, The, 75
Freethinker, The, or *Essays on Ignorance*, 75
Freethinker, The, by J. Baker, 75
Friendship's Offering, 237, 239, 261, 262

Gallerie des Modes, La, 206
Gallery of Fashion, 204–6; 223
Garrick, David, 116, 137, 174
Garrick, Mrs, 117, 136
Gazetteer, The, 114
Gem, The, 237
Gems of Beauty, 250
Gentleman's and Lady's Magazine, The, 157

Gentleman's & Lady's Magazine in French & English, 155

Gentleman's & Lady's New Magazine, The, 118

Gentleman's & Lady's Museum, The, 155

Gentleman's Journal, or the Monthly Miscellany, 31, 131

Gentleman's Magazine, or Monthly Intelligencer, The, 79–81; 91; 125; Elizabeth Carter contributes, 134–5; advocating Sunday Schools, 188

Gentlemen's & Ladies' Diary & Palladian, The, 50

Genuine Letters of Henry & Frances, 164

Giles Gingerbread, 108

Gill, Mrs, 27

Giradin, Madame Emile de, 261

Goldsmith, Oliver, 111, 113–15; *Lady's Magazine*, 119–21; *Busy-body and Bee*, 119–21; *British Magazine*, 124–6; pirated, 126; Deserted Female, 199

Goodwill, Jasper, 106–7

Goody-Two Shoes, 108

Gore, Mrs Grace, 246, 250, literary earnings, 251; 256–7

Gothic vogue, 132, 169–70; 211

Graces, The, 238

Grand Magazine of Magazines, The, 125

Grand Magazine of Universal Intelligence, The, 125

Gregory, Dr, 35

Griffeth, Mrs, 164

Griffiths, Ralph, 111–13

Griffiths, Mrs, 111

Grover, Mrs, 27

Guardian, The, women's interests, 55; extracts in *British Classics*, 156

Guthrie, Thomas, 80

Gwillim, Mrs, 27

Halifax, Marquis of, 30, 33–5

Hall, Mrs S. C., 257, 261, 262, 264

Hall, S. C., 157; *quoted* 193; on Maria Edgeworth and Scott, 202; on Miss

Mitford, 232; *The Amulet*, 239, 240; on Lady Morgan, 255

Halsband, Robert, 90

Harriet Stuart, 111, 117

Harris, Benjamin, 64

Harris, Mrs Elizabeth, 64

Harrison, James, 155–6

Hastings, Lady Elizabeth, 42

Hatchards, 198

Haydon, Benjamin Robert, 157

Haywood, Eliza, 72–4; *The Parrot*, 78; 87; *Female Spectator*, 95–103; second novel-writing period, 111; *Young Lady*, 107–8

Heath, Charles, 155, 241, 242, *Book of Beauty*, 244, 249; death, 261

Heath's Book of Beauty, see *Book of Beauty*

von Heideloff, Nicolaus Wilhelm, 204–6

Hemans, Mrs, 197, 257, 262

History of Booksellers, A, 110

History of Lady Julia Mandeville, 116

History of Oroonoko, or the Royal Slave, 20, 123

Hofland, Mrs, 257

Hogg, James, 237, 240

Holcroft, Thomas, 172

Holland, Vyvyan, *quoted*, 205

Hood, Thomas, 237

Hook, Theodore, 240, 256

Howitt, Mary, 197, 262

Hughes, Jane, 80–1

Hudson, Mr, song composer, 131

Humphrey Clinker, 113

Hulton, bookseller of Birmingham, 113

Hunt, James Henry Leigh, *quoted*, on Miss Burney, 136; on Minerva Library, 168–9; on Mrs Inchbald, 172; on John Bell, 180, 182, 186, 218; on Boldini, 185; contributes to *Ladies' Pocket Magazine* 234; on Lady Blessington, 249

Huntingford School for Industry, 195

Hutton, Charles, 51–2; 156–7

Idalia, or The Unfortunate Mistress, 73

Idler in Italy, 250

Illustrated London News, 258
Imperial Magazine, The, 125; 126
Inchbald, Elizabeth. 138, 172–3; acts in Mrs Cowley's play, 174; Mary Wells and *The World*, 182; *profile in Lady's Monthly Museum*, 211
Instructions for Cutting Out Apparel for the Poor, 194–7
Italian, The, 169

Jacobin imprints, 191
Jane Austen in Bath, quoted, 173
Jenny and Jemmy Jessamy, 104
Jerdan, William, 246, 247, 250
Jerrold's Magazine, 258
Jewsbury, Mary-Jane, 197
John Bull, 240, 252, 256
Johnson, Mrs of Kensington, 27
Johnson, Mrs E., 184–5
Johnson, S., 185
Johnson, Dr Samuel, 36, 57, 80; praise of Charlotte Lennox, 117, 126; prologue to Kelly's play, 118; *Universal Chronicle*, 125; *The Idler*, 125; and Anna Williams, 126; on Elizabeth Carter, 135; on Mrs Montagu, 135; Blue Stockings, 136; *Rambler*, 137
Johnson's Sunday Monitor & British Gazette, 184–5, 189
Jones, Griffith, 124
Joseph Andrews, 103
Journal de la Mode et du Gout, 220
Journal des Dames et des Modes, Le, 234
Journalism for Women, quoted, 272
Journals, The, 55–7
Justinier, Mrs, headmistress, 187
Juvenile Forget-Me-Not, The, 257

Kames, Lord, 203
Kavanagh, Julia, quoted, 169
Keepsake, The, 159, 236, 238–9, 241–4, 250; dealings with contributors, 258–9; last number, 261
Kelly, Hugh, 118–19, 128
King, Dr William, 62

Kirby, Joshua, 187
Knight, Charles, quoted, 156, 177, 218
Kotzebue, A. von, 173

Lacedaemonian Mercury, The, 26
Lackington, bookseller, 164
Ladies' and Gentlemen's Diary, 50
Ladies' Cabinet of Fashion, Music & Romance, 263, 266–71
Ladies' Catechism, The, 37
Ladies' Companion (Lane's), 164
Ladies' Complete Pocket-book, The, 159
Ladies' Diary, The, 45–52; rival by Carnan, 108; 134, 156–7
Ladies' Dictionary, The, 28–9
Ladies' Fashionable Repository, The, 264
Ladies' Journal, The, Dublin, 77
Ladies' Library, The, 70–1
Ladies' Mercury, The, 26, 31, 32
Ladies' Magazine, The (Jasper Goodwill), 106–7, 151
Ladies' Mirror or Mental Companion, 164, 238
Ladies' Monthly Magazine & World of Fashion, 230
Ladies' Museum, The (Lane's), 159–62; 164, 238
Ladies' Museum, The, 210
Ladies New & Elegant Pocket Book, The, 164, 238
Ladies' Pocket Magazine, 234
Lady's and Gentleman's Diary, or Royal Almanack, 156
Lady's Curiosity, The, 107
Lady's Daily Companion, The, 162–4
Lady's Gazette, of Fashion, The, 264
Lady's Magazine & Museum of Belles Lettres, 210, 227
Lady's Magazine, The, or Universal Repository (1733), 81, 86
Lady's Magazine, The, or Compleat Library (1738), 83
Lady's Magazine, The (1759–63), 121–4
Lady's Magazine, The (from 1770), 121; 128–41; first serial story, 138; on Sins of

Society, 139–41; plagiarized by Wheble, 142; letters to the Editor, 148–50; notices to contributors, 149; plagiarists reprimanded, 149–50; advertisements, 150; contents formula, 150–1; criminal trial reports, 151–4; publishes *Our Village*, 232; contents of 1816, 264

Lady's Monthly Museum, The, 175; 210–17

Lady's Museum, The, 117–18; 121, 264

Lady's Pocket Magazine, The (1830–5), 264

Lady's Weekly Magazine, The, 104

Lady's New & Elegant Pocket Magazine (1795), 156

Lamb, Charles, 168, 179, 234, 238

Lanchester, Madame, 208, 220

Landmarks of a Literary Life, 262

Landon, Laetitia E., 232, 234; her work and life, 244–8, 250, 253; compared with Sydney Morgan, 256, 262

Landor, Walter Savage, 238, 250, 262

Lane's Leadenhall Library (Minerva), 113, 168, 170

Lane, William, 113, 154, 159; *The Novelist*, 163; novel publishing and libraries, 164–9; 238

Lennox, Charlotte, 111, 117–18, 126

Letters between Amelia in London & her Mother in the Country, 224

Letters for Literary Ladies, 201

Letters from a Lady of Quality to a Chevalier, 73

Letters of Education, 201

Letters on Female Education, addressed to a Married Lady, 201

Letters on the Improvement of the Mind, 201

Letters to my Son, Lord Chesterfield, 34

Lettres Portugaises, 71

Lewis, M. G., 132

Libertine, The, 19

Libraries, circulating, 110–11, 113, 154, 164, effect on book sales, 165; provincial and seaside, 165; Charles Dickens on, 167; John Bell's, 179–80; Hazard's of Bath, 192; 201

Library, John Newbury's Juvenile, 108

Library of Fiction, or Family Story Teller, The, 197

Life and Errors, John Dunton, 26

Lindsey, Rev. Theophilus, 188

Literary Anecdotes of the 18c., quoted, 45, 111, 144

Literary Gazette, The, 246, 247

Literary Magnet, The, 197

Literary Women of England, quoted, 24, 175, 197, on L.E.L., 246

Literary Souvenir, The, 197, 238, 239, 245

Lloyd, Robert, 125

Locke, John, 40

Lockhart, John Gibson, quoted, 74, 240, 241

London & Paris Ladies' Magazine of Fashion, 234, 264

London Journal, The, 258

London Magazine, The, 80, 90, 125

London Mercury, The, 26

Loose Hints upon Education, 203

Lost Lover, The, or *Jealous Husband*, 58

Love Child, The, 173

Lover, The, 56

Lover and Reader, The, 56

Lovers' Vows, 173

Lytton, Bulwer, 246, 250; of Mrs Gore, 257; contributor to the Annuals, 262

Lucius, by Mrs Manley, 63

Maberly, Mrs, 262

Macaulay, Catherine, 201

McLean, George, 247

Magazin de Modes, Mrs Bell's, 226, 227

Magazine a la Mode, The, 155

Magazine of Domestic Economy & Family Review, The, 197, 264, 272

Magazine of Female Fashions of London & Paris, The, 207–8

Magazine of the Beau Monde, The, 264

Maginn, Dr, 247

Maidenhead Lost by Moonlight, 74

Maids, Wives, & Widows Penny Magazine, 271

Mangall, Miss Richmal, 202

Manley, John, M. P., 58

Manley, Mary de la Rivière, 57–63; 73, 93, 94, 137

Manley, Sir Roger, 57

Malcolm, James Pellor, *quoted*, 38

Mallet, Mrs, 27

Malthus, Mrs S., 63

Mansfield Park, 173, 193

Marriage, 32–6; Lord Halifax's *Advice*, 34; Mary Astell's attitude to, 42–5; directions for in *Ladies' Diary*, 47–9; Steele's attitude to, 53–5; Mrs Haywood condemns arranged marriages, 98; chastity before, 119; Blue Stockings conception of, 138; out of social strata, 212

Marryat, Charles, 250, 262

Martineau, Mrs, 269

Masham, Lady, 40

Masqueraders, The, or *The Fatal Curiosity*, 73

Matthews, Charles, 258

Matrimonial Magazine, The, 155

Maxfield, Mrs, 27

Meddler, The, 125

Melbourne, Lord, 232, 243, 253, 262

Memoirs of a Certain Island Adjacent to Utopia, 73

Memoirs of a Coxcomb, 90

Memoirs of a Magdalen, 118

Memoirs of a Woman of Pleasure, 90, 111

Memoirs of Rivella, 63

Memoirs of the Life of Mrs Sumbel, late Wells, 182

Micrososm of London, 207

Midgeley, Dr, 57

Middlemarch, 236

Midwife, The, 108

Minerva Press, 113, 154, 164–8; Leigh Hunt's opinion, 168; 201; pocket books, 238

Mirroir de la Mode, 208

Mitford, John, 232

Mitford, Mary Russell, 199, 232, 257, 264

Mode Elegant, La, or *World of Fashion*, 230

Moll Flanders, 74

Monk, The, 132

Molloy, J. Fitzgerald, *quoted*, 239, 251

Montagu, Mrs Elizabeth, 86, 135, 137

Montagu, Lady Mary Wortley, 35, 86–92

Monthly Mirror, The, Reflecting Men & Manners, 164

Monthly Miscellany, The, 79

Monthly Review, The, 111

Monthly Visitor, The, 197

Moore, Doris Langley, *quoted*, 206

Moore, Thomas, 241, 243

More, Hannah, 71, 116, 136; as playwright, 173; accused of plagiarism, 173; *Cheap Repository Tracts*, 190–4; dedication in *Female Preceptor*, 198; *The Strictures*, 203; novelist, 137

Morison, Stanley, *quoted*, 227, 228

Morgan, Sir Charles, 253

Morgan, Lady, 232, 246, 250, 253–6, 269

Morley, Countess of, 252

Mortality figures, 18c., 85

Morning Post, The, 178–9

Most Gorgeous Lady Blessington, The, *quoted*, 251

Mothers and Daughters, *quoted*, 251–2

Motteux, Peter Anthony, 31

Mysteries of Udolpho, The, 132, 169–70

Napoleon, Prince Louis, 260

National Register, The, 223

New Atlantis, The, 58–9; 63; copied by Mrs Haywood, 73; 110

Newcastle, Margaret, Duchess of, 20–1

New Bon Ton Magazine, The, 232

New British Ladies' Magazine, The, 232

New Lady's Magazine, The, 121, 144–8

New Monthly Belle Assemblée, 264

New Monthly Magazine, The, 232, 239, 243; L.E.L.'s contributions, 245; Lady Blessington's contributions, 249

New Novelists' Magazine, The, 155

Newbury, John, 108, 117, 118, 124, 156

News of the World, The, 223

Nichols, John, 45, 111, 144
Nicholson, bookseller of Cambridge, 113
Night-Walker, The, 27
Noble's Circulating Library, 111
Nonsense of Commonsense, The, 86, 88–92
Norris, Dr, 27
Northanger Abbey, 57, 170, 193, 212
Northern Antiquities, 132
Northern Heiress, The, 72
Norton, Hon. Mrs, 227, 242–4, 246; literary earnings, 251; 253
Notes & Queries, 26
Novelist, The, or Amusing Companion, 163
Novelists' Magazine, The, 155
Novels, romantic, 72–4; potted for magazines, 106; mid-18c., 110–11; library novels satirized by Goldsmith, 113–15; initial publication in magazines, 118, 126; gothic, 132, 211; by instalment, 118, 126; epistolatory, 71, 138; as drugs, 154; women novelists' and their miseries, 215; silver-fork novels, 251, 256
Novice of St Dominic, The, 253
Nutt, Mrs, 27

Observer, The, 157
Oeconomy of Charity, The, 188
Old English Baron, The, 132
Old Maid, The, 116
Opie, Mrs, 257
Oriental tales, 132, 211
Orphan Riviv'd, The, 66–7
d'Orsay, Count, 249, 261
d'Orsay, Harriet, 249
Osborne, Dorothy, 22, 26, 88
Our Village, 232
Owenson, Sidney, *see* Lady Morgan

Paine, Tom, 191
Palladian, The, 50
Pamela, 33, 89, 103, 138
Pardoe, Miss, 269
Parents' Assistant, The, 161

Parrot, The (1728), 77–8; (1746), 103
Pegasus, 55
Percy, 137, 173
Peregrine Pickle, 126
People's Journal, The, 258
Petit Courier des Dames, Le, 232, 234
Phelan, Charlotte, E., 197, 272
Philanderer, The, 117
Phillips, Ambrose, 75
Picturesque Annual, The, 257
Pilkington, Laetitia, 92–4
Pilkington, Matthew, 93
Pix, Mary, 24–5
Place, Francis, *quoted*, 132, 150
Plebeian, The, 56
Pocket books, 159–64, 238
Pocket Magazine, The, or Elegant Repository of Useful and Polite Literature, 156
Poetical Album, The, 197
Polite Repository, The, 164
Polwhele, Rev. R., 36
Pope, Alexander, 73, 87, 134
Popping, Sarah, 64
Porters, the Misses, 156
Powell, Mrs Elizabeth, 64–6
Power, Marguerite, 261
Power of Love, 110
Practical Education, 201
Princess, The, 269
Priestly, bookseller of Leeds, 113
Prince of Wales, 179, 180
Prior, James, *quoted*, 121
Prisons, debtors, 93, 157, 181, 224
Proclamation Society, 191
Protestant Post-Boy, The, 64
Proctor, Bryan Waller, *see* Barry Cornwall
Public Magazine, The, 125
Public Characters, on Mrs Cowley, 174; on Mrs Robinson, 175; 1800–1, 178; of *The World*, 181; of Mary Wells, 182; of Mrs Inchbald, 211
Public Ledger, The, 118, 124
Pym-Hales, Caroline, 162

Quarterly Review, The, 243, 254

Questions, The, 202
Quizzical Gazette, The, 232

Radcliffe, Ann, 132, 169–70
Raikes, Robert, 188
Rambler, The, 116, 137
Ramsay, Allan, circulating library, 110
Rash Resolve, The, 73
Reader, The, 56
Reading, John, 69
Recamier, Madame, 208
Recollections of Literary Characters, 115
Record of Fashion and Court Elegance, 208
Records of Love, 38, 67–71
Rees and Britton, *quoted*, 154, 224
Reeve, Clara, 132
Reflections and Maxims (Rochefoucauld), 19
Reflections on Marriage, Mary Astell, 44
Reformed Coquet, The, 72
Reminiscences of Literary London, *quoted*, 154, 224
Repository of Arts, Ackermann's, 224–6
Reynolds, F. Mansel, 242
Reynolds, Sir Joshua, 136
Richards, Mrs, 27
Richardson, Samuel, 33, 71, 89, 103
Rienzi, 232
Ritchie, Leitch, 261
Rivals, The, 167
Robins, Joseph, 234
Robinson, Mary, 175–6, 181
La Rochefoucauld, duc de, 19
Romance and Reality, 246
Romance of the Forest, 169
Rosina, 116
Royal Female, The, 125
Royal Mischief, The, 58
Royal Ladies' Magazine, The, 264
Royal Slave, The, 20; potted in *Lady's Magazine*, 107
Rowlandson, Thomas, 224
Roxana, 74
Runaway, The, 174
Ruskin, John, 262

Sadleir, Michael, *quoted*, 35, 248
Saint Clair, 253
Saint James's Chronicle, The, 173
Sault, Richard, 27, 57
Sayings & Doings, 256
Scott, Sir Walter, 74, 199; and Miss Edgeworth, 202; criticized in *Lady's Monthly Museum*, 214–15; 239, 241; in *Book of Beauty*, 250; *parodied in Lady's Magazine*, 264
School for Wives, 174
Schools, boarding, 37–9; 200–1, 212; the Misses More's, 137, 175; Mrs Justinier's, 187; charity, 188; industrial, 192, 195; Sunday, 188, 192–3; 194–7; the Misses Lance's, 246
Scourge, The, 232
de Scudery, Mlll, 74
Secret History of Queen Zarah, The, 58
Secret Memoirs, 110
Secret Memoirs & Manners of Several Persons of Quality of Both Sexes, 58
Seduction, 32–3; in *Ladies' Diary*, 48–9; in *Female Preceptor*, *199–200, 213*; in *Ladies' Cabinet*, 266–7
Sentimental Journey, A, 131, 145
Sentimental Magazine, The, 155, 201
Serious Proposal to the Ladies, A, 40
Servant's Magazine, or Female Domestic's Instructor, The, 272
Seward, Anna, 174
Shadows of the Old Booksellers, *quoted*, 156, 218
Shoberl, Frederic, 239, 240
Shute, Mrs, 27
Sicilian Lover, The, 175
Sicilian Romance, The, 169
Singer, Mrs, 27
Sitwell, Sacheveral, *quoted*, 205
Skipton, Sir Thomas, 58
Smallpox, 87–8
Smart, Christopher, 108
Smith, Charlotte, 169, 177–8
Smollett, Tobias, 111, 113, 114; edits *British Magazine*, 124–6; 132, 169

Society for Promoting Christian Knowledge, 188
Society for Promoting Sunday Schools, 151
Society for the Suppression of Vice and Immorality, 191
Sophia, 118, 126
Southey, Mrs (Caroline Bowles), 197
Southey, Robert, 239, 240
Sowle, Mrs Stacey, 64
Spectator, The, 53–5; 56–7; 87; essays purloined for *Ladies' Magazine*, 107; extracts in *British Classics*, 156
Spinster, The, 56
Stacey, Mrs, 27
Steele, Richard, 33, 35, 53–7; *Ladies' Library*, 70–1; *Conscious Lovers*, 76–7; criticized by Lady Mary Wortley Montagu, 91–2
Stanhope, Hon. Mrs Caroline, 121
Stanhope, Rev. Charles, 121, 144–8; 181
Stamp Duty, *note*, 51; 64
Stationers' Company, The, 46, 156
Stephanoff, F. P., 242
Sterne, Laurence, 131, 170, 173
Stillingfleet, Benjamin, 136
Stokes, John, 185
Stothard, Thomas, 155, 238
Strictures, The, 137, 203
Stuart, Daniel, 179
Such Things Are, 172
Sue, Eugene, 261
Sumbel, Mrs (Mary Wells), 181–3
Sunday Monitor & London Recorder, 185
Swift, Jonathan, 30–1; of Mrs Manley, 59, 63; *resigns* from *Examiner*, 62; and Mrs Popping, 64; of Mary Davys, 72; of Mrs Haywood, 73; friend of the Pilkingtons, 93

Talbot, Mrs Catherine, 137
Tatler, The, 53–7; spurious number, 60; extracts in *British Classics*, 156
Taylor, Mrs, 27

Tea Table, The, 74
Tempest, Mrs, 27
Temple, Sir William, 22, 26, 30, 88
Tennyson, Lord Alfred, 261
Thackeray, William Makepeace, 250, 257, 261
Theatre, The, 56
Thompson, Mrs, 115
Thrale, Mrs, 127, 180
Timperley, C. H. *quoted*, on John Bell, 186
Tipper, John, 46–52
Tipper, Mrs, 27
Tonna, Mrs, Charlotte E., 197
Topham, Capt. Edward, 180–2
Town Talk, 56
Toulman, Camilla Dufour, *see* Crosland, Mrs Newton
Townsend's *Quarterly Selection of Parisian Costumes*, 232–4; 264
Treatise on the Education of Daughters, 117
Trimmer, Sarah, 187–90; 197; memoir in *Female Preceptor*, 197–8
Trollope, Mrs, 269
Trotter, Catherine, 24, 81
Turkish Embassy Letters, 87
Turkish Spy, The, 57
Turner, J. M. W., 156
Two Quiet Lives, *quoted*, 88
Tytler, James, 157–8

Universal Chronicle, The, 125
Universal Library, 110
Universal Museum, The, 127
Unsexed Females, The, 36

Vindication of the Rights of Women, 35, 201
Virginity, attitudes to, 32, 36
Visiter, The, 75–7

Walpole, Horace, 73, 132, 169
Walpole, Sir Robert, 88, 92
Wandering Spy, The, 63
Wanderings of Warwick, The, 177
Ward's Miscellany, 197

Watts, Alaric, 239
Wavil, Mrs, 27
Webb, S., 80
Weekly Magazine, The, 125
Weekly Medley, The, 64–6
Weekly Mirror, The, 157
Wells, Mary, 181–3
Wesley, John, 26
Wesley, Samuel, 26, 27
Westmacott, Charles Molloy, 252
Wheble, bookseller, and publisher, 142, 149
Whisperer, The, 59
Whitchurch, Mrs, 27
Wife, The, by Mira, 104, 108
Wilberforce, William, 191, 193
Wild Irish Girl, The, 253
Williams, Anna, 127
Williams, Jane, *quoted,* on Catherine Cockburn, 24; on Mrs Robinson, 175; on Mary-Jane Jewsbury, 197; on L.E.L., 246
Wilson, Harriette, 177
Winchelsea, Lady, 20

Winter, Mrs, 27
Winter's Wreath, 241
Wollstonecraft, Mary, 35, 201
Woman, quoted, 272
Woman and her Master, 255
Woman, or Ida of Athens, 253
Woodforde, Nancy, 204
Woodstock; or the Cavalier, 214
Word to the Wise, A, 118
Wordsworth, William, 236, 241, 250
Wortley, Edward, 35, 87
Wortley, Lady Emmeline Stuart, 242
World of Fashion, The, 228–30; competition of the Annuals, 234–5; 264
Wray, Mary, 70
Wright, bookseller and librarian, 110
Wynne, John Huddlestone, 126, 144

Young Ladies' Miscellany, The, 75
Young Lady, The, 107–8
Young Widow, The, 271–2

Zoffany, John, 206

GEORGE ALLEN & UNWIN LTD
Head Office: 40 Museum Street, London, WC1
Sales, Distribution and Accounts Departments:
Park Lane, Hemel Hempstead, Hertfordshire

Athens: 7 Stadiou Street, Athens 125
Barbados: Rockley New Road, St. Lawrence 4
Bombay: 103/5 Fort Street, Bombay 1
Calcutta: 285J Bepin Behari Ganguli Street, Calcutta 12
Dacca: Alico Building, 18 Motijheel, Dacca 2
Hornsby, N.S.W.: Cnr. Bridge Road and Jersey Street, 2077
Ibadan: P.O. Box 62
Johannesburg: P.O. Box 23134, Joubert Park
Karachi: Karachi Chambers, McLeod Road, Karachi 2
Lahore: 22 Falettis' Hotel, Egerton Road
Madras: 2/18 Mount Road, Madras 2
Manila: P.O. Box 157, Quezon City, D-502
Mexico: Serapio Rendon 125, Mexico 4, D.F.
Nairobi: P.O. Box 30583
New Delhi: 4/21-22B Asaf Ali Road, New Delhi 1
Ontario, 2330 Midland Avenue, Agincourt
Singapore: 248C-6 Orchard Road, Singapore 9
Tokyo: C.P.O. Box 1728, Tokyo 100-91
Wellington: P.O. Box 1467, Wellington, New Zealand